Echoes of
OKLAHOMA
SOONERS
FOOTBALL

Echoes of OKLAHOMA SOONERS FOOTBALL

The Greatest Stories Ever Told

Edited by Mark Stallard

TRIUMPH
BOOKS

Library of Congress Cataloging-in-Publication Data

Echoes of Oklahoma Sooners football : the greatest stories ever told / edited by Mark Stallard.
    p. cm.
Includes bibliographical references.
ISBN-13: 978-1-57243-874-3
ISBN-10: 1-57243-874-6
    1. Oklahoma Sooners (Football team)—History. 2. University of Oklahoma—Football—History. 3. Sports journalism—Oklahoma I. Stallard, Mark, 1958–

GV958.U585E24 2007
796.332'630976637—dc22

2007008275

This book is available in quantity at special discounts for your group or organization. For further information, contact:

Triumph Books
542 South Dearborn Street
Suite 750
Chicago, Illinois 60605
(312) 939-3330
Fax (312) 663-3557

Printed in U.S.A.
ISBN: 978-1-57243-874-3
Design by Patricia Frey
All photos courtesy of AP/Wide World Photos.

CONTENTS

FOREWORD

When I was in junior high I worked in a shoe store in Miami, Oklahoma. I was a good worker, but on Saturday afternoons in the fall—1:00, to be precise—I'd slip back to the storeroom, where I hid a little transistor radio, and listen to the Sooners play. I was just starting to play football myself at that time, but as I listened to Bob Barry call the games—and he's still announcing the OU games today—I used to think how great it would be if I had the opportunity to play football at the University of Oklahoma. So I guess you could say I was always a Sooners fan.

In high school a group of us would go to the Oklahoma games, paying a dollar each for a ticket, sit in the south end zone of the stadium, and watch the Sooners play. It was very exciting to me. I still remember seeing Gale Sayers of Kansas and all the other great players from around the Big Eight play. It didn't matter if the Sooners won or lost—they usually did win, though—I just wanted to be a part of it; I wanted to be a part of the great football tradition at Oklahoma. I thought, "How great would it be if I had the opportunity to go play there?"

So Oklahoma was where I wanted to go to school. In 1965 OU had one of the worst seasons in their history, finishing with a 3–7 record. Gomer Jones, who had followed Bud Wilkinson as the head coach of the team, resigned, and Jim Mackenzie left Arkansas to coach the Sooners. The thing is, he had been recruiting me hard to come to Arkansas and I was very close to signing with the Razorbacks because they were on top of their game at that time and the Sooners were down.

When he was recruiting me for Arkansas, Mackenzie said to me, "You don't want to go to Oklahoma. I know it's your dream, but they're going to be in a transition period and you'll go through four years of that. If you come to Arkansas, you'll play with a winner immediately." But when he became the head coach at OU, he called me and said, "Forget all that stuff about Arkansas. You need to follow your dreams and go to Oklahoma."

And that's what I did. It was the best decision I ever made.

Things worked out well for me, but you know, this is a special place. A lot of great players set the high standard at Oklahoma in the 1930s, '40s, and '50s. And I think all of us as players respect that tradition when we come here. For me personally, it was four great years and even today, and I'm almost 60—I'm still very close to the program.

At the end of my senior season I won the Heisman Trophy. I was presented the award on a Tuesday, but we still had one more game to play the following Saturday against Oklahoma State, who had a pretty good team that year. It was a big game because there was a rumor that if we didn't win, they might fire the entire coaching staff, a staff that included head coach Chuck Fairbanks and assistants Barry Switzer, Galen Hall, and Larry Lacewell—just some great coaches. As players we knew that these coaches were the best available and we needed to keep them at Oklahoma. It turned out to be a difficult week to prepare to play the game because of all the stuff that went with winning the Heisman: the interviews, appearances, and others things that can cause distractions. But we worked extremely hard and went to Stillwater ready to battle the Cowboys.

I'll never forget the first time we lined up on offense and I looked up—their field runs east and west—and there was a big sign the Oklahoma State students had put up that said "Steve Who? Won What?" referring of course to me winning the Heisman. It seemed like any time we had the ball heading east, I'd look up at that sign and it gave me a little extra motivation.

I carried the ball 55 times that day, which was an NCAA record, and we ended up winning the game by one point. I was in great condition and was used to carrying the ball a lot, and I averaged carrying the ball 33–35 times a game my entire career. My senior year, though, there were games where I carried the ball more than 50 times, including that OSU game. Late in the Oklahoma State game we were coming off our own goal line and I had carried the ball eight, 10, 12 times in a row—incredible. And I was worn out.

One thing you never do, especially on offense if you have momentum in a game, is to call timeout. But I could hardly breathe. I said to Jack Mildren, our quarterback, "You've got to call timeout," and he did. Then Jack went to the sideline and put on the headphones to talk to Coach Switzer.

"Who in the hell called timeout?" Switzer screamed at Jack. "You don't call timeout!" And Jack told him, "Coach, Steve called timeout because he's dying." And Switzer became irate. He said something to the effect of, "You tell that big son of a bitch to keep carrying the ball; he can rest after the game." So I continued carrying the ball and we won the ballgame, 28–27.

Recently, a reporter here in Oklahoma wrote that if a player carried the ball 55 times in this day and age, they'd have a congressional investigation. But that was what I was trained to do. My entire career at Oklahoma I ran out of the I formation. I was conditioned for it. I tell people who ask, "How can you carry a ball 55 times in a game?" that it was easy because I carried it 100 times in practice.

One thing is very important to me and I feel strongly about it; I won the Heisman because I had great teammates, great coaches, and I played for a great school. People have asked me about winning the Heisman as an individual award, but to me it was never an individual award. I had some of the greatest teammates you could ever play with: fullback Mike Harper, tight end Steve Zabel, center Ken Mendenhall, guard Bill Elfstrom, and two great quarterbacks, Bob Warmack and Mildren, to name just a few.

So that's important to me when I look at the Heisman Trophy, to think of my teammates and coaches and remember how it is as much their trophy as it is mine. I won it because of the great players I lined up with at Oklahoma. We had three first-round draft choices from the team my senior year.

Oklahoma football has never been about one coach, one specific team, and certainly not one player. It's about tradition, winning, and pride—all the things that have made the University of Oklahoma's football program the best in the country. You'll find many stories about the Sooners' greatest players, teams, and coaches in this collection of articles about OU's storied and glorious football program, articles that show how the team evolved to and sustained greatness.

I'm so proud to have been a part of it.

—Steve Owens
1969 Heisman Trophy winner

Uwe von Schamann and Bud Hebert celebrate von Schamann's game-winning field goal in the Sooners' now legendary 29–28 triumph over Ohio State during the 1977 season.

Section I
THE GAMES

The Daily Oklahoman

LONGHORNS DEFEATED BY SOONERS ON BOYD FIELD

The game was played a little differently during the first decade of the 20ᵗʰ century, but it doesn't mean Oklahoma fans didn't enjoy a good whipping of the Longhorns as much as they do today. The Sooners walloped Texas and easily won the 1908 contest. This game story ran in The Daily Oklahoman *on November 14, 1908.*

Outclassed, Texas University Athletes Lose Championship Contest after Many Victories at Home, 50–0

Norman, Oklahoma, November 13—Oklahoma University, by playing perfect football every minute of the 70 played, had a walkaway with the big Texas team. The Oklahoma boys played their very best, which resulted in nine touchdowns and five goals for them, or a score of 50–0.

Texas played hard but were too slow and while unable to get themselves through the Sooners' line for any gains, the Sooners seldom failed to make good gains.

Twice during the game it looked as though Texas might score, once when by a long punt they had gotten the ball within five yards of OU's goal, and again when Dyer, the Longhorns quarter, got a fumble near the Texas goal line and ran 60 yards, only to be captured by Douglas.

Only once in the first half and but three or four times in the second half did Texas make her downs. The Sooners line was impregnable and the only gains the Longhorns made were on forward passes and punts.

Duncan, right end, and Dyer, quarter, did the best work for Texas while there was not a man on the Sooners team that does not deserve special praise for his work.

The game was the cleanest ever played here. There was not one word of wrangling. The Texans did their best and took their defeat like men. Texas can be proud of putting out a team who are at least gentlemen.

The Sooners were penalized twice as often as the Longhorns, but the penalties were all just and the umpire acted perfectly fairly. Texas

2

won the toss-up and took advantage of the wind and by a long kick, a punt, and a penalty on OU, got the ball near the Sooners' goal. They failed on a place kick from the 25-yard line.

OU punted out and Texas punted back to the Sooners' 10-yard line. Wantland took the ball and went through the Texas line and outran two Texans the whole length of the field for the first touchdown after nine minutes of play. Armstrong kicked goal.

Six minutes later, after good gains by Capshaw, Roy Campbell, and Douglas, Capshaw broke through the Longhorns' line 40 yards for a touchdown. Armstrong failed for goal.

Texas kicked off past the goal line. OU kicked out to the center of the field. Texas punted for 45 yards. Wantland went 20, then big Douglas, without interference, knocking Texans right and left, gained 30 yards. Oklahoma was penalized and Douglas recovered the 15 yards.

Texas by two successful forward passes, a punt, and a penalty against OU got the ball within two yards of the Sooners' goal line and got a touchdown. Texas, as usual, failed to make any gain against the Sooners' line and punted. Narn carried the ball 15 yards, Capshaw 30, Douglas 10, Wolf 15, and Capshaw 20 for a touchdown. Armstrong kicked goal.

Texas kicked off but 15 yards and recovered the ball and worked a forward pass for 20 more. Captain Wolf got a Texas man with the ball and ran him five yards toward the Sooners' goal.

OU punted for 60 yards, and then for the first time the Texans made their downs.

Half ends with score 17–0.

Between halves Professor D.W. Ohem, professor of geology here, started a snake dance and about 300 men followed his lead. After dancing all over the field, they all threw their hats over the goal post.

Texas kicked off in the second half. Stitler made 20 yards for Texas, OU got touchback and gains by Campbell, Douglas, and Wantland. Douglas carried the ball over the line for a touchdown. Armstrong kicked out to Wantland and then kicked goal.

The Sooners then drove the ball right back to Texas's line, and Ralph Campbell carried it over for a touchdown. Armstrong kicked out to Wantland but failed to kick goal. Again after gains by Capshaw, Douglas, Campbell, Roberts, and Armstrong, Key Wolf captured a fumble and converted it into a touchdown. A Texas man got away in a clear field but was run down by Ralph Campbell in 40 yards. Armstrong kicked goal.

Again Texas punted a few minutes later for 40 yards and Wantland this time kicked his last goal.

The score now stood 45–0 and it was so near dark that the ball in play could not be seen. Ralph Campbell made 40 yards. Sooners fumbled and Over ran 60 yards for Texas, to be captured by Douglas.

OU by straight line backs made a touchdown and failed to kick goal. Sooners carried their players off the field with a score of 50–0.

Lineup
Sooners—Roy Campbell, center; English, LG; Wolf, RG; Douglas, LT; Ralph Campbell, RT; Walling, RE; Narn, quarter; Wantland, RH; Capshaw, LH; Armstrong, full.

Longhorns—Barleny, center; Truett, LG; Stieler, RG; Feldlake, (capt) LT; Wolf, RT; Duncan, LE; H. Leonard, RE; Dyer, quarter; Estell, RH; Slaughter, LH; Walker, full.

Sooners coach, Bennie Owens; Longhorns coach, Montzentine; referee, Dr. H.H. Cloudman, Vermont; umpire, Jack Allen, Harvard; field judge, St. Claire.

Thompson was substituted as center, Roberts RH, and Long RG in second half. Jones took H. Leonard's place at RE.

Touchdowns: Wantland, 2; Capshaw, 2; Douglas, 1; Ralph Campbell, 3; Key Wolf, 1; Armstrong, 2.

Two 35-minute halves.

The students are having a big celebration and torchlight parade tonight.

 *The Daily Oklahoman*

SOONERS TAKE VALLEY TITLE IN FINAL GAME

The Sooners joined the Missouri Valley Conference in 1920 and promptly won the conference championship. Oklahoma finished the season with a route of Drake to take the title—the only blemish on their record was a tie against Kansas State. It was the last championship team Bennie Owen coached at OU.

Drake Falls Before Heavy Oklahoma Team by Score of 44 to 7.

Des Moines, Iowa, November 25—Unmasking a baffling assortment of forward passes perfectly received by fleet forwards, Bennie Owen's Sooners won the Missouri Valley championship here this afternoon by decisively defeating Drake 44–7. This is the first year in the Valley conference for Owen's protégés.

After a 7–7 tie with the Kansas Aggies last Saturday on the Sooners' home field, a much closer game was expected; but the mixing up of new plays combined with the perfect work of the heavy Oklahoma line showed that the "Cowboys" had again the old form that they possessed in 1918 and had shown in the Washington, Missouri, and Kansas games this year.

Drake Line Holds

In spite of the light Drake line, the Sooners men were unable to tear through it with much success and early in the game resulted to Bennie Owen's old standby, the famous "Oklahoma aerial attack."

After that Drake never had a chance to win, the Owen machine tearing up the Des Moines gang in the last half for a score of 28 against their opponents' 7.

Oklahoma outplayed and outgeneraled Drake and clinched its claims to the Missouri Valley Conference championship. Oklahoma made one gain of 50 yards by the aerial route. On the next down, on Drake's 2-yard line, White went across for a touchdown. The long pass was made after two attempts had failed.

Davis Kicks Goal

The first scoring was early in the first period, after an exchange of punts, when Oklahoma carried the ball to Drake's 22-yard line and Davis kicked goal from there. Both sides lost ground frequently in attempting to gain for the remainder of the period.

In the second period, after Oklahoma gained 15 yards by a pass, Hill made an additional 20 yards through right tackle and went across the line. White kicked goal. Play was more or less even until near the close of the period, when White intercepted a pass by Drake and was stopped on Drake's 23-yard line. A pass from White to Johnson was good for the next Oklahoma touchdown. White failed to kick goal.

Drake Territory Invaded

The third period opened with frequent line bucking, Drake gaining in that manner. Oklahoma, however, by passes worked well into Drake territory and Haskell scored, White kicking goal. The period ended on Drake's 15-yard line.

Oklahoma forced the playing in the fourth period and Morrison soon made a touchdown and in a few minutes Johnson went across for another. White kicked successfully both times.

Drake Scores on Fumble

Drake's only touchdown came when Oklahoma lost the ball on its 20-yard line by a fumble and Drake made a gain around end, through right tackle and the line, Niggemeyer scoring and Clayton kicking goal. Play was kept near the center of the field until Oklahoma made its 50-yard pass. White to Tyler, and White then went across and kicked goal. Lineup:

Oklahoma	Position	Drake
Luster	LE	Pendy
Johnson	LT	Amme
Mckinley	LG	Tilmont
Hamm	C	Marsh
Deacon	RG	Lutz
Smoot	RT	Hornaday
Haskell	RE	Sherer
Davis	QB	Clayton
Hill	LH	Allen
White	RH	Niggemeyer
Swatek	FB	Young

Substitutions
Oklahoma: Edmondson for Deacon; Ogilvia for Davis; Morrison for Swatek; Marsh for Luster; Tyler for Haskell; Ross for Smoot; Cullen for Edmondson.

Drake: Denton for Tilmont; Woodhead for Sherer; Long for Pendy; Sarif for Marsh; Wado for Woodward; Woodhead for Wade; Gibbon for Health.

Touchdowns: Oklahoma: Johnson, 2; Hill, Haskell, Morrison, White, 1.

Drake: Niggemeyer, 1.

Goals from touchdown: White, 5; Clayton, 1.

Field goals: Davis, 1.

Score by Quarters

OK University	3	13	7	21–44
Drake	0	0	0	7–7

Punts: White, 10 times for an average of 34 yards.

Attempted passes: Oklahoma, 26; completed 11 for 185 yards. Drake, attempted 12; completed five for 60 yards.

Yards gained in scrimmage: Oklahoma, 240; Drake, 82.

Yards lost in scrimmage: Oklahoma, 61; Drake, 52.

Penalties: Oklahoma, six for 50 yards; Drake, two for 30 yards.

First downs: Oklahoma, 33; Drake, 8.

Fumbles: Oklahoma, 3; Drake, 4.

Lost ball on downs: Oklahoma, 1.

Punts returned: Oklahoma, 67 yards; Drake, 0.

White kicked off 15 times for an average of 55 yards; Clayton, five for an average of 40 yards.

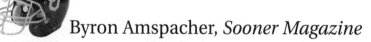

Byron Amspacher, *Sooner Magazine*

SPORTS REVIEW—1939 ORANGE BOWL

With a perfect 10–0 record and a defense that had allowed just 12 points all season, the Sooners had high hopes for a victory when they arrived in Miami in 1939 for the school's first-ever bowl game against Tennessee. The Volunteers soundly dashed OU's hopes for a win and captured the Orange Bowl, 17–0. Byron Amspacher wrote this article on the game for Sooner Magazine.

While Oklahoma football fans are still wondering what hit the undefeated Sooners football team at Miami, where it dropped an Orange Bowl game to Tennessee, 17–0, Coach Tom Stidham is already thinking about spring practice and next season.

After the loss, the first in 15 games for the Big Six champions, Stidham had only this comment to make to reporters: "I've got just one thing to say, boys. We had to get it sometime, and we got it today. We'll just rub this off and start next year against SMU."

No one has yet been able to give a satisfactory answer as to just what happened to the Sooners, pride of the Big Six and Missouri Valley sector, in that January 2 game at Miami. Although Tennessee had by far the best team met by the redshirted Sooners all year and the best team on the field that day, Oklahoma put on perhaps its worst exhibition of the year.

The game was marred all the way through by rough play and penalties, with both sides giving and taking in one of the hardest games ever fought.

Tennessee was brilliant. No team could have beaten the Vols that day. It was the opinion of practically every writer present that the victors were the best team in the nation and could have taken care of other bowl winners without trouble.

The blocking of the orange-shirted Tennessee team was unbelievable to Sooners fans, who thought that the blocking of the Oklahoma team was perfection itself. On every play a horde of Tennessee men seemed to pop up out of the ground and mow the Sooners down.

But while the Oklahomans were having trouble functioning as a team, several players turned in outstanding individual performances, and Hugh McCullough, triple-threat back, was especially bright.

Here is what Sid Feder, Associated Press writer, had to say about McCullough's performance:

"It was Hugh McCullough, as game a gridder as ever came down the pike, who played the hero's role all the way for the Sooners.

"He played 58 of the 60 minutes and did about everything one man could to stop the terrific Tennesseans. The only trouble was there weren't 10 others like him on the field for Oklahoma this warm afternoon.

"He passed, he ran, he kicked (and how), and he played plenty of defense. Then, two minutes before the finish, when the scoreboard showed 17–0 and nothing mattered anymore, Tom Stidham took him out.

"Both packed sides of this colorful Orange Bowl boomed applause as he limped off. His right leg was hurt, one sleeve of his jersey had been ripped clear out, but one and all admitted that young Mr. McCullough was quite a lad with that pigskin."

Jim Hopkins, sports editor of the *Oklahoma News*, also had praise for the performances of McCullough and several other Sooners players. Here is what he had to say:

"Despite the brilliance of those two Tennessee backs [Wood and Cafego], two major football coaches said Hugh McCullough of Oklahoma was the best player on the field. I have thought all season that McCullough is the most underrated player of the year.

"He stayed in Monday's rough contest 58 minutes. While there, he did all of the kicking, passing, signal-calling; most of the ball carrying; and much of the tackling. He took some severe jolts and came back for more.

"Dick Favor, a reserve blocking back; guard Ralph Stevenson; Frank Ivy, reserve end; were other Sooners whose work stood out against a preponderance of brilliance on the Tennessee side." While Tennessee was ripping down the field for long gains, Oklahoma's attack, which had been good all year for a touchdown or two when necessary, never did get started.

Handicapped from the start by the absence of two of their best running backs, Howard "Red Dog" McCarty and Bill Jennings, the Sooners lost another valuable asset right at the start when Earl Crowder, senior blocking back, was injured.

And while the running game was slowed down to a trot, Coach Stidham's boys also had trouble getting their passing attack to function. Finally, when it didn't really matter, the Sooners drove down to the Vols' 19-yard marker with a series of sharp passes, but it just wasn't their day, and the attack bogged down.

But while the football team had a disastrous day, Oklahomans who made the 1,500-mile trip to Miami were treated to a colorful spectacle at the game. Here is how one writer described it:

"A holiday pageant so packed full of color that it looked like a carefully designed Hollywood set was set in motion by the parading bands in red, orange, white, blue, yellow, green, totaling 1,700 players."

The 150-piece Sooners band just about stole the show in pregame parading. It was chosen as the official bowl band and led the parade on the Saturday before the game. The efficiency and sportsmanship of the Sooners band was widely praised by Tennessee partisans as well as by neutral observers in Miami.

Seven Sooners players made their last appearance on the gridiron in an Oklahoma uniform in the Tennessee game. They were McCullough, Waddy Young, All-American end; Jim Thomas, guard; and Gene Corrotto, Crowder, Otis Rogers, and Raphael Boudreau, backs.

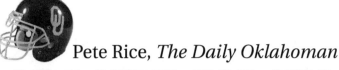

Pete Rice, *The Daily Oklahoman*

OU BOUND FOR SUGAR BOWL AFTER HOLDING OFF AGGIES 19–15 IN FOOTBALL THRILLER

A Bedlam Series classic, the Sooners received their first major bowl bid of the Bud Wilkinson era after holding off the Aggies in 1948. Pete Rice reported the action for The Daily Oklahoman.

North Carolina Is Sooners' Foe in New Orleans Classic; A&M Accepts Delta Bowl Bid

Stillwater, Oklahoma, November 27—The University of Oklahoma Saturday night accepted a bid to play North Carolina in the Sugar Bowl in New Orleans New Year's Day, following a 19–15 win over Oklahoma A&M.

The Aggies accepted a bid to meet William & Mary in the Delta Bowl in Memphis New Year's Day.

Grabbing a two-touchdown advantage early in the second quarter, the Sooners escaped with the important victory, barely able to hang on to their lead by the skin of their teeth as the Aggies put up a furious last-ditch fight to the delight of an estimated 30,000 chilled, rain-soaked fans making up Stillwater's largest football throng in history.

The Aggies, beaten only twice previously this season and rated a three-touchdown underdog by the experts, ran at will against the strong Sooners line during the second half and, while wasting three scoring chances, became the first team to outdistance Oklahoma in statistics this year.

The Cowboys proved their forwards just as rugged as the touted Sooners, playing a courageous battle with guard Darrell Meisenheimer and tackle J.D. Cheek as the ringleaders up front.

Thomas Is Stopped

The Aggies stopped Junior Thomas, Oklahoma's league-leading ground gainer, for a net of 53 yards in 10 tries Saturday as Jack

11

Mitchell took over the ball-carrying leadership for the Sooners. Limping late in the game and sharing his quarterback duties with Darrell Royal, Mitchell led the Sooners with 98 yards in 16 carries, but it was big Jim Spavital of the Aggies who ran best on the slippery field.

Spavital, who broke the game open for the Aggies with a 57-yard sprint down the sidelines in the third quarter, romped off 102 yards in 16 tries. He also scored the other Aggie tally on a 10-yard pass from quarterback Jack Hartman.

The overall team figures showed Oklahoma netting 254 yards, only seven of which were by air, and the Aggies on top with 312. The Cowboys hit eight passes for 68 yards and were only three yards off Oklahoma's rushing pace.

Drizzle Still Falls

With the slow, six-hour-old drizzle still falling, Oklahoma marched to a score on its first possession, moving from the kickoff 83 yards for the touchdown. The drive took 16 plays with Lindell Pearson, the Sooners' top scorer of the day, hitting the middle for the final four with five minutes gone in the game.

Les Ming, a Sooners place-kicking specialist who could easily have been the goat of the game had the Aggies converted one of their late scoring opportunities, muffed the conversion, his eighth miss in 46 tries this year.

Late in the opening quarter Oklahoma started a 64-yard drive that took only three plays and a penalty to accrue into a six-pointer. Starting off the march with a five-yard assessment against the Aggies for delaying the game, Thomas swept his right end for 21 yards.

Pearson Goes

Pearson then made 24 through the middle and on the next play Mitchell danced across from the 14 with only 40 seconds of the second quarter gone.

Ming, who missed two of three conversion attempts Saturday, needed two tries to hit this one. The first kick was wide but the Aggies were offside again, giving him the second chance to put Oklahoma in front, 13–0.

After an exchange of punts, Toy Ledbetter of the Aggies came up with one of his three fumble recoveries. Pearson dropped the ball on an attempted pitchout play and the Aggie covered the pigskin on Oklahoma's 33. It took 11 plays for the Cowboys to score their first tally. The payoff pitch, and the 10th pass of the drive, was a 10-yard flip from Hartman to Spavital, and Hartman hit the conversion to cut Oklahoma's margin to 13–7 at halftime.

Both teams opened up at the start of the last half; the Sooners forced the Cowboys to kick and drove 63 yards to score with a little more than two minutes gone.

Two-Play Drive

It was a two-play drive, Leon Heath from Hollis hitting the middle for 13 yards before Pearson broke into the clear on an off-tackle play and outraced the Aggies secondary on a 50-yard touchdown sprint.

That put Oklahoma ahead 19–7, but very quickly it turned into a much closer ballgame.

Ledbetter returned the Oklahoma kickoff 20 yards to the Aggies' 43, and on the first play from scrimmage Spavital turned in the most beautiful run of the day, a 57-yard jaunt down the sideline during which he sidestepped two Sooners tacklers and literally leaped away from Jim Owens, the last Oklahoma defender, on the 27-yard line.

There was still less than four minutes of the second half gone when Spavital turned in his sensational sprint, and that was all the scoring until the last second of the game.

The Aggies had threatened thrice in the late minutes, driving into Sooners territory twice and recovering a fumble on the Sooners' 2. But each time the Cowboys got their backs to Oklahoma's 10-yard stripe, they bogged down, and each time Oklahoma punted out of danger. That is until there were 16 seconds remaining. Then, with fourth down and the ball on their own 3-yard stripe, the Sooners sent Royal into deep punt formation. He skipped around in the end zone, wasting time before giving the Aggies an intentional safety. Six seconds were left to go when Royal was downed and officials ruled the Cowboys offside again. So the Sooners ran the same play, Royal hitting the ground in the end zone just as the gun went off.

The Associated Press

SKEIN ENDS AT 47

The Sooners' 47-game winning streak—as daunting today as it was in 1957—was ended by an unassuming Notre Dame squad. This is the account of the game published by the Associated Press.

Oklahoma Toppled as [Dick] Lynch Scores from 3 in the Final Quarter

Norman, Oklahoma, November 16—Oklahoma's record streak of 47 football victories was ended today by a Notre Dame team that marched 80 yards in the closing minutes for a touchdown and a 7–0 triumph.

Oklahoma, ranked number two in the nation and an 18-point favorite, couldn't move against the rock-wall Notre Dame line and the Sooners saw another of its streaks shattered—scoring in 123 consecutive games.

The defeat was only the ninth for the Oklahoma coach, Bud Wilkinson, since he became head coach at Oklahoma in 1947. It virtually ended any chance for the Sooners of getting a third straight national championship.

Although the partisan, sellout crowd of 62,000 came out for a Roman holiday, they were stunned into silence as the Sooners were unable to pull their usual last-quarter winning touchdowns—a Wilkinson team trademark.

Rousing Cheer for Irish

As the game ended—when Oklahoma's desperation passing drive was cut off by an intercepted aerial—the crowd rose as one and suddenly gave the Notre Dame team a rousing cheer.

It was a far cry from last year, when the Sooners ran over Notre Dame, 40–0. The victory gave the Irish a 3–1 edge in the five-year-old series dating back to 1952.

The smashing, rocking Notre Dame line didn't permit the Sooners to get started either on the ground or in the air.

The Sooners were able to make only 98 yards on the ground and in the air just 47. Notre Dame, paced by its brilliant, 210-pound fullback

Nick Pietrosante, rolled up 169. In the air the Irish gained 79 yards by hitting nine of 20 passes. Bob Williams did most of the passing for Notre Dame.

Notre Dame's touchdown drive, biting off short but consistent yardage against the Sooners' alternate team, carried from the 20 after an Oklahoma punt went into the end zone.

Sooners Call First Team

Time after time Pietrosante picked up the necessary yard he needed as the Irish smashed through the Oklahoma line. Notre Dame moved to the 8 and the Sooners first team came in to try to make the third Sooners goal-line stand of the day.

Pietrosante smashed four yards through center and Dick Lynch was stopped for no gain. On the third down, Williams went a yard through center.

Then Lynch crossed up the Sooners and rolled around his right end to score standing up. Monty Stickles converted to give Notre Dame the upset and end collegiate football's longest winning streak.

The closest Oklahoma could get to Notre Dame's goal was in the first quarter, when the Sooners' alternate team moved to the 3 before being held on downs.

In the third period, brilliant punting by Clendon Thomas and David Baker kept Notre Dame back on its goal line, but the Sooners couldn't capitalize.

Thomas sent punts down on the Notre Dame 15 and 4, and Baker put them down on the 3 and 7.

This time there were no breaks as Notre Dame shook off last week's jitters, which saw the Irish fumble away the ball five times in losing to Michigan State, 34–6.

Pietrosante gained almost a third of Notre Dame's rushing yardage as he made 56 yards on 17 carries. Lynch was just two yards behind with 54 in 17 carries. The best an Oklahoma player could muster was 36 yards in 10 tries. This was made by Thomas.

Williams completed eight of 19 passes for 70 yards. In Oklahoma's last-minute desperation drive, quarterback Bennett Watts made two of three aerials for 31 yards.

Notre Dame was the last team to beat Oklahoma, at the start of the 1953 season on the same field on which it smothered the Sooners today. Then coach Frank Leahy's Irish beat Oklahoma, 28–21. The next game Oklahoma and Pittsburgh tied at 7–7. Then the Sooners set sail through the 47 games until Terry Brennan's Irish stopped the string today.

Wilkinson, the nation's winningest active coach, had amassed 101 victories in his 10 years at Oklahoma. There were three ties.

Oklahoma started as if it would stretch its string. It marched the first time it got its hands on the ball from the Sooners' 42 down to the Irish 13. But the big Notre Dame line stiffened on the 13.

Oklahoma continued to play in Notre Dame territory the rest of the first quarter. It had another chance when a fumble, with nine minutes gone, was recovered by guard Dick Corbitt on the Notre Dame 34. However the Sooners were stopped cold and finally Baker had to punt on fourth down.

In the second quarter another Sooners drive got down to the 23, but on the first play of the second quarter Carl Dodd fumbled. The ball was punched around in the Sooners backfield and Pietrosante finally smothered it on the Notre Dame 48.

Then Williams started his passing attack to three different receivers and piloted the Irish down to the 3 with first-and-goal. Pietrosante picked up a yard in each of two plunges, Frank Reynolds went to the one-foot line, and then Jim Just was held for no gain.

Later Notre Dame came back with its bruising ground game and moved to the 16. With fourth down Stickles came in for his fake place kick, but instead Williams hit Just on the 6 for a first down. It was then on the second play that Reynolds's pass was intercepted by Baker in the end zone.

Notre Dame (7)
Left Ends—Royer, Prendergast.
Left Tackles—Puntillo, Geremia.
Left Guards—Schaaf, Adamson, Sabal.
Centers—Schultz, Sullivan, Kuchta.
Right Guards—Ecuyer, Djubasak.
Right Tackles—Lawrence, Nagurski, Dolan.
Right Ends—Stickles, Wetoska, Colosimo.
Quarterbacks—Williams, Izo, White, Hebert.
Left Halfbacks—Reynolds, Doyle.
Right Halfbacks—Lynch, Just.
Fullbacks—Pietrosante, Toth, Lima.

Oklahoma (0)
Left Ends—Stiller, Coyle.
Left Tackles—Searcy, Thompson.
Left Guards—Northcutt, Oujesky, Gwinn,
Centers—Harrison, Davis.
Right Guards—Krisher, Corbitt.
Right Tackles—D. Jennings, Lawrence, Ladd.
Right Ends—Rector, S. Jennings.
Quarterbacks—Dodd, Baker, Watts, Sherrod.

Left Halfbacks—Sandefer, Boyd, Hobby.
Right Halfbacks—Thomas, Carpenter, Gautt, Fellow.
Fullbacks—Morris, Rolle.

Score by Quarters

Notre Dame	0	0	0	7–7
Oklahoma	0	0	0	0–0

Touchdown—Lynch (3, run). Conversion–Stickles (1).

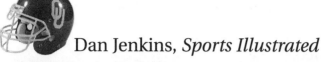

Dan Jenkins, *Sports Illustrated*

THIS YEAR'S GAME OF THE DECADE

The pregame hype before the 1971 OU-Nebraska game—the true Game of the Century—was immense. The Thanksgiving Day game more than lived up to its expectations as Nebraska slowed the powerful Sooners offense just enough to leave Norman with a win, the Big Eight championship, and, ultimately, the 1971 national championship. Sports Illustrated *featured the two teams on their cover before the game and Dan Jenkins wrote this excellent article on the two teams and the Game of the Decade hype.*

Nebraska and Oklahoma, the top-ranked teams in the nation, meet next week in the kind of epic battle that turns up in college football with delightful frequency.

In college football there is this thing called the Game of the Decade and it always seems to be lurking in the doorway, like a Nebraska Cornhusker in a funny red hat or an Oklahoma Sooner in a funny red vest. A Game of the Decade is a rather special kind of contest, something on the order of a Crucial Showdown or a Battle of Giants or maybe even a Game of the Century. And no matter how often they play one, a Game of the Decade is a combination of all that is wonderful and insane about college football.

It develops slowly. It starts out with a couple of teams like Nebraska and Oklahoma beating everybody in sight by six or seven touchdowns early in the season. As a result—and this is an essential ingredient—the two teams are ranked high in the national polls, preferably first and second. Then around mid-October everybody realizes that Nebraska and Oklahoma are not going to lose a game until late in the year when they meet each other. In, of course, a Game of the Decade.

As far as the 1971 supergame is concerned, it took a vastly surprising Oklahoma team to create the excitement. In early September it was obvious that Nebraska would hardly be exercised until Thanksgiving Day in Norman, when there would be this minor irritation, this remote

18

possibility of an upset should the Sooners get high enough. That was fine, and Nebraska started off as expected—by burying everybody. Even Bob Devaney was moved to admit that his Cornhuskers might win a few.

While this was going on, though, Oklahoma was turning out to be more of a sprint relay team than a football team, and when the Sooners ran circles around three excellent foes—USC, Texas, and Colorado—on successive Saturdays, it suddenly occurred to a lot of people that on November 25 there was going to be another Game of the Decade.

Now the two teams are there, as last week Nebraska bruised its way over Kansas State 44–17 and Oklahoma sprinted past Kansas 56–10. So, next week, get set for number one Nebraska (10–0) against number two Oklahoma (9–0) in still another of college football's gigantic, colossal, breathtaking, polldown Battle of Giants. Maybe even Game of the Century.

One of the most important things to understand about these games is that they are sometimes more nerve-tingling before they get played than after they are over—when all of the players, coaches, and fans, plus town, region, and state of the winning school are stopping downtown traffic and when the losers are looking for a high ledge. Any old footballwise observer knows there is no more miserable creature in the world than a man whose team has lost a Game of the Decade, even on a fluke play, and at the same time there is nothing in the world more insufferable than a man whose team has won a Game of the Decade, even by pure theft.

As Darrell Royal of Texas once observed, "It's the fans who make it bigger than it is. For the players and coaches, it's just a big game. For some fans, it's something they might have to live with forever."

To be rather sticky about it, there are two different kinds of Games of the Decade. There is the mini-Game and there is the real Game. In the first a contest develops between a couple of teams that simply appear to be the best of the year, regardless of their records; teams that may have lost or tied one along the way—as, for instance, the USC-UCLA happening of 1967.

The second kind is larger and less frequent, but it has happened before. The teams involved should be undefeated and ranked numbers one and two, and they should meet late in the season. Which is to say that Nebraska and Oklahoma haven't invented anything. There have been many such classics, well-remembered by historians, the most famous of which are listed here.

The Nebraska-Oklahoma Game of the Decade seems to fall most comfortably into a category including these gems: Texas-Arkansas '69, Notre Dame–Michigan State '66, Notre Dame–Army '46 (which in some ways is in a class all by itself), Michigan-Minnesota '40, and

TCU-SMU '35—games that were colorfully known, in order, as The Big Shootout, The Game of the Year, The Game of the Century, The Battle of Giants, and The Aerial Circus.

History tells us a few things we might expect from Nebraska and Oklahoma. For instance, it is a good bet that the game will be exciting, full of suspense. The home field seems to mean little, since visitors have won as many Games of the Decade as they have lost. Nor does being a favorite mean much, since the underdog has won half the time. The most revealing fact of all is that the team most reliant on the forward pass tends to lose. This could be taken as a bad omen for Nebraska. But it is also true that the team that wins the biggie usually does it with the aid of a pass—somewhere, somehow.

It emerges that the average number of Games of the Decade in, alas, a decade is four. Roughly every other season one comes along, one with the necessary ingredients of a long and proper buildup, unbeaten opponents, a national honor at stake, and, when possible, some glamorous stars, if not an O.J. Simpson or a Bubba Smith or a Tom Harmon or a Glenn Davis and Doc Blanchard, at least a Jerry Tagge, a Jack Mildren, a Greg Pruitt, or a Johnny Rodgers.

The decade that produced the most big games between number one and number two teams was the 1960s. Virtually every season, in a bowl if nowhere else, a number one met a number two, or at least a number three. But the best single season for Games of the Decade was 1935 when there were three that captured the fancy of everyone. First, at midseason, Notre Dame and Ohio State, undefeated and untied, met at Columbus, and the Irish won in the last minute, 18–13. A few weeks later Princeton and Dartmouth, undefeated and untied, met in a blizzard at Palmer Stadium, and the Tigers romped 26–6.

With these two Games of the Decade out of the way, the nation turned to a new area that was struggling for attention, the Southwest. Thus, on November 30, a week after Princeton-Dartmouth, 40,000 converged on a 24,000-seat stadium in Fort Worth for a TCU-SMU encounter that would decide the Rose Bowl invitation and the winner of the Knute Rockne trophy for the national championship.

All of the world's leading football authorities, including Grantland Rice, were present that day in a bewildered Texas city to get bewildered themselves by a fellow named Sam Baugh, who threw 43 passes, an unheard-of number in those days. SMU won, despite Baugh, in a 20–14 classic decided on a sensational pass play, while people drove their automobiles through wire fences in order to get near the field.

These days, happily, no such measures are necessary in order for even 40 million people to watch a Game of the Decade. Most of the games have been turning up on television, and so will Nebraska-Oklahoma, at 2:30 EST—check your local listings.

This particular Game of the Decade will match two teams as different as sprinters and weight lifters. Nebraska is a complete team, coupling a well-balanced attack with an iron defense. Oklahoma is all offense, most of it rushing out of the fashionable wishbone T. Nebraska likes to probe and hammer, run and pass, work toward field position, and hold that line. Oklahoma only wants the football, and it will almost collapse that line in order to get it, the theory being that the Sooners will simply outscore you.

The statistics are telling on both sides. Devaney's Cornhuskers have allowed only 172 yards per game—best in the United States—and a mere 6.4 points per game, while offensing for 441 yards per game.

Meanwhile, Oklahoma has rushed for 481 yards per game, has a total offense of 563 yards per game, and has scored 45 points per game—all tops in the country.

Nebraska thinks of itself as a team without stars, but stars have emerged. Jerry Tagge, the quarterback, is a star. He is big, strong, can pass to perfection, read defenses, and lead. Johnny Rodgers is a game-breaker at running, catching, and returning.

When Tagge passes and Rodgers catches, Nebraska can strike as quickly as Oklahoma does when Jack Mildren keeps the football or pitches it out to Greg Pruitt, Joe Wylie, or Roy Bell on the triple option.

Both Tagge and Mildren are way up there in total offense for the year, but they got there by different routes. Tagge has passed his way, Mildren has run, but each can do the other better than one might suspect. Interestingly, the touchdown ratio for each player is nearly equal. By throwing and running, Tagge and Mildren have accounted for 20 and 21 scores, respectively. And that's what counts. For all the fame of Auburn's Pat Sullivan and Washington's Sonny Sixkiller, Tagge and Mildren might be the two best college quarterbacks in the land—certainly the most complete.

As for blazing Pruitt's impressive rushing statistics (1,423 yards in nine games), Nebraska can counter with those of Jeff Kinney and Gary Dixon, who share the same position, Nebraska's I-back. Together they've gained 1,257 yards, most of it the hard way, but always churning forward. This means Nebraska runs, too.

In a sense, the game will match two different attitudes and systems, Nebraska representing the old, Oklahoma the new. In an era when the triple option and wishbone are dominating the style of play, Nebraska has stuck with an I formation and all the variations Devaney can devise.

Oklahoma's wishbone is more than the name, however. Coach Chuck Fairbanks, who installed it after last season began, has more speed than any team that has ever tried to play it. Pruitt is a streak, and so are Wylie and Bell. And Mildren is a player for whom the attack is perfect. He is a strong, fast, savvy operator who understands the offense. He reads the options and has the knack of being able to pitch the ball a greater distance—sometimes 20 yards out to Pruitt—with more accuracy than any quarterback who has run it.

As both teams believe in their abilities to move the football, the question then is which team seems more capable of slowing down the other. Statistics would indicate that this edge belongs to Nebraska. But Oklahoma has played stronger teams outside the conference, like USC and Texas. So maybe the statistics are misleading.

Bringing it down to their five common opponents in the Big Eight, one can find edges for both. Oklahoma scored more points. Nebraska has a stiffer defense. They both won easily every week.

The one alarming figure in Oklahoma's disfavor—and one that surely gives hope to every Nebraskan—is the outrageous number of times Oklahoma has fumbled. The Sooners have managed to lose almost three fumbles per game—but without slowing down.

Can Oklahoma lose three fumbles and beat Nebraska? Probably not. But can Nebraska outscore an Oklahoma wishbone that does not lose three fumbles? Probably not.

The answer to the enigma then lies in faster, more deceptive Oklahoma's ability to operate the most devastating attack in football today. Nobody really stops the triple option, because it has the enemy outnumbered. It stops itself. If the Sooners do not stop themselves, then they will win something that might be called—hey, gang, why not call it the Game of the Decade?

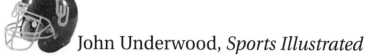 John Underwood, *Sports Illustrated*

NEVER TOO LATE FOR THE SOONERS

Barry Switzer and his boys showed the Buckeye State a little Oklahoma magic in 1977 and left Ohio State fans wondering how they lost to the Sooners. Sports Illustrated *covered the classic OU win.*

In a wild and sometimes woefully inept affray, Oklahoma lost a 20-point lead and its flashy backs lost the ball four times, but it was Ohio State that lost the game on a last-gasp field goal.

On the Oklahoma sideline Barry Switzer is laughing. Why is Barry Switzer laughing? With six seconds to play, Switzer's team is losing to Ohio State 28–26. The game is in Columbus, Ohio, where, as one Oklahoma coach observed respectfully, even the stadium looks like Woody Hayes—wide and old and menacing. The 88,119 spectators, mostly Ohio State fans, are invoking Woody's wrath on the Sooners, on whom at this desperate moment the sky appears to be falling as well. That sky is bloated with rain and gray as wet aluminum. Switzer's matted blond hair and laughing face stand out.

So, on the field, does the lank and limby and somewhat incongruous figure of the Oklahoma place-kicker, standing apart from the huddled Sooners at about the Ohio State 35. The kicker is a 21-year-old with a Smiling Jack mustache. His name is Uwe von Schamann but his teammates call him "Von Foot." As the last chance the Sooners have, Von Foot is being encouraged by the Buckeye fans to grab his own throat. "Block that kick! Block that kick!" they scream. Ohio State has called a just-before-the-kick timeout in order to get this encouragement going and to give Von Foot additional time to think about the enormity of his task. Von Foot is not choking, however. In mock orchestration, he is *leading* the Ohio State cheer, his arms upraised and his forefingers flourishing.

And Switzer, laughing out loud in a giddy release of tension, says to his assistants on the Oklahoma sideline, "What the hell are we doing in this profession?"

The record will show that Uwe (pronounced YOO-va) "Von Foot" von Schamann then soccered a 41-yard field goal through that immense volume of low atmosphere and high pressure. The record will not show that it was a statement made as emphatically as a cop ringing a doorbell, a booming, authoritative kick, high and far and dead-center true, winning the game for Oklahoma with three seconds to spare. Switzer kissed Von Foot when he came off the field. A sentimentalist, Barry.

What might be made of such an ending—besides reaffirming that what Switzer is doing in this profession is standing it on its ear, having now won 44 of 49 games in just four seasons and three games as the Sooners' head coach—is that this first-ever meeting of the two winningest teams in the past quarter century of college football had a significance, a meaning beyond the score. A triumph, say, of Youth and Loose over Age and Uptight.

Switzer is 38, Hayes is 64, and they make the oddest of couplings. Hayes, an almost Caesarean figure, does not give interviews; he grants audiences. Though a charming and thoughtful conversationalist, Woody automatically veers off when talk wanders too close to the intimate workings of his football team (injuries, game plans, other classified stuff). By contrast, on Friday night in Columbus, Switzer and his defensive coordinator, Larry Lacewell, were among the last to leave a pregame party at John Galbreath's Darby Dan Farm. (Hayes had made a brief but impressive talk in which he said "winning is the epitome of honesty," and slipped away.)

The game itself was certainly no vindication of one system or style over another. It was, rather, a hair-raising example of what only too rarely happens when you get a lot of good players on one field at one time, on teams contending for the national championship but having to cope with breaks and twists of fortune so violent that it is impossible to play conservatively.

It was a contest both marvelously played and exquisitely flawed (eight turnovers, six by Oklahoma). It was a bruising, helmet-rattling (not to mention body-injuring, for six Sooners and Buckeye regulars went down during the course of play) blockbuster of a game filled with flashes of inspiring resourcefulness and incredible bungling. It was a game neither team should have lost. Or won.

Different, that's what it was. Different because Oklahoma is different. (No, Oklahoma is *wild*.) And Ohio State is different. Ohio State? Different? Ah, you'd be surprised.

"All football coaches are pragmatists," Hayes said on Friday, sitting quietly and alone in a classroom where he teaches his freshman players "word power" (from a book, *Word Power Made Easy*, by Norman Lewis). "They go with what works." What Hayes is working on this year is an expanded offense that makes exciting use of the skillful

Rod Gerald at quarterback and pragmatically compensates for the fact that the Buckeyes do not have the traditional two-and-a-half-ton truck that usually lines up at fullback for them. It did not take Oklahoma by surprise, but Ohio State ran option plays three out of four times Saturday and looked competent—even nifty—doing it.

Neither does Hayes rip out the headphones anymore when George Chaump, his offensive coordinator, calls a pass from the press box, because even Woody thinks Gerald can throw. There is still no power word in Hayes's book for *often*, however, and while a dozen passes were called, only six were actually launched by Gerald and his backup, Greg Castignola. The first four (by Gerald) were incomplete; the last two, by Castignola, were caught, one for a touchdown. There is no telling how much more success (if you want to call it that) Ohio State would have had throwing, had it dared to be so radical. Oklahoma, under Lacewell, plays a stunting, gambling style of defense, and Lacewell virtually conceded the Buckeyes the forward pass. "If Ohio State wants to pass, let them," he said. "Maybe they'll throw it in the ground."

One still got the impression the ball was flying around all afternoon. It was, only it wasn't being passed. Mainly it was being fumbled by Oklahoma. "We need a new category for statistics," says Lacewell. "Pitchouts attempted and pitchouts completed."

Even Switzer jokes about it because, though they don't always hold on to the ball, the Sooners have, in quarterback Thomas Lott and running backs Billy Sims, Elvis Peacock, and Kenny King, perhaps the fastest backfield that ever lined up. "But 24 fumbles in three games, and we lose 17 of 'em," says Switzer. "And still we're 3–0. It's unbelievable."

What makes it even more astonishing is that Lacewell's—not to say Oklahoma's—pride and joy, the Sooners defense, lost its blood scent. Or, more accurately, its bloodlines. Suddenly last season Lacewell had to learn to live without the Selmons and the Shoates and the Jimbo Elrods and the other All-Americans of past championship teams. The Sooners defense went limp. In a game with Colorado, Switzer got on the headphones to Lacewell. "He'd never called me before," Lacewell recalls. "He always left me alone. But Colorado was marching up and down the field. He said, 'Lacewell, can't we do something to slow them down?' I said, 'No.' He said, 'Oh.'"

Things haven't gotten much better this season. Before the game in Columbus, Lacewell speculated that Ohio State coaches seeing films of Oklahoma's first two games with Vanderbilt (a 23-point yield) and Utah (24) would have been hard put to find an area they *wouldn't* want to attack.

Having established Oklahoma as a team that (a) fumbles, (b) passes poorly, and (c) plays defense with a kind of creeping neurosis, but (d) wins, one is required to add to the assessment the effect that Switzer's personality has had on the team. After successive big-score losses to Oklahoma State and Colorado last year, Lacewell was stunned to hear Switzer tell the squad, "We got 'em right where we want 'em." Which proved to be the case. The Sooners whipped Kansas State, then Missouri, and the following week they dumped Nebraska 20–17.

Against Ohio State, much as they did in beating Nebraska with last-minute thunderbolts in 1976, the Sooners experienced a transformation. Trailing 28–20 with six-minutes–plus to play, when fumbling could no longer be tolerated, Oklahoma did not fumble. When crucial passing was called for, the Sooners passed adeptly. And when the defense positively had no choice, it rose up.

The game in Columbus was played virtually on one end—the downwind end—of the field. Going up to his press-box seat beforehand, Ohio State's Chaump watched the 20-mph gusts whip trash upfield from the south end zone. "I'd rather it rain," he said soberly.

What Chaump meant was that Ohio State no longer has the strong kicking game that becomes essential in bad weather. Oklahoma, on the other hand, had Von Foot, who also punts. Oklahoma won the toss and chose to kick off with the wind. Von Foot put the ball out of the end zone. His first four kicks landed in the same general area. Ohio State never got to run one of them back.

The Buckeyes did not get beyond their 29-yard line in the first quarter, and by the time the teams changed goals Oklahoma, striking swiftly, had accumulated 17 points largely as a result of the spectacular, hurdling runs of Sims and Lott's counters to the strong side. For the next two periods Ohio State played with the wind at *its* back. Von Foot had scored the only points that were to be made in the south end zone early in the second quarter on a 33-yard field goal to make it 20–0. Then it was the Buckeyes' turn. An 80-yard drive and the deficit dropped to 20–7. A fumble recovery on the Oklahoma 19 and a Gerald option run inside right end and it was 20–14.

Ohio State squandered three more chances after Oklahoma turnovers on the Sooners 20-, 33-, and 23-yard lines but then drove 48 yards after a third-down quick kick into the wind by Peacock to go ahead 21–20. Shortly afterward a Sooners pass by number two quarterback Dean Blevins was intercepted at the Oklahoma 33 and Ohio State moved in on Castignola's touchdown pass to make it 28–20.

From that point on, stress worked a miracle cure. The Sooners never made another mistake. Actually, the defense had played well from late in the second quarter, victim only of the offense's largesse (mostly life-or-death pitchouts). The Sooners sought to force Gerald to keep the ball, not because they thought he could not hurt them but because they thought he should be tested. "A matter," said Lacewell, "of choosing your poison."

As it developed, Gerald was knocked out of the game late in the third quarter and spent the rest of the afternoon embracing an ice pack. Before that, linebacker Daryl Hunt had played a tune on him. Hunt's responsibility on the option was Gerald alone. The first time he got to him, after the ends had sealed off the outside pitch and left Gerald to go it alone inside, Hunt whacked him solidly and stripped him of the ball. "It's going to be like that all day," Hunt told Gerald as he helped him up.

In the fourth quarter the wind was again in Oklahoma's sails, and Blevins was at quarterback for the last, breathtaking rally. (Oklahoma's Lott, like Ohio State's Gerald, had been put out of the game with an injury.) On third down at the Oklahoma 46, Castignola was walloped successively by stunting tackles Dave Hudgens and Phil Tabor. The ball popped free. Middle guard Reggie Kinlaw, the best of the "new" Oklahoma defenders, came under the stunt to recover it at the Ohio State 43.

Oklahoma scored in 12 plays. Blevins, who had been booed to tears in the opener with Vanderbilt when he started in place of the injured Lott, passed 10 yards to split end Steve Rhodes for the mover. Then, on a fourth-down play at the Ohio State 12, Blevins kept the Sooners' hopes alive by staggering the cadence on his count, drawing middle guard Aaron Brown offside. The play was stacked up, but the penalty gave Oklahoma a first down at the 7. Peacock scored on a fourth-down option from a yard and a half out but couldn't get in on the two-point conversion, and it was 28–26.

Von Schamann's ensuing onside kick may have been anticipated by everybody in the stadium, but it was perfectly executed. Von Schamann sliced the ball hard off a Buckeye in the front line—a back inserted to improve the chances of fielding the predictable kick—and the ball caromed free just over the 50. Mike Babb dived on it for Oklahoma.

On first down Blevins got man-to-man coverage again on Rhodes and hit him for 18 yards to the Buckeye 32. From there he worked carefully on the inside legs of the option, deliberately keeping to the middle of the field and working the clock down. With six seconds to play, the ball was on the 23, and Von Foot was ushered into the game.

At that moment, if Switzer was asked, could he explain what caused him to suddenly laugh out loud? Probably not. But Larry Lacewell could. Old Barry had 'em where he wanted 'em.

Larry Dorman, *The Sporting News*

A BUTT-KICKING IN MIAMI

Barry Switzer claimed the third and final national title of his coaching tenure at OU in this Orange Bowl showdown against Penn State. The Sooners stuck it to the Nittany Lions and won handily, as reported by Larry Dorman for the January 13, 1986, issue of The Sporting News.

Oklahoma Found Ground for Motivation

Miami, Florida, January 1—From the time they stepped off the team plane at Miami International, wearing coats and ties and walking tight-lipped past reporters and TV lights directly to their team buses, the contingent from Penn State University appeared to be in trouble.

There was just something, well, stiff about both the Nittany Lions' demeanor and that of their coach, Joe Paterno.

All of this proved a fitting portent. The team's number one ranking was slipping away from the beginning of Orange Bowl week. Then the last vestiges were yanked rudely away on New Year's Day by an Oklahoma team that was the antithesis of the slow, ponderous, and tight Nittany Lions.

There is a fine line between teams with character and teams *of* characters. Penn State has character. Oklahoma, it turns out, has both.

Oklahoma won the mythical national championship by defeating Penn State, 25–10, aided by Tennessee's 35–7 thrashing of the University of Miami in the Sugar Bowl. But events during the week helped shape some of the events on the floor of the decrepit old dowager that is the Orange Bowl.

For openers, Sooners linebacker Brian Bosworth said one of the Penn State coaches insulted him while the two teams were on a boat ride around Miami. That definitely boggles the mind.

"He told me I wasn't a linebacker, at least not by Penn State standards," Bosworth said. "He said he didn't like me or my style of play. Well, that kind of attitude ate at me. It pumped me up until the game became my personal vendetta. I wanted to go out and kick somebody's butt."

He did that—13 tackles and a lot of intimidation.

The Sooners drew further motivation from press accounts of what was going on in New Orleans, where the University of Miami was preparing for its game with Tennessee. Oklahoma players read about the Hurricanes' nocturnal cruising of the French Quarter and their daily assurances that they would beat Tennessee and be voted number one, and they recognized the same pattern that had gotten them defeated by Washington, 28–17, in the Orange Bowl a year earlier.

"We did all the same stuff," Bosworth said. "We could tell they were in for it."

Then there was Oklahoma quarterback Jamelle Holieway, who generated the feeling in most quarters that he was a cookie-cutter likeness of the Thomas Lotts and J.C. Wattses who have quarterbacked Oklahoma in the past—great runner, no passer.

Penn State designed a defense just for him. It worked—to an extent. Holieway was tackled for 41 yards in losses for a net gain of one yard. So all he did in the game was give Oklahoma a lead it never relinquished by—get this—passing. A bomb to tight end Keith Jackson gave Oklahoma a 10–7 lead and the Sooners never looked back.

"I love to put it up," said Holieway, a precocious freshman. "Running is fine, but hitting the bomb—well, there's nothing like it."

That's something Penn State quarterback John Shaffer would know little about. His biggest completions (in a game in which he was on target on 10 of 22 passes for 74 yards) went to Oklahoma players. Sooners safety Sonny Brown picked off a Shaffer overthrow in the second quarter and returned it 31 yards to set up the second of an Orange Bowl–record four field goals by Tim Lashar.

On Penn State's next series, Shaffer hit Sooners safety Tony Rayburn, who returned it 34 yards to set up the Lashar field goal that gave Oklahoma a 16–7 lead.

With the Nittany Lions driving with the opening kickoff of the second half, Shaffer underthrew a ball into double coverage. Smith got his second interception of the night and Penn State was done.

Had it not been for a Holieway fumble that set up Massimo Manca's field goal before halftime, the game never would have appeared close. The Sooners got another field goal courtesy of a Penn State fumble. Fullback Lydell Carr, who had been pounding all night, finally broke a 61-yard run to shovel the final spade of dirt onto Penn State's grave.

"This hurts only because I can't believe that one person could do so much to cause a team to lose," Shaffer said. "I hurt because I could see my teammates on defense playing their hearts out and all I could do was run three plays and get off the field."

It wasn't all Shaffer's fault. Maryland by two points, Alabama by two points, Syracuse and Boston College by four points each—all of those close calls for Penn State during the 1985 campaign came back vividly in the wake of the Sooners' relatively easy victory.

Penn State's charmed existence simply came to an end at the hands of a better team. Paterno will have 106 of the 116 players he brought to Miami back next year. He admitted that he learned something from this trip: he had his team practice more for this game than any other bowl in his 20-year tenure, and maybe that wasn't the right approach.

The Nittany Lions finished the season third in both wire-service polls, two notches below their ranking entering the Orange Bowl. Maybe they knew when they got off the plane that there were a couple of teams in the country better than they.

Oklahoma's Barry Switzer, the coach of one of those teams, is savoring life at the top once more—maybe more than he did during the 1974 and 1975 national championship seasons, because he now knows how fleeting it is.

"Humility," he said, "is only seven days away in this profession."

Roy S. Johnson, *The New York Times*

OKLAHOMA RALLIES AND EARNS BERTH IN ORANGE BOWL

November 23, 1986. Oklahoma had Nebraska's number throughout most of Barry Switzer's career at OU. As they had so many times against the Cornhuskers, the 1986 Sooners came from behind and broke the hearts of Nebraska fans again to take the Big Eight title and an Orange Bowl berth.

It was a comeback fitting for such a long and emotional rivalry. Struggling for most of the contest, and down by a touchdown with just over four minutes remaining, the Oklahoma Sooners snatched the Big Eight championship from the grasp of the Nebraska Cornhuskers today with a furious rally that ended in a 20–17 victory before 73,198 shocked spectators.

With one minute, 22 seconds remaining in the game on a clear, cool day, the Sooners capped a 94-yard, game-tying drive with a 17-yard touchdown pass from Jamelle Holieway to Keith Jackson, the All-American tight end. Then, with six seconds left, Tim Lashar kicked a 31-yard field goal that gave the Sooners (10–1) their third consecutive berth in the Orange Bowl on New Year's Day.

"We've done it so many times that we believe if we stay close, we can win any ballgame," said Barry Switzer, the Sooners coach. "We expect that."

Jackson, who had caught only 11 passes for 316 yards all season, caught three today for 87 yards and a touchdown, including a 41-yarder in the closing seconds that set up the game-winning kick.

"They probably spent all week preparing for our running game," said Jackson, a junior. "Who prepares for the OU passing game? They didn't, and it cost them the game."

Holieway, a sophomore, recovered from a shaky start and finished with six completions in 12 attempts, with one interception, for 147 yards and a touchdown.

For the Cornhuskers, who fell to 9–2, it was an ending that extended their string of frustration against the Sooners. It was their fourth consecutive defeat in the series. They will play in the Sugar Bowl against either Louisiana State or Alabama.

"We Just Choked"

"This year I felt we had the best team; we just choked," said Danny Noonan, Nebraska's All-American middle guard. "It's frustrating because we gave up the big play. You can do that against Iowa State, but not against Oklahoma."

It was indeed a day in which the Cornhuskers played better overall. Behind the timely play of Steve Taylor (nine completions in 20 attempts for 141 yards, one touchdown, and 79 yards rushing), Nebraska was the dominant team. The Cornhuskers stifled the Sooners' vaunted wishbone, harassed Holieway into mistakes, and took a 17–7 lead 1:12 into the second half on a 25-yard pass from Taylor, a sophomore, to Rod Smith.

But from there, the Sooners defense, ranked first in the nation, took command. "Intimidation," said Brian Bosworth, the Sooners' vocal linebacker who finished with a game-high nine tackles. "If you don't talk trash, then you don't have confidence in your team. After a while, we had Taylor second-guessing himself, and that worked in our favor."

Passing the Test

It also gave the Sooners offense enough time to regain its composure. With three turnovers in the second half, it looked like they were just overmatched by an emotional Cornhuskers defense that was ranked second in the nation. But with 4:10 remaining, Holieway began what his coach called "a great test," guiding the Sooners from their own 6.

Holieway, who also gained 94 yards rushing, carried the ball three times in the drive. But the biggest plays were a 35-yard completion to Derrick Shepard that took Oklahoma to the Nebraska 32, and the touchdown, which was supposed to be a lob pass to Jackson in the end zone.

A tie would have given the Sooners the conference title outright, which is why, Switzer said, they did not attempt a two-point conversion.

Forcing Nebraska to punt, Oklahoma took over at its 35. After making a first down and then being pushed back by a holding penalty, the Sooners faced third-and-12 from their 37.

Oklahoma ran a play that left Jackson covered by a defensive end, Broderick Thomas, instead of a faster cornerback. Jackson then made an acrobatic one-handed catch and ran out of bounds at the 14 to set up the winning kick.

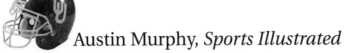

Austin Murphy, *Sports Illustrated*

SOONER BOOMERS

The Sooners surprised the college football world in 2000, beating Florida State in the Orange Bowl to capture the school's seventh National Championship. Austin Murphy reported on the Sooners' dominant performance for Sports Illustrated, *January 8, 2001, issue.*

Near-Perfect Execution by a Crunching Defense Clinched an Unbeaten, Untied, Unbelievable Season for Oklahoma

What was Carol Stoops whispering to her husband? Was she wishing him luck? Reminding him to floss? Knowing she wouldn't speak to him for about 12 hours, she'd staked him out on Wednesday morning in the back of a banquet room at the Oklahoma team hotel in Miami Beach. When the meeting broke, Bob Stoops lagged behind to share an embrace with his wife. "We're going to win," said Carol, her eyes welling with tears. "I know it."

"I know it too," said Bob, the Sooners' coach. "It's our destiny."

To other people, the only thing that seemed preordained going into the Orange Bowl, which pitted Oklahoma against heavily favored Florida State in a battle for the national championship, was that the game would be marked by a ton of offense. The 11–1 Seminoles had averaged 42.4 points and a nation's-best 549.0 yards per game going into this season finale against the 12–0 Sooners, who had averaged 39.0 and 429.3. After practice four days before the game, Stoops had listened patiently to a litany of reasons why his team would struggle against Florida State, then cut off a reporter and said, "Hey, we have some athletes, too, you know."

Now the world knows. With an audacious, ingenious defensive game plan that utterly befuddled Chris Weinke, the Seminoles' Heisman Trophy–winning quarterback, Oklahoma held powerful Florida State to one measly safety in a 13–2 victory that earned the Sooners their seventh national title.

God bless the Sooners, for by winning they spared America an off-season of bickering over Miami and Florida State, who likely would have been co–national champions had Oklahoma lost.

Hurricanes fan: "We beat you in the regular season, so we're the real national champs."
Seminoles fan: "Yeah, but Washington beat you, so by your logic, the Huskies are number one!"

That debate, mercifully, is moot. The Sooners, who entered the Orange Bowl as 11-point underdogs, are the undisputed champions, having pulled off perhaps the most stunning postseason victory since Penn State picked off Vinny Testaverde five times to beat Miami in the 1987 Fiesta Bowl. That Florida State was listed as such a heavy favorite didn't offend the Oklahoma players as much as make them feel comfortable, for the Sooners hadn't been favored in most of their other big games this season. "If the oddsmakers decided who won," said Stoops two days before the Orange Bowl, "we'd be 7–4."

While Oklahoma sought merely to win the game, the Seminoles, who had won last year's championship, had grander ambitions. They spoke of a desire to make history, of becoming the first Florida State team to win back-to-back national titles. They craved recognition, in the words of linebacker Tommy Polley, as "one of the best teams in the history of college football." Instead, they ended up losers, a result that surprised Stoops less than anyone else on earth.

A quick story about the Sooners coach. In order to goose attendance at the exhibition opener of the Sooners softball team last February, Stoops was invited to take batting practice. He faced Jennifer Stewart, an All-American left-hander who would lead Oklahoma to the 2000 NCAA title. Stewart was throwing gas. To the crowd's amusement, Stoops couldn't do much with her first 10 pitches, whiffing on some, dribbling others toward the mound. Instead of leaving the batter's box when his turn was over, he turned to softball coach Patty Gasso and said, "I want 10 more cuts." Whereupon he started making solid contact. "I took her to the fence," Stoops said with a smile.

This anecdote isn't meant to illustrate the 40-year-old Stoops's athleticism—he was a four-year starter and two-time All–Big Ten safety at Iowa from 1979 through '82—or the erosion thereof. It's intended to highlight Stoops's distinguishing characteristic, a rock-solid belief in himself, which has infected everyone else in the Oklahoma football program. Stoops has exuded this confidence throughout the two years it has taken him to transform the Sooners from the moribund mess he inherited in December 1998 to national champions. It was on display last week when reporters asked him how on earth his players could hope to match up with the team speed of the Seminoles. "No one has described us as slow, either," he responded.

Don't think the Sooners didn't take heart in the fact that before taking over at Oklahoma, Stoops had served three years as defensive coordinator at Florida. The suffocating pressure defense he installed in

Gainesville, the so-called Stun 'n' Done, complemented the Gators' Fun 'n' Gun offense and helped Florida win the 1996 national title. The Gators' victim in the championship game? Florida State, which fell 19 points short of its season scoring average in that 52–20 defeat. While preparing for the Orange Bowl, Stoops and his staff took some comfort knowing that the Seminoles had changed their offensive schemes precious little over the last four years.

Then again, four years ago Weinke was in his sixth season of riding the bus as a minor leaguer in the Toronto Blue Jays organization, not in his third year of directing one of the most prolific offenses in Florida State's history. Sitting in a makeshift film room at the Fontainebleau Hilton Hotel in Miami Beach the day before the game, Mike Stoops—Bob's little brother and co–defensive coordinator—spent yet another worried hour studying video of the 28-year-old Weinke, who'd occupied Mike's thoughts and haunted his sleep for a month. As Weinke completed pass after pass on tape, Stoops sighed and said, "I wish he'd gone in the NFL draft last year."

Weinke may be wishing the same thing after Wednesday night. So superbly did the Sooners' defenders disguise their coverages, Weinke could not find his rhythm, even while completing 25 of his 51 passes for 274 yards. He also threw two interceptions and coughed up the fumble that led to Oklahoma's only touchdown.

Indeed, the game's key matchup was the Seminoles' formidable passing game versus the Sooners' pass defense. Oklahoma won the battle with execution and trickery. The Sooners went with five and six defensive backs most of the night, daring Florida State to run. (The Seminoles couldn't, mustering only 27 yards on 17 rushes.) Oftentimes, nickel back Ontei Jones would start about five yards from the line of scrimmage, then, just before the snap, sprint back into deep coverage. Jones and free safety J.T. Thatcher would blitz on one play, then fake a blitz on the next. "It seemed like they had radar," said Florida State wideout Antrews Bell after the game. "Everything we tried, they were ready for."

Bell and his fellow receivers didn't do Weinke any favors, dropping several balls, including one in the end zone by Robert Morgan with the Sooners clinging to a 6–0 lead in the fourth quarter. Looking on from the Seminoles' sideline, flinching at every muffed ball, was Marvin "Snoop" Minnis, who had caught 63 passes and scored 11 touchdowns for the Seminoles this season. On December 20, four days after walking in Florida State's graduation ceremony and, in theory, receiving his degree, Minnis learned that he'd failed two courses and had been declared academically ineligible for the championship game.

"It was a big shock," said a heartsick Minnis four days before the game. "I failed research methods and criminology"—the latter being a particular problem, considering Snoop's major, criminology. "It's not like I didn't go to class or didn't do my work," he said. "I went to class every day and turned in all my papers. But I guess I messed up the exams. It had to be that."

Snoop's absence had the added consequence of preventing the Seminoles from running as much no-huddle offense as they would have liked to. Because that up-tempo style is so taxing on the receivers, said Florida State offensive coordinator Mark Richt, "You've got to have at least six receivers, and you're better off with eight." With Snoop out and Bell nursing a sore hamstring, the Seminoles were, in effect, down to five.

Even if Minnis had played, Oklahoma's defense would have been up to the challenge. In the final month of the season it had grown accustomed to bailing out the Sooners' sputtering offense. After leading Oklahoma to October victories over Texas, Nebraska, and Kansas State, quarterback Josh Heupel cooled considerably. One of his worst outings came at Texas A&M on November 11, when he was flummoxed by the soft umbrella zone that the Aggies unveiled just for him, and threw three interceptions. With the Sooners trailing 31–28 in the waning minutes of that game, Oklahoma middle linebacker Torrance Marshall picked off a pass and ran 41 yards for the winning touchdown.

Watching the game on television in Miami, Hurricanes backup linebacker Sheven Marshall suddenly found himself being cursed by his teammates. They were giving him good-natured grief for being a blood relation of the player whose heroics for the Sooners had pre-served Oklahoma's undefeated season—and thus prevented Miami from facing Florida State in the Orange Bowl (Torrance is Sheven's older brother).

Torrance Marshall is as well-traveled as Heupel, whose tortuous journey from his native Aberdeen, South Dakota, to Norman (with two stops in Utah) has been generously documented. Marshall's route from South Florida to a captaincy in Norman was no less circuitous. Unable to make the grades he needed to qualify for a scholarship at Miami, Marshall packed his bags for Kemper Military School and College in Boonville, Missouri, where he was required to "square" his food—bringing his fork straight up from his plate, then straight across into his mouth—but permitted to take the most direct route to the ball carrier. He made 182 tackles in two seasons and in 1997 became the first junior college All-American in Kemper's history. Even after return-ing to Florida and putting in an extra semester at Miami-Dade Community College, he failed to meet Miami's academic require-ments. He then chose Oklahoma over Kansas State. With the Sooners he has proved a perfect complement to stellar weakside linebacker Rocky Calmus.

It was a first-quarter interception by Marshall, the Orange Bowl's MVP, that led to Oklahoma's first points, a 27-yard field goal by Tim Duncan. Astoundingly, those were the only points the Sooners would need to clinch their first national crown since 1985.

The game had been over for an hour when a sudden downpour forced the celebrating Heupel family off the field. In a tunnel in Pro Player Stadium, Heupel spotted a close friend, Patrick McClung, a minister in Norman. Despite the deluge the two friends walked to midfield and knelt in prayer. Losing the Heisman to Weinke had stung Heupel more than he had let on. All along, however, he had said he would trade that storied doorstop for a national title any day.

Now that the day was upon him, he wept openly, his tears mingling with the rain as he thanked the Almighty for allowing him and the Sooners to fulfill their destiny.

Berry Tramel, *The Daily Oklahoman*

WELCOME BACK, OKLAHOMA

It had been a few years since the winner of an OU-Nebraska game had claimed the conference championship. In 2006 the two longtime powers met in Kansas City and, like so many times in the past, the Sooners conquered the Huskers and captured the Big 12 title.

Kansas City, Missouri, December 3—The clock ticked down on a remarkable game in a remarkable season, and standing in the bottom row, behind the Oklahoma bench, his body freezing but his spirits soaring, Sooners fan Mike Stamp held aloft his sign: "Upon Further Review: The OU Sooners Are Big XII Champs."

Nice irony. Witty slogan. Just didn't go quite far enough.

These Sooners are more than kings of Middle America college football. They are, quite simply, back. Back from the mediocrity of 2005. Back from the loss they didn't deserve at Oregon and the loss they most certainly did in Dallas. Back in the saddle of national prominence.

OU beat Nebraska 21–7 Saturday night in the Kansas City cold, capping an amazing turnaround from a wild season of Rhett Bomar and Gordon Riese and Adrian Peterson.

"It's great to be so young and perform the way we did in a big game; lets everyone know Oklahoma football is back," said Sooners safety Nic Harris. "We're back!"

Back in September, Harris was burned by Oregon's winning touchdown pass after a replay fiasco. Saturday night he had one of OU's three acrobatic interceptions and beamed as the Sooners celebrated at the final gun.

He's come a long way in three months. So have the Sooners.

"Really proud of 'em," said OU president David Boren. "I'm as proud of 'em as I am the national championship team, considering all they've overcome."

Not so very long ago, quarterback Paul Thompson was a backup flanker. Now he's a championship quarterback, joining the legions of

Davis and Lott, Watts and Bradley, Holieway and Heupel, Hybl and White. Now he's the leader who brought the Sooners—headed for the Fiesta Bowl and who knows how high a national ranking—back onto the national stage.

"It's crazy, man," Thompson said. "It's a dream come true. I definitely wanted to be a leader of this team and leader of a Big 12 championship."

Thompson was a caretaker at times during OU's seven-game winning streak that led to first place in the South Division—but not Saturday.

The Sooners and Cornhuskers didn't play the slobber-knocker game expected. Both teams had to throw to move the ball, and Thompson threw it better than Son of Sooner Zac Taylor, Nebraska's QB, thanks in large part to pass-catching whiz Malcolm Kelly, the game's best player.

The Sooners won with a few big pass plays and stingy defense all night long. Nebraska reached OU territory in 11 of its 14 possessions but scored only on a 21-play drive after an interception.

"You gotta credit Oklahoma's defense," said Cornhuskers coach Bill Callahan. "They were stalwart on every front. They played championship defense."

This will not go down as one of the more dominant Sooners teams. But it might go down as one of the more special.

This team played with its back to the wall all season and with its back to the wall all Saturday night. The Huskers kept punting OU deep into its own territory, kept clamping the Sooners' running game.

Yet never did Nebraska seem on the verge of a rally. Never did the Huskers threaten to win this one.

Here are the words [Bob] Stoops used postgame to describe his squad: *super competitive, resilient, great will,* and *determination.*

"Maybe we're not in a position where we're blowing people out by 30," Stoops said. "But that's okay. There's a lot of different ways to win. We trust our defense in tight situations, and our offense comes up with plays when we have to.

"Incredibly competitive."

Back in the front row, a Texas fan, proudly wearing his burnt orange gear, stood behind the OU bench and, as the final seconds ticked off, he placed the OU cap atop his head—a solid salute.

Moments later, when the yellowed field finally was clear of celebrants, Arrowhead Stadium bid bon voyage with Sooners fan Toby Keith's "How Do You Like Me Now?" played over the loudspeaker.

College football likes these Sooners plenty. Welcome back, Oklahoma.

Steve Owens is widely considered the best inside runner in Oklahoma's proud history of running backs.

Section II
THE PLAYERS

 Bennie Owen

LETTER TO THE COLLEGE FOOTBALL HALL OF FAME

The Sooners have had 142 football All-Americans—still, somebody had to be first, and for OU it was Claude Reeds, who earned the honor in 1913. Oklahoma's legendary coach, Bennie Owen, wrote the following letter in 1956 to the College Football Hall of Fame about Reeds and his career with the Sooners.

November 30, 1956

Mr. George E. Little
Executive Secretary
Football Hall of Fame
Rutgers University
New Brunswick, New Jersey

Dear Mr. Little:
I coached at Oklahoma 22 years, from 1905 through 1926, and Claude Reeds, our fullback of 1910, 1911, 1912, and 1913, was the best football player I coached or saw during that period. I enthusiastically recommend him for the Hall of Fame. I realize he did not make Walter Camp's All-American, but I doubt if that's important. Most players in our area were poorly publicized then.

Reeds was honored in 1931 when the late John C. Grover, a Kansas City lawyer who officiated all over the Missouri Valley area for a quarter of a century (he was a great friend of C.E. McBride, sports editor of the *Kansas City Star,* who usually officiated with Grover), selected an all-time all-Valley 11 printed in the *Star.* Grover's all-time backfield had Tommy Johnson of Kansas at quarterback, Chuck Lewis of Missouri and Dick Rutherford of Nebraska (he blocked for Ray Chamberlain) at halfback, and Reeds at fullback. Grover began his description of Reeds by writing, "…the tall, dark-haired, quiet, unassuming Claude Reeds of Oklahoma."

Summing Reeds up, he was a perfectionist. He made everything look dead easy. He was a clean player, a popular player, and a sportsmanlike player. He always made his grades and he graduated. He had football intelligence. He was hard to hurt and played well in any kind of weather. A hurdler in track, he had plenty of speed afoot and speed of reflexes, too. Offensive blocking was his forte. He was the best shoulder blocker I ever saw. He is still accounted the university's finest punter of all time. He was superb defensively either as a tackler or on pass defense. He liked physical contact so well that we used him at end in three 1912 games and he was great. He threw the first long forward passes we ever used in 1912 against Jumbo Steihm's Nebraska Cornhuskers at Lincoln (a full year before Notre Dame used the pass against Army) and almost beat Nebraska. He could buck like a fullback or run the broken field like a half. Best of all, the harder the game, the harder Claude played.

He came to us in 1910 as a freshman fullback, 20 years old, 6'2" tall, and weighing 170. Against Texas that year he had the bad luck to foul a punt obliquely for a kick of only four yards. Disgusted with himself, he didn't get to kick again until we held Texas for downs on our 1. Then Claude not only kicked us out of the hole (fields were 110 yards long in those days) but he kicked a punt that measured 107 yards from the line of scrimmage, counting the roll. He booted it 20 yards over the head of the Texas safety. He was always at his best in times of crisis. In 1911 we finished all-victorious with our fastest backfield of all time and Reeds was our fullback. He kicked so fast we put him only eight yards back of center. As a blocker he sometimes got two and three opponents on the same run. We used him as a runner off long punt formation that year and he was virtually unstoppable. He ran with his back horizontal and his knees up around his ears and started very fast because of his track experience.

At the time of our 1911 game against Oklahoma A&M, the Aggies had not scored on us since we began meeting them in 1904. However, we fumbled and Comstock, their end, picked up the ball in full running stride and took off for the goal. Reeds pulled in behind him, four yards back. Comstock was fast but so was Reeds and besides, he was thinking of that no score tradition. He caught Comstock from behind and pulled him down on our 4, and we held them for downs, making them wait three more years for their first touchdown against us.

In our first game of all time against Nebraska, Steihm's team beat us 12–9 at Lincoln. But Reeds's punts stranded them so deeply near their own goal that their drives had to go almost the full length of the field and we eventually stopped many of them. Reeds also pegged the first long forward passes we ever used, one to Billie Clark, our tackle, to set up our first touchdown. In the final minutes Reeds threw a long pass to Courtright, our half, that Courtright caught on Nebraska's 6, but had the bad luck to drop as he was tackled. Nebraska recovered, or we might have defeated them—and they had a wonderful team.

Reeds's final season was 1913. He was so good that Missouri refused to let us use him in our game at Missouri that year, alleging he had played against them in 1910. (They were mistaken. It was his brother, Artie.) However he played all the other games. Against Kansas he ran 28 yards to our first touchdown from long punt and bucked eight yards for our second as we won 21–7. After that game the *Daily Kansas*, the Kansas University school paper, wrote, "Oklahoma just walloped us.... Their greatest player came out of every scrimmage smiling and then went through us or around us for another gain. Well, we've no cause for bitterness and there's no use trying to stop lightning, you know." We had a mud game with Oklahoma A&M that year and won it 7–0 with Reeds plowing over for the only touchdown. Then came his final game, against a strong, undefeated Colorado team at Oklahoma City on the muddiest field I ever saw. All day Claude had punted on third down, wiping his kicking foot off on some fellow player's jersey. Early in the second quarter he did it again on third down and retreated. But instead of punting, he ran wide from long punt and cutting back a dozen times and switching the ball from one arm to another and stiff-arming, he ran 70 yards to a touchdown in his final game, kicking mud six feet high, and we won 14–3.

Claude operates a big farm today about 15 miles west of here near Newcastle, Oklahoma. He must be close to 66 or 67 years old now but still looks tall and lean as ever. After he graduated here, he coached very successfully for many years at Central State Teachers' College of Edmond, Oklahoma, about 40 miles north of Norman.

Sincerely yours,

Ben G. Owen
530 Elm
Norman, Oklahoma

CHECK SIGNALS? WHY, THAT'S SO EASY!

The first OU quarterback to earn All-American status, Jack Mitchell was also a great punt returner. He capped his career with the Sooners by being named MVP of the 1949 Sugar Bowl. Harold Keith penned this article on Mitchell at the end of the 1948 season for The Daily Oklahoman.

But Life of Quarterback Is No Snap, Mitchell Admits

Norman, Oklahoma, November 16—Jack Mitchell, Oklahoma psychology major, came out of the classroom with three books under his arm and a big quid of chewing gum in his mouth.

Fleeing the reporter, he tried to sidestep. But the crowded corridor was no broken field. So Jack Mitchell, the psychology major, had to admit he was Jack Mitchell, Oklahoma football quarterback, and consented to answer questions.

How come he always has time to call a play in the huddle, then come to the scrimmage line, look over the defense, check the original signal, and call a new play without getting caught by the 25-second rule?

"That's easy," Mitchell said. "We don't stay in the huddle long. Our line has a lot of hustle and team spirit. They're rarin' to go. They leap from our huddle to the scrimmage line, sometimes running over me en route. Usually we're standing at the scrimmage line with the play all called up, waiting for the referee to put the ball down, blow his whistle, and start the 25-second count."

How many times in each game did he check the signal called in the huddle?

"That depends on the opposition," says Mitchell. "If they haven't changed their defense, we don't check the signal at all. But if they change defenses, we'll probably check the signal, calling a new one to fit the new defense.

"We checked it four out of five times against Texas Christian because its tackles and linebackers shifted lots. We also checked lots against Nebraska. We were trying to send our plays away from Tom Novak, their roaming linebacker. He's tough."

What's the most fun in football for a quarterback?

"Outmaneuvering the opponents, if you can. It's fun catching a tackle out of position, thinking he's got the play stopped. Sometimes they outmaneuver you."

What hurts a quarterback's pride most of all?

"Not being able to score in the scoring zone. It's the quarterback's fault if his team can't punch the ball over after you get close to the goal. That's where you get beat."

Didn't he ever get hoarse shouting all those signals?

"You bet! At the Missouri-Oklahoma game here two weeks ago, the crowd roared so loud I had to turn around and yell the signals two or three times to each side of our line.

"In the Texas game, the Cotton Bowl turf was so dry and dusty, my throat was sore after the game. A quarterback has to get his voice in shape just like a singer. I used to go out in the country and practice hollering our charging signal."

How did it feel to run back a punt 70 yards to a touchdown against Missouri?

"Swell, but there ought to be some better way to spotlight the blockers. Myrie Greathouse, our fullback, threw the key block on that play. The Missouri end would have hit [Darrell] Royal and me just as we were handing off if Greathouse hadn't rolled him.

"Few of the 40,000 persons at the game saw Greathouse throw that block. All the newspapers missed it. That's not right. Fans don't realize that a lineman prides himself just as much on throwing a good block as a back does on making a good run.

"T formation centers ought to get more plugs, too. Pete Tillman, our center, does a great job keeping opposition linemen off the quarterback until the quarter can move out."

What does a quarterback like best to do after a game?

"I like a big malt and a hamburger at Eddy Davis's restaurant. Or we get together with the other married players and relax, or sit around and play bridge. We usually play the football game over, too."

Does a quarterback worry about his signals while he's at home?

"You bet. I worry all the time. Will the defensive linemen in the next game crosscharge or slant? Will their linebackers shoot the gap? My wife, Jeanne, also a psychology major at Oklahoma, helps rehearse me.

"She makes me review our best long yardage plays, our best short yardage plays, and our passing down stuff against all the different defenses. We're both worrying plenty about this battling Kansas team this week."

Meanwhile the Sooners put in some heavy-duty work Tuesday in preparation for the Kansas game in Lawrence Saturday.

Coach Bud Wilkinson sent his first and second stringers through a scrimmage against the scrubs but said he wasn't too well pleased with their performance.

The Sooners also stressed pass defense, operating against Kansas plays. Punting and punt returns rounded out the session.

Harold Keith, *The Daily Oklahoman*

VESSELS WINS HEISMAN TROPHY

The first Sooner to win the Heisman Trophy, Billy Vessels was also a two-time All-Conference selection. He rushed for 1,072 yards and scored 108 points in 1952. The Daily Oklahoman *ran Harold Keith's story on the player after Vessels won the prestigious trophy.*

Sooners Ace Voted Nation's Top Star

Norman, Oklahoma, November 25—Billy Vessels, Oklahoma's swift-cruising senior halfback from Cleveland, Oklahoma, has won the Heisman Memorial Trophy, college football's greatest individual award.

The honor came as a shock to Vessels.

"What? You're kidding! I didn't either! Gee ... I can hardly talk." That was his comment when he was notified in the Sooners dressing room before practice Tuesday that he had been voted the award that is presented annually to the most outstanding player in the country.

Harry H. Kennedy, chairman of the Heisman Trophy committee, made the announcement Tuesday from New York. Kennedy telephoned university president George L. Cross Monday to say that Vessels was running strongly and might win. Tuesday afternoon he again phoned to say that Vessels had won.

Vessels polled 98 firsts, 91 seconds, and 49 thirds for a grand total of 525 votes.

Vessels has scored 16 touchdowns and has one game left to play, against Oklahoma A&M on Saturday. He has rushed 960 yards and ranks second in the nation in that department.

Vessels is the first winner from the Big Seven conference.

Catlin 10th, Crowder 12th

Jack Scarbath, Maryland quarterback, was second with 367 votes and Paul Giel, Minnesota halfback, was third.

Coach Bud Wilkinson's Oklahoma team placed two other men in the top 12; center Tom Catlin finished 10th and quarterback Eddie Crowder 12th.

Donn Moomaw of UCLA was fourth in the poll, followed by Johnny Lattner of Notre Dame, Paul Cameron of UCLA, Jim Sears of Southern California, Don McAuliffe of Michigan State, Don Heinrich of Washington, Catlin, Leon Hardeman of Georgia Tech, and Crowder.

Nationwide Poll

The Heisman Trophy winner is determined by a national poll of America's sportswriters, sportscasters, and telecasters. It is awarded annually by the Downtown Athletic Club of New York.

John Heisman, for whom the trophy is named, lived from 1869 to 1936. He played football at Brown and Pennsylvania and for 37 years was coach of eight different colleges, including Pennsylvania, Georgia Tech, and Auburn, and was Rice Institute's first coach.

He was twice president of the American Football Coaches Association, one of the organizers of the original New York Touchdown Club, and its first president. He was also the first director of the Downtown New York Athletic Club, one of the oldest amateur athletic clubs in the country.

To Attend Dinner

Vessels, Coach Wilkinson, President Cross, and Governor Johnston Murray are all being invited to attend the dinner at the club December 2 when the award will be made. Wilkinson, as Vessels's coach, will speak.

The Oklahoma player will face a busy schedule on that day. At noon he will meet the New York press. At 4:00 PM he will meet the newsreel men. At 5:15 he will meet a group of high school All-Star football players. At 6:15 he will be guest of honor at a reception.

The awards dinner starts at 7:15. An awards ceremony at the gymnasium starts at 9:00, and at 10:15, New York time, he will again receive the award during a national radio broadcast. All of this will occur at the sponsoring club.

Previous winners of the Heisman Memorial Trophy are:

Jay Berwanger, Chicago
Larry Kelley, Yale
Clint Frank, Yale
Davey O'Brien, Texas Christian
Nile Kinnick, Iowa
Tom Harmon, Michigan
Bruce Smith, Minnesota

Frank Sinkwich, Georgia
Angelo Bertelli, Notre Dame
Leslie Horvath, Ohio State
Felix "Doc" Blanchard, Army
Glenn Davis, Army
John Lujack, Notre Dame
Doak Walker, Southern Methodist
Leon Hart, Notre Dame
Vic Janowicz, Ohio State
Dick Kazmaier, Princeton

Brian Bishop, *Sooners Illustrated*

PRODIGAL SON

Is there any larger legend from the annals of OU football than Joe Don Looney? The mythic-like running back played only one full season for the Sooners—no matter, his legacy endures. Looney's storied time at Oklahoma was profiled by Brian Bishop for Sooners Illustrated.

Joe Don Looney Still Leaves a Haunting Memory in Sooners Lore

"He was like something streaking across the sky. You see it once and you're not gonna forget about it. Joe Don could do everything on a football field; he could do anything with a football, including autograph it; he could do all the things little boys dream of doing in front of roaring and adoring crowds. He could—but he didn't want to. So he didn't."

—Bill Looney, Joe Don's uncle

In some ways the story of Joe Don Looney parallels a story in the Gospel of Luke about a brash, rebellious son who, upon barely reaching maturity, approaches his father and prematurely asks for his inheritance.

But while there are similarities, Looney's story is much more complicated.

Author Doug Looney (no relation) wrote in "The Greatest Player Who Never Was," his 1995 *Sporting News* piece on Looney, "He grew up wild as the Texas wind in Fort Worth, eventually wandered into an Oklahoma junior college, and subsequently transferred to the University of Oklahoma, where his star was born as an extraordinary running back. And then he became the first-round draft pick of the Giants. During those years in Norman and in the pros—between 1962 and 1969—he captured the nation's attention. Indeed, he had a stranglehold on the public's fascination. The 'finest football player ever' wasted it all."

Where did Joe Don come from, and why is a man who was perhaps the "most talented" remembered instead as one of the most exasperating, unique individuals in the history of sport?

It's both complicated and perplexing, but the short of it was that Joe Don Looney was born in 1942 as the first and only child of Don and Dorothy Looney of Fort Worth, Texas, who from almost the first day of their marriage did not see eye to eye on many issues, particularly those concerning success and social status.

Don had quite an impressive athletic résumé of his own, first as an All–Southwest Conference end at TCU and later as an All-Pro for the Philadelphia Eagles, where he led the NFL in reception yards in 1940 as a rookie. His second season, 1941, ended with the bombing of Pearl Harbor, when suddenly professional football was not very important, and Don joined the Army Air Corps, after a brief time with the navy.

After his military service in 1945, Don returned to the friendly confines of Tarrant County, where he purchased and operated a Gulf service station with a small house behind it. Much to the dismay of Dorothy, the Looney's would call the modest frame house home.

A service station owner was not exactly what Dorothy had expected when she and Don met during his days as a football star at TCU, and again when he was subsequently drafted by the Eagles, along with TCU star and 1938 Heisman winner Davey O'Brien. However the war took away some of Don's prime earning years and, in the days before lucrative network television contracts, professional football players, even All-Pro players, rarely made the kind of money that private business paid. Don had not been able to save a large nest egg from his short stint in professional football; the service station might not have been a status job, but he saw it as his best opportunity to make it as his own boss.

Don's dogged determination in his small business eventually did pay dividends. He was also an accomplished high school referee who rose quickly through the ranks to college ball and finally as an NFL referee.

A frequent customer of Looney's Gulf service station was Fort Worth oilman Ralph Lowe. Lowe, reputed to be a lover of "fast horses and fine women," also enjoyed wagering on sporting events. Although Lowe saw Looney as a hardworking young man, the fact that Don was now an NFL referee and former player could offer potential insight, and a competitive edge on NFL betting lines. Lowe offered Looney a job as his associate and advisor in public relations. Dorothy was ecstatic that she no longer needed to hide Don's profession from acquaintances and friends. He was now in the oil business, and she was going to see he made the most of the opportunities.

Regardless of the original intent of Don's hire, there is nothing to suggest that Looney ever knowingly supplied Lowe with any NFL information or that Lowe ever asked him to. Don's primary responsibility was to use his considerable charm to secure favorable drilling contracts for Lowe, and that he did.

As they prospered, Don had increased responsibilities in the West Texas fields around Midland, where he wanted to move the family in order to have more time at home. Dorothy steadfastly refused, as they were beginning to make headway by getting on all the right lists in Fort Worth, where her bridge parties were keeping her plugged into the proper social circles. The tension between the two continually ate away at Joe Don, who found communication with both parents complex and attention from either of them even more difficult.

Gradually Joe Don retreated to his bedroom, the sanctuary of many lonely children, where he became somewhat of a recluse and spent hours reading and listening to music. He made a few friends with other boys who found themselves in similar domestic situations, and together they explored unusual and strange books on bodybuilding, yoga, politics, mysticism, and all kinds of subjects considered extraordinary in the postwar '50s.

Before his sophomore year in high school, all parties involved were in favor of Joe Don leaving Fort Worth for boarding school. The family selected Admiral Farragut Academy in Florida, where Joe Don and his burgeoning disciplinary problems were relocated in 1957.

At Farragut, Joe Don played organized football for the first time. Although his distaste for authority waxed, young Looney did find some consolation in an atmosphere that accepted his growing interest in bodybuilding. But one year of this unlikely union was enough strain for both Looney and the Farragut administration, and in the summer he returned to Fort Worth, where he enrolled at Paschal High School.

However, in 1958 Texas high school rules prevented any transfer student from playing varsity in his first season after a transfer. Therefore, Looney was relegated to the "B" team, where he easily dominated as a result of natural ability, speed, and a self-induced, year-round training program that consisted of running and weight lifting. His accomplishments were not lost on Paschal coaches, whose expectations for the Panthers' '59 season soared with every "B" game exploit.

"We knew what we had. We were just waiting for him to get eligible," said Paschal coach Bill Allen.

In some ways his year at Farragut Academy only reinforced Looney's hypothesis that authority could be challenged without serious consequences. After all, he had managed to defy many of the rules at a military institution without expulsion, proving his theory that life without rules is possible.

When Looney returned to Fort Worth after his year of boarding school, any meaningful relationship between mom, dad, and son deteriorated even further. Don was still away from home the majority of the time and Dorothy was now accustomed to daily activities on her own. Joe Don reacted accordingly, setting up a refuge in the basement that included a weight room. There he could entertain friends, work out, and read in peace.

The anticipated '59 season, Joe Don's senior year, got off to a slow start when Looney elected to skip two-a-days, forcing Coach Allen to call Looney and request that he join the team.

"What's the point?" Looney theorized. "I'm in great shape and I know the plays."

That Looney "logic" would manifest itself several more times over the next decade, with similar results each time.

However, hindsight now indicates that the beginnings of Looney's bizarre behavior and anxious acts were often Joe Don's desperate attempts to make contact with his dad and penetrate a barrier between the two that was almost void of interaction. Although the target of the behavior would often change, the objective was attention. This pattern would repeat itself and magnify in intensity over the next 20 years.

Looney finally reported to the Panthers squad before the first game, but due to his boycott of two-a-days, Allen refused to make him first-team immediately, slowly moving him into a more prominent position. Although Looney eventually led the team to a successful season and a win over archrival Arlington Heights, his rather short high school career was not enough to incite any serious consideration from college recruiters.

It was time to choose a college, and Looney finally was successful at sending his dad a message that could not be ignored. Joe Don announced that he had decided to enroll at Texas. Don was livid. Finally there was communication between the two, as Don emphatically declared that he was not going to fund the tuition of any Longhorn.

Joe Don momentarily had the attention he craved. At least Don's emotional explosion indicated that he did care about something in Joe Don's life. A compromise of sorts was reached when Looney promised that if he were ever to play football, it would not be at Texas, but at TCU.

With that promise and a prayer, Joe Don headed to Austin in the fall of 1960 where Looney was rushed by Kappa Sig, considered to be the pinnacle of UT "cool" at the time. The Kappa Sigs moved Looney to the top of their rush chart when the good-looking freshman punched out a rival Fiji in front of the Phi Gamma Delta house. Unfortunately, Looney was learning that extreme behavior sometimes brought extreme rewards.

Looney quickly gained a reputation around UT and Austin for a variety of performances and deeds—not all of them good. On the bright side, Looney was asked by the Texas track coach to join the squad, and said that he was the finest natural runner that he'd ever seen. Looney was flattered, but worried that track might interfere with his escalating social life. However, joining the team would give him access to a rather large weight room, so Looney accepted.

But there were also allegations of destruction, threats, and disciplinary probation—enough so that wealthy and influential Kappa Sig alumni in Austin directed the fraternity to cut Looney loose before initiation. Although Looney was having the time of his life, it never occurred to him that he had to attend class, and five Fs and the Kappa Sig expulsion sealed his fate at Texas.

So Looney returned back home to TCU, where he finally rewarded Don with a stated intention of following in his footsteps and playing football for the Horned Frogs. However, neither father nor son was aware that a Southwest Conference rule, meant to discourage transferring within the conference, would bar him from playing at TCU for two years. So Joe Don, who was now convinced that playing football might actually give him the attention he sought, enrolled at Lawton's Cameron Junior College, where his academic exploits at Austin were ignored.

True to form, and testing the system, Looney was late for his first practice at Cameron. Instead of ignoring it, Aggie head coach Leroy Montgomery was fuming with this unknown talent and proceeded to dress him down in front of the squad. Surprisingly, Joe Don relished the moment. He knew Montgomery cared. After the coach stopped, Looney extended his hand: "Coach Montgomery—nice to meet you."

According to Joe Don, it was the beginning of the best relationship he ever had with a coach.

The Cameron squad was a perfect collection of misfits and malcontents, and Looney loved the attention and the camaraderie. His on-the-field exploits landed Cameron in the Junior Rose Bowl his sophomore season. No team from the Midwest had ever made the game, much less won it. The Aggie squad did so by defeating California's Bakersfield Junior College squad, 28–20, before a record crowd of 45,000. Joe Don noticed the attention he received from the press and the crowd and was hooked.

Oklahoma also noticed Looney. Jay O'Neal, former quarterback under Bud Wilkinson, was now one of only five assistants on the 1961 staff, and tells about recruiting Joe Don.

"We'd never heard of Joe Don Looney before the Junior Rose Bowl game. But when Cameron went out there and won it, we naturally were interested in how and why. I obtained some film and it wasn't hard to see a big back that could run faster than anyone on the field. He also could punt a football a mile high. We'd only gone 5–5 the year before, and believe me, we were looking for players."

Other schools noticed as well. USC, Alabama, Kentucky, and others immediately requested an audience. But it didn't matter. Looney had a secret dream that OU coaches were totally unaware of.

Oklahoma played the University of Texas on national television each fall. Joe Don figured that he could exorcise all of his life's demons and at the same time send a "How you like me now?" message to all of his friends and foes, if he were only allowed to introduce himself in a crimson uniform during the pregame buildup on national television as, "Joe Don Looney—Fort Worth, Texas."

O'Neal gives more insight on Looney's recruitment process.

"At the time, there were no scholarship limitations. So there was really no risk on our part. And, although I knew he was an intelligent kid, I honestly didn't think he'd make it. It was a long shot because his GPA was horrid due to that one semester at UT. I believe he had to have 19 hours of B or better in order to be eligible. Twelve units were about a semester's load, and 19 meant he'd also have to go to summer school. The odds were against him even showing up in Norman."

Looney told O'Neal and Cameron coach Montgomery that he was heading to Norman. Montgomery advised against it because Wilkinson had never recruited a junior college player before. When O'Neal told Looney that he'd have to really get serious in the classroom to even be eligible, Looney replied, "Don't worry, Coach. I'll make it."

O'Neal accepted the pledge and then told Looney to report to Norman on August 28. That would allow for two-a-days and 15 practices before the opener with Syracuse on September 22.

When Looney arrived in Norman, he was 6'1" and 205 pounds in a day where most backs were 20 pounds lighter.

"We thought he was a guard," one teammate said, "and were shocked when we learned that this guy was a back."

Joe Don was not greeted by Wilkinson, but only by a series of Bud's regimented instructions and signs of where to report at what time. Of course, this was not exactly the welcome that Looney longed for, and he declared that "no sign was going to tell him what to do."

Bud and Joe Don were at odds before ever setting eyes on one another.

The next insult was when Looney saw the first edition of the Sooners depth chart, released by Wilkinson four days before the opener. Looney was listed as third-team fullback even though he knew he was far better than those listed above him. After all, he had won every race when the squad was lined up and ran 40- and 60-yard sprints.

O'Neal explains, "Our offensive system was based on timing. No matter how big or fast you were, you had to get the timing between the quarterback and running backs down to perfection, or the offense just wouldn't work. Our quarterbacks had to learn the precise mannerisms and movements of each back. That took time. To think that any player could come in here and mesh with our quarterback after 15 practices was foolish.

"We also had different substitution rules. They were complicated, as football was moving from one-platoon football, where players went both ways. When Looney arrived, if you took a player out of a game on either side, generally he could not return for the rest of the quarter. So there was far more to it than 'who's the best' at any given position."

Apparently, Looney did not bother to learn the rules, or more likely, he simply chose to disregard them. But the bottom line was that Looney resented what he saw as Bud ignoring him, and it brought back many of the painful memories of relationships that he'd struggled through with his family.

All Sooners fans know what happened next. Every one of the 55,000 that were at Owen Field on September 22, 1962, can recall the moment, and millions of others not in attendance can as well.

Syracuse was ahead, 3–0, running the clock and driving for another score with less than three minutes left in the game. A stunning tackle by John Tatum forced a fumble and gave the Sooners life some 70 yards from the goal line. The distance looked more like 70 miles, as OU's offense had done little that day.

Looney, who had been sitting on the bench all day, suddenly jumped up and spoke his first-ever words to Wilkinson. "Put me in, Coach, and I'll win the SOB."

A stunned Wilkinson took Looney by the elbow and said, "Tell Monte [Deere] to give you the ball outside."

On his first carry, Looney gained a first down on a plunge up the middle. Then, with 2:07 remaining, Deere called "fullback sweep left" and, on his second carry as a Sooner, Looney ran to the outside, saw it blocked, and cut back inside, where he was surrounded by six Syracuse players. Somehow, he escaped and took off for a 60-yard touchdown and Oklahoma won, 7–3. A legend was born.

After the game, much like Barry Switzer 20 years later after a performance by a similar athletic enigma (Marcus Dupree), Bud was reluctant to discuss the performance, fearing that it would only be disruptive to his team. After several minutes the press began to question Wilkinson about the game-winning run.

"My view of the play was obscured. I'll have to see it on film before I'm able to respond," Wilkinson said.

The comment, quickly relayed to Joe Don, cut like a sword. He had come to Oklahoma because of the attention it would afford him, and now his coach was refusing to give him his due.

However, O'Neal says that behind closed doors all the coaches were indeed impressed.

"We sat around and agreed that it was one hell of a run," and they agreed that Looney would have to get more opportunities.

Later that season, Looney did get more opportunities and did not disappoint. Against Kansas, he uncorked a similar 61-yard run in the third quarter with OU trailing, 7–0. The Sooners won that game, 13–7.

He was also instrumental in other big wins as OU won the Big Eight and played Alabama in the Orange Bowl. Looney ended the season with 852 yards on just 137 carries. He led the nation in punting with a 43.4-yard average, had seven catches for 119 yards, and scored 10 touchdowns while garnering All-Conference and All-America honors.

Despite the spectacular on-field success, Coach Wilkinson and Looney were traveling apart at roughly the speed of light. Dorothy would send Joe Don every article or mention of OU and/or Wilkinson that was printed in the *Fort Worth Star-Telegram* or *The Dallas Morning News*. She encouraged him to stand up for himself—in hindsight, maybe not such good advice.

There was much speculation in 1963 that Wilkinson would run for political office. Looney, encouraged by Dorothy's not-so-subtle hints, would surmise that Wilkinson was being two-faced, asking the team for commitment, while at the same time considering abandonment. Of course, nothing that Wilkinson could have done would have helped. Looney was simply convinced that Wilkinson didn't like him and was determined to fight back.

For football coaches, there were certainly bigger distractions than Joe Don Looney.

"We were very busy in the off-season preparing for the upcoming spring and next year," said Jay O'Neal. "We weren't really aware of too many problems with him. During the season, things were pretty regimented and there's just very little time to even notice. But during the spring, we had no formal off-season program and idle time was probably not a good thing for Joe Don. I think he packed his bags at least once and was thinking about leaving in the spring. But things pretty well cooled down by year end.

"The next time I heard from Joe Don was in early August, when he called me and asked if he could report at 227," O'Neal said. "I believe we had given him a weight of 202. He's due to report in three weeks and here he's 25 pounds over! My first reaction was to tell him that 227 was too heavy. He wouldn't be able to run. Looney then told me, 'Coach, I think I may be faster.' I said, 'Joe Don, what have you been doing?'"

While most athletes worked during the summer to earn money for the upcoming school term, Looney, who was not hurting for money, had drifted down to Baton Rouge, Louisiana, to lift weights at Alvin Roy's gym. Among avid weight lifters, there were tales of amazing feats coming from disciples of Roy. Just a few years earlier, the LSU Tigers had won their first national championship with several Roy devotees, including Heisman Trophy winner Billy Cannon.

In fact, Looney had fudged on his weight when he called O'Neal in August. Instead of weighing 227, Joe Don actually left Baton Rouge clocking in at 235. Roy's gym was one of the first to introduce anabolic-androgenic steroids to athletics on a widespread scale. (Steroids were not illegal and most people did not consider them a health risk at the time.)

"We didn't think about drugs," said O'Neal. "We were pretty ignorant of those types of things, as weight training was in its infancy at the time and used by very few teams. All we knew is that Looney reported back looking like Superman. And when we lined them up and ran them, he still outran everyone."

One of his best friends, end John Flynn, confirms that Joe Don "went to Baton Rouge before his senior year and got all 'roided up. He got so big he couldn't receive. And he started arguing about everything."

Joe Don—his aggression more than likely fueled by behavior-changing steroids—was becoming a team problem. Wilkinson was still unaware of one of Looney's reasons for even coming to Norman—the chance to show up old enemies on national TV by announcing, "Joe Don Looney—Fort Worth, Texas."

So the final blow may have unsuspectingly come in the second week of the season as OU and number-one-ranked USC squared off in the L.A. Coliseum. The game was shown on national television and at the time it was customary for the network to allow each team to introduce its top 13 to be announced live, on camera, before kickoff. Joe Don's name was not on it.

Looney was incensed, and pouted, but still played well enough to score on a double reverse that beat Southern Cal, 17–12. During the contest wide receiver Lance Rentzel recalls that Joe Don told Wilkinson, "Take me out. My biorhythms are out of sync."

Looney then sat on the bench motionless. After quite a while, he jumped up and announced, "Coach, my biorhythms are fine. Put me in."

Bud did, and Looney ran "61 trap" for a touchdown.

Following USC, OU had a week off before their "Game of the Century," number-one-versus-number-two showdown with Texas. Looney, still sulking, decided to visit several old Cameron buddies who were playing at Tulsa. But Looney announced his plans to no one and was AWOL from the team meeting Sunday evening. Bud quickly moved to end the insubordination with a face-to-face meeting with Looney.

Neither party was completely satisfied, and the issue was left somewhat unresolved. But the bottom line was that Joe Don was increasingly unwilling to play defense, practice, listen, cooperate, or go to meetings. All he wanted to do—and did—was run with the ball, if his karma was right.

As the Cotton Bowl approached, perhaps Looney recognized that it would be his last chance to realize his "Joe Don Looney—Fort Worth, Texas" introduction dream on national television. Regardless of the reason, he seemed to play that day with little enthusiasm, gaining only four yards on six carries, as Texas defeated OU, 28–7.

That week Wilkinson informed his staff that Looney would be dismissed from the squad.

Jay O'Neal recalls the staff meeting.

"There was little discussion, but I think we all understood why. It was not a single incident, but the fact that regardless of his talent, his disruptive behavior was detrimental to the team. Bud did not discuss it with us beforehand—make no mistake, Bud ran the show. He probably talked it over with Gomer [Jones], but it was announced and then we proceeded on to the next item of business."

The dismissal was front-page headline news around the state. When the press demanded and pried for an explanation, Bud at first said it was by team vote, although none had been held. It was also suggested that a scuffle in practice with an assistant coach was the reason, although most discount that as a very minor and somewhat common incident. The excuses may not have been entirely true, but they were probably easier than retelling an entire litany of discretions.

> "The Giants thought that he was the greatest talent they ever had—but football is war without casualties. The necessary resolve, the willingness to follow orders, the esprit de corps, are the same in war and in football."
>
> —Frank "Pop" Ivy

Wilkinson may have given up on Joe Don, but he was still an attractive talent to professional football. Allie Sherman, head coach of the New York Giants, recognized his potential.

"He had it all. I mean all," said Sherman. "He was more than just size. He was more than just speed. He was wonderfully built big legs, huge torso, could deliver a blow. He had slashing, veering power, agility, acceleration. He had body control like [Walter] Payton—only with power. He could bust that first tackle, then go 14 to 24 yards more. He could catch the ball. He was bright. He had vision. There wasn't a single thing he didn't have."

The Giants made Looney their number one pick in the '64 draft, and he received a $40,000 signing bonus and a $25,000 salary. Almost immediately, Looney was making a name for himself off the field. During the first week of training camp, curfew was relaxed one evening and the team was allowed to enjoy several hours of freedom. Looney chose to remain in his room and read. The next evening an 11:00 PM curfew was in force, and Looney reported 10 minutes late only to find a note on his pillow instructing him to report for an audience with head coach Allie Sherman.

Looney immediately knocked on Sherman's door, where the coach tried to calmly explain the importance of team rules to his number one draft pick. After a mild talk, Sherman informed Looney that the transgression also carried a $50 fine.

"But Coach," Looney responded. "I was in my room all night last night while everyone else was out. Do I get a credit for that?"

Perplexed by this Looney logic, Sherman dismissed Joe Don and summoned quarterback and fellow Texan Y.A. Tittle—perhaps the foremost player in pro football at the time—to go down to Looney's room and point out that the rules were in the best interest of the team.

Tittle was accomplished at evading rushing defenders, but he was not prepared for what came next, as he explained to Joe Don that even he had to abide by curfew rules.

"Mr. Tittle," said Joe Don, "you mean they still check on you to make sure you're in bed?"

Y.A. replied, "Yes, they do."

Looney then asked, "You're 37 years old and have been in this league 17 years, and they do that?"

"Yes, they do."

"Mr. Tittle, you're 37 years old and have been in this league 17 years, and you still don't know when to go to bed?"

Tittle left Looney's room as perplexed as Sherman had been moments before, and returned to knock on Sherman's door. When Sherman opened the door, Tittle asked, "Coach, why do we have a curfew?"

From there it deteriorated, as Looney lasted all of 28 days with the Giants and was traded to the Colts, then the Lions, the Redskins, and finally, the Saints.

While with Detroit, Looney skipped a training-camp practice session, electing instead to stay in his dorm room. Lions assistant coach Joe Schmidt, who would later become head coach, thought it might help to show Joe Don a softer side, and he went to talk to Looney.

"You ought to come to practice," Schmidt said. "You're part of the team. You'll get fined."

"Joe, how long you've been doing this?" Looney asked. "Going to practice every day?"

"Fourteen years," Schmidt replied.

"Joe," Looney said, "you ought to take a day off once in a while."

Many similar stories were collected from each camp over the next six years.

Otto Graham coached Looney during his time with the Redskins with the same predictable results: disputes, confrontations, and mediocre performances.

"He was a strange individual," Graham said. "No one could communicate with him. I knew he was a questionable person to have on my team, but he was such a great talent."

Each of the five NFL coaches who had Joe Don thought he could handle him. Tom Fears, who was head coach of the '69 Saints, Looney's last stop, said, "Looney had more potential than anyone who ever played the game."

Dan Devine said of the two best kickoff returns he ever saw, one was by Gale Sayers, the other by Looney.

So was Joe Don the greatest ever?

Said Devine, "On occasion, he certainly did perform like it."

In an earlier interview with *Sooners Illustrated*, Looney was asked about stories that he might have been the greatest, had he played to his potential. Responded Joe Don, "In my life, I wasn't supposed to be a great football player. Obviously, it never happened. Something always came up."

Most agree Joe Don never liked the game much.

"He had more of a sandlot philosophy about football," said friend Roger Parker of Houston. "He just wanted to play and have fun. The further he went in football, the less fun he had."

Joe Don once told Parker, "The only value in football is fun. So when you play it for money, it loses its value."

Joe Don left football, briefly served in Vietnam, was discharged from the army, and literally traveled the world in search of himself and some sort of enlightenment for at least a decade. Outside of the NFL, Looney never had a job. His dad kept him going. He probably made $200,000 in the NFL, but it was spent sooner rather than later.

Roughly the decade between 1970 and 1980 was ruined by drug abuse in almost all stops, including Peru, New York, India, California, Mexico, and Texas. It included a good deal of time spent in Hong Kong, living abroad while preparing for a sail around the world with a boyhood friend, Gatlin Mitchell. It was here that he seriously took up yoga and quickly shed over 45 pounds in a fury of diet and enemas, then suddenly abandoned Mitchell, the boat, and his dream.

He also, of course, spent seven years following an Indian swami named Baba Muktananda, who was known as the "guru's guru." Looney served as a bodyguard for Baba and also kept Vijay, an elephant, in the remote village of Ganeshupuri, India.

When introduced to the United States in 1970, Baba Muktananda was still largely unknown. His Siddha Yoga meditation movement quickly took root in the fertile soil of American minds searching for something deeper than materialism.

But if materialism is what Looney and his peers were fleeing, they obviously overlooked, or ignored, some glaring inconsistencies in Baba's own life.

In eight short years, from 1970 to 1982, Muktananda's followers had built him 31 ashrams, or meditation centers, around the world. When crowds saw the guru step from a black limousine to a waiting Lear jet, it was clear to all but his most devoted followers that the diminutive, orange-robed Indian had become enlightened to American-style success.

Even Looney's father paid Baba $100 a month. The guru assigned Joe Don to take care of the elephant in order to teach Looney humility. The authority-hating Joe Don was totally devoted to Baba, who told him what to do every moment of every day.

Go figure.

Says Bill Looney, "You get out of the realm of the ordinary and defy the order of the day, people will remember you."

Presently, the elephant died and Joe Don said he was glad.

Later, in 1982, after allegations of a sex scandal became more than rumor, and Joe Don became somewhat disillusioned with the Swami, Baba died, and Looney returned to Alpine, Texas—remote and isolated, 70 miles north of the Mexican border. Here, 18 miles south of Alpine, in the shadows of Cathedral Mountain, he purchased 33 acres and constructed a strange geodesic dome house heated by solar power, with its water and electricity generated by a windmill.

But it was a different Joe Don.

Sometime in the early '80s, Looney was gradually able to free himself from the grip of drugs. Looney was able to admit that he'd tried many forms of mysticism and religion and had been quick to fall for frauds and charlatans. But somehow he considered it all a part of his general education and personal development, which allowed him to discard the excess of inherited baggage in the pursuit of a happiness that was custom-tailored to his own needs.

Slowly, Joe Don became more tolerant and began reconciling with family and friends. In Alpine, population 5,455, he befriended cowboys, misfits, and plain folks in and around the community. Not one person there had an unkind thing to say about him.

For the first time in his life he enjoyed doing ordinary things with ordinary people. He bought a motorcycle and enjoyed the feeling of freedom it afforded him. He followed high school football and the Sul Ross University women's basketball team. In 1983, Joe Don attended his first football alumni reunion at OU, and would also return in 1984 and again in 1987.

But foremost, Joe Don sought a relationship with his divorced parents, and his daughter Tara, born in 1968 during his brief marriage (1967–69) to Peggy Collins, whom he remained more or less dedicated to throughout his turbulent life and wanderings in the 1970s.

In 1988, Joe Don announced to both Don and Dorothy that he was going to build them a house on his property, where he expected them to reconcile and live. Surprisingly, his mother and dad did not object to the strange and tender request. And soon all three were working together, although not always in harmony, on the project, ultimately funded, of course, by Don's money.

September 24, 1988, was to be the annual running of the Lajitas Raft Race, a wild river race for homemade rafts run down the Rio Grande, about an hour south of Looney's home. Looney and several other locals built and entered their raft under the team name "Las Animales."

The race was scheduled to start at 9:00 AM and Joe Don and Las Animales teammate Tom Connor decided to ride their motorcycles down Highway 118 to the Rio Grande early that morning.

Joe Don overslept and the pair left Looney's home a bit late. They would have to step it up a bit in order to make the 9:00 AM start.

Somewhere along the way—about 10 miles north of Study Butte— Tom lost sight of Looney's motorcycle in his rearview mirror. It would be almost an hour before Joe Don's body was found, almost without a scratch and still wearing his helmet, lying under a mesquite bush about 50 yards off of 118.

Finally, Joe Don Looney, who had truly declared peace with the world, after 45 years, was at peace.

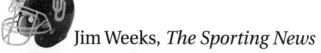

Jim Weeks, *The Sporting News*

PRIDE PROPELS OWENS, SOONERS' LINE-SMASHER

Nobody ran the ball harder or more often than Steve Owens, OU's second Heisman Trophy winner. The bruising back carried the ball 958 times in three seasons for 4,041 yards and 57 touchdowns for the Sooners. In addition to winning the Heisman, Owens was also named The Sporting News' *Player of the Year in 1969.*

Norman, Oklahoma, December 13—Steve Owens charged down the steep, red-carpeted ramp into Oklahoma's U-shaped football stadium.

No one cheered the man who was to be *The Sporting News'* Player of the Year.

It was Friday afternoon, and the Sooners were beginning a weekend ritual as much a part of playing football at OU as skinned elbows, praise for winning, and criticism for losing.

The 60,000 seats at Owen Field were not occupied, as they would be the next afternoon.

The powerful Owens and his teammates will work out just enough to get thoroughly warmed up and get the feel of things. Then they will board buses to spend the evening in Oklahoma City.

"It's really sort of a big deal," said Owens of the evening away from the University of Oklahoma campus. "You get away from all the activities and you have a chance to think about the next day."

The day of the game, Owens will wake up about 8:30 and Mike Harper, Sooners fullback and his Friday-night roommate for the last two years, will get the morning paper.

"We like to find out how Miami and Jenks did," Owens said, referring to the high schools where he and Harper played.

"I really started thinking about coming to OU when I was working in a shoe store in Miami in 1962," Owens said, recalling that he had heard much about Sooners greats, but really hadn't followed OU until that year.

"I remember we had a radio on in the store and Joe Don Looney ran 60 yards for a touchdown to win the Syracuse game. I wanted to be like him."

In some ways, two people never have been so much alike and yet so different. Few people question either's skill as a college running back. But Looney may be best remembered for the controversy surrounding his dismissal from the team the year after that big play. Owens will be remembered as the greatest inside runner in OU's proud history.

Harper a Super Blocker

Harper, a baby-faced, humorous, three-year starter, has contributed to Owens's feats. The Jenks senior received more attention as a blocker than many college backs receive scoring touchdowns. "Steve's going to give me half of the Heisman Trophy," Harper said with a big smile.

Soon the team will eat breakfast, although Owens will eat only about one-third of his prime steak. "I usually go into a game weighing about 205 pounds. I like to feel hungry. What do they say? 'A hungry bear always fights better.'

"You really get the feel of things going back into Norman," said Owens, watching the thousands of fans wending their way to the stadium.

Owens has been building up the "feel of things" for a week.

"I start thinking on Sunday about the team we're going to play," he said. "Then Monday afternoon we hear the scouting report and I start getting emotionally ready. I look at films all week, sometimes even take them home at night.

"One of the main things I study is their personnel and what they do. I look for their tendencies on a third down and one yard. It helps me to know which way and how to cut on a certain situation."

Then the game was on and Owens needed all the strength, savvy, and determination he had mustered during the last week and the years of preparation.

"This year they keyed more on me and our running game," he said. But he gained 1,523 yards rushing to wrap up the NCAA title and wound up his college career with 3,867 yards.

Steve Takes a Battering

"It was really a strain on everyone. They put nine guys up there and there weren't blockers for everyone. I got hit by two or three guys on every play," said Owens, who carried the ball nearly 30 times a game this season, including 55 times in his final appearance, and broke the national single-game and career records for such things.

"You come out with cuts and bruises, and that's all right because I think I hand some out, too. I expect to get hit—that's the way football is. And I really don't mind it as long as I'm able to defend myself," he said.

Owens cradles the football in both hands almost as though he were carrying a small child. Another of his outstanding traits is that he hardly ever fumbles. He charges into the mass of grunting, battling players, knocking people aside, hurdling, twisting, lunging, diving for more yardage.

"I got hit more and more after I was down this year. I looked out for it, but there's no way to protect yourself when you're down. My back really took a beating from those helmets. But I expected it."

Owens carried the ball more than 700 times on rushing plays in his college career and never missed a game.

"I got tired and I got beat up, but I never considered quitting. When my leg was hurt against Wisconsin, I thought the pain was a little sharper than usual, but after I got up and kept playing, it didn't bother me. After the game, I couldn't even walk to the bus.

"I guess I shouldn't have played the next week against Pittsburgh. Coach Fairbanks said it was up to me. I guess I had too much pride not to play, but I couldn't do the things I normally do." He gained only 104 yards and scored only three touchdowns, and *Sports Illustrated* named him national back of the week.

Owens has gained 100 or more yards in each of 18 straight games since the opening contest of his junior season. Each week he set a national mark for consecutive games over 100 yards.

He nearly missed the mark against Colorado this season, getting over the 100 total only on the next to the last play of the game and scoring a touchdown on the final play. His run was finally stopped at 71 yards by Nebraska.

"The other guys on the team were really aware of the 100-yard record," Steve said. "It didn't mean that much to me. I think you can gain 50 yards and play a great game. But they wanted me to set a record that wouldn't be broken. It became an obsession with them."

For a player who was the center of publicity even during his sophomore season, Owens was remarkably popular and respected by his teammates.

He was one of the OU cocaptains this season and didn't take the honor or the publicity lightly.

"Steve Owens is a great football player because he goes 100 percent in every practice," said OU offensive coach Barry Switzer. "He learns a little bit every day and becomes a little bit better."

"Personal pride is my driving force," Owens said. "I want to be a better football player. I'm not just competing with myself. If I gain 180 yards this week, I want to gain 200 the next week.

"I have an obligation to the other players, too. If they can see that I can joke around in practice, why shouldn't they? There are always people not on the team that are ready to criticize people in my position. I don't want them to have a chance to say anything bad about me.

"I thought I was a better football player this year. We had Roy Bell [sophomore halfback] going on sweeps and I had to block. I never had to block before."

Sooners coach Chuck Fairbanks is not the type to call players *super* or *great*. But he almost slips when talking about Owens.

"Owens always plays a great game," Fairbanks said early this season. "What can you say that hasn't already been said about him?"

Then after the Sooners bowed to Kansas State, 59–21, in a shocking upset that shook the Big Eight Conference to its foundation, Fairbanks found out what else can be said.

He Never Quits Trying

"I never have seen a player try so hard on every play," Fairbanks said after viewing the game films. "He's a little bit better player than I thought he was."

The next week, Owens carried the ball 53 times for 248 yards and four touchdowns in OU's 37–14 win over Iowa State.

Owens, twice Big Eight Conference scoring and rushing leader and holder of eight conference and 14 OU records, tries to keep things in perspective.

Before he won the Heisman Trophy, Steve said: "Think of the small percentage of players who are being considered. That's a great honor.

"It hurts when people don't believe me when I say I would trade the Heisman Trophy for a 10–1 or 9–1 season."

After a game, Owens will visit with prospective recruits. He doesn't look like a hero. He is tired. He looks like he shaved with a broken bottle, his lower lip is nearly twice its normal size, and his back hurts.

He and his wife, Barbara, will seek the sometimes quiet of their apartment, only to find 35 well-wishers there rehashing the game. Owens may not even know some of them.

The Owenses have been married three years and it hasn't been easy. There's little or no financial help from home. Barbara works at a local bank.

Owens is now more concerned about Barbara's new set of china than his aching back or a chance to relax. "We saved a long time to get that," he said.

Owens's unlisted telephone number is called about as often as his number on the field. "We get more calls than ever now," he said.

But Owens is beginning to realize that such things go with being a heralded athlete. He's not really complaining

"I wouldn't trade my four years at OU for anything. OU football has done more for me than I ever could do for it."

Berry Tramel, *The Daily Oklahoman*

LITTLE BIG MAN

He might have finished second in the Heisman Trophy voting to Nebraska's Johnny Rodgers, but Greg Pruitt was second to none during his career at Oklahoma. The Sooners mighty mite was a two-time All-American, running for 3,188 yards and scoring 41 touchdowns. Berry Tramel wrote the following article on Pruitt in 1999.

OU's Pruitt in a Class by Himself

The starting flanker was moved to second-team halfback and told to consider it career enhancement.

Greg Pruitt wasn't buying it.

"I remember very clearly trying to figure out how I was going to get the ball more on the bench," Pruitt said.

September 1970, and the Oklahoma Sooners had just abandoned the veer for the wishbone. Flankers were needed elsewhere. Pruitt's skilled hands and swift legs were of little use in an offense that treated wide receiver like a penal colony.

All of which explains why Pruitt's cell phone rang Friday, heralding the news that the 47-year-old mighty mite had just been voted into the College Football Hall of Fame.

The most terrifying element in the most terrifying offense ever to hit college football finally will be enshrined.

"I guess there was a time I thought I had the kind of career that would get me in," Pruitt said. "I was pretty confident that would happen. I had a time frame in mind. That time frame came and went."

That's how Pruitt ran in 1971. He came and went. He was the original hello/good-bye halfback at OU. In that remarkable '71 season Pruitt gained 1,665 yards on 178 carries. Those were the days before calculators, but legend has it that's a 9.4 yards-per-carry average.

The guy who came to Oklahoma as a half-pint wide receiver left it as a halfback legend. In the most remarkable four-game stretch in OU history—against Southern Cal, Texas, a Colorado team that finished number three in the nation, and Kansas State—Pruitt gained 905 yards on 69 carries.

Maybe I'm missing something, but it seems Pruitt's legend has faded over time. His remarkable numbers written off as products of clueless defenses. His image reduced to a mere speedster running track meets in open field.

Which is rubbish. He was fast and tough and skilled. Pruitt was the rarest of players: an underrated superstar. Steve Owens broke records. Joe Washington swiped breaths. Billy Sims won a Heisman and should have won another. Marcus Dupree was a bionic man-child.

None were better than Pruitt. He dazzled as a Sooner, then dazzled as a pro. In 12 NFL seasons, mostly as a Cleveland Brown, he further proved his worth. Of all the OU running backs, Pruitt was the best on the planet's highest level.

Pruitt was in town Monday to host his second annual celebrity golf tournament for the Legacy, a grief center for children in downtown Oklahoma City. He commutes between his Cleveland home and his Houston sports agency business, but he was drawn back to Oklahoma by the 1996 bombing and last year lent his support to the Legacy.

"I do it for my favorite audience, which is kids," he said.

Pruitt was a kid himself in 1969, when he came to Norman. Barry Switzer swears Pruitt was 5'6", 150 pounds the first time the coach saw his future star.

Switzer was skeptical: "For everyone who turns out to be Greg Pruitt, there are thousands of little, quick guys who can't play."

Pruitt could play. At a recruiting workout, Pruitt caught passes from future teammate Jack Mildren, and head coach Chuck Fairbanks asked offensive coordinator Switzer for a report.

"I think he's better than Eddie Hinton," Switzer said, which remains the highest praise a Sooners pass catcher can receive.

Pruitt passes out the praise himself.

He calls Mildren the best wishbone quarterback of them all. A coach on the field. A guy who took hits all game long and couldn't be intimidated. An innovator.

To wit, Pruitt recalls all the times Mildren cut upfield for substantial yardage, then pitched the ball to a trailing halfback. He asks how often we saw that after Mildren, and the answer is: not much.

Pruitt also lauds Switzer, who in 1970 convinced Fairbanks to switch to the 'bone, which only shook college football for the next 20 years.

To those who still claim Switzer was merely a recruiter and not a coach, Pruitt offers a story.

In '72, against Oregon or Utah State (Pruitt's memory is fuzzy), the Sooners encountered an option-stopping play for the first time.

The cornerback came across the line, went directly for the trailing halfback, and tackled the man awaiting a pitch.

At the next timeout, Switzer immediately shifted gears. The next time, he told the blocking halfback, slow up and wait for a pitch from Mildren. A pitch to the blocking back was a weird twist, and sure enough, the next time Pruitt was bushwhacked, he lay on the ground laughing as a teammate dashed downfield for a long gain.

Those Sooners, Pruitt swears, were well-drilled and well-coached. And well-led.

Pruitt's elation at the Hall of Fame news was tempered by the knowledge that Switzer, for the first time, was eligible but not inducted.

Switzer never was Pruitt's head coach, but like many players from the late '60s and early '70s, Pruitt is devoutly committed to him anyway.

Pruitt said when he came to OU from Houston, "I was a hard guy to get along with; Switzer managed to make me see the light."

Switzer has no reputation as a disciplinarian, but Pruitt disputes the myth. Switzer gave Pruitt an attitude adjustment—not through screaming, but through caring.

"Some coaches never get close with their players," Pruitt said. Switzer did, and it worked for hundreds of Sooners, Pruitt among them.

Back to that 1970 season. Pruitt was a benchwarmer the first three games of the wishbone era, getting only eight carries.

But then he scored the winning two-point conversion in a victory over Iowa State. And followed with a three-touchdown game against Missouri. Pruitt was back in the starting lineup.

A splendid trivia question: What halfback started ahead of Pruitt at OU? Everett Marshall, who was a fine player.

But no Greg Pruitt.

Few were.

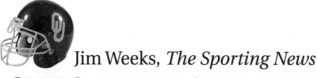 Jim Weeks, *The Sporting News*

SIMS AND LOTT MEAN LOTS OF WINS FOR SOONERS

The heart and soul of the Sooners wishbone offense in the late 1970s, 1978 Heisman Trophy winner Billy Sims and his quarterback, Thomas Lott, piled up the yardage and the wins for Oklahoma. Sims was the third Sooner and just the sixth junior to win the prestigious award. The Sporting News *ran Jim Weeks's article on the two stars.*

Norman, Oklahoma—They say Thomas Lott can't pass and Billy Sims shouldn't be flying.

Nevertheless, when it comes to football, you're doing fine, Oklahoma.

With senior quarterback Lott operating the wishbone magic to near perfection and junior halfback Sims providing explosive running, the Sooners may be headed for another Big Eight Conference championship and even the mythical national championship.

Lott and Sims are the keys to another powerful Oklahoma offense. And they get plenty of help from a German-born soccer-style place-kicker and a defense made up of an unusual combination of super-stars and former offensive backs.

The Sooners appear to be on another collision course with Nebraska in the matchup that seems to settle the Big Eight Conference championship each year.

Already Oklahoma has defeated four teams that have been ranked in the nation's top 20 this season.

And Sims, who has averaged more than seven yards a carry and rushed for more than 100 yards in every game except one, has become one of the leading candidates for the coveted Heisman Trophy.

That's not surprising to those who follow Oklahoma football.

Four years ago, Sims was the object of one of the hottest recruiting battles in this part of the country when he came out of tiny Hooks, Texas, as the second-ranked rusher in Texas high school history.

But Sims played behind All-American Joe Washington as a freshman in 1975. And the next two years he was hampered by injuries. In fact, in 1976, Sims played in only one game and gained another year of eligibility when the Big Eight ruled him a hardship case.

Sims gained the reputation as a flier because he likes to leap head-first over the line near the goal line and even hurdle opponents anywhere they can be found. He says he uses techniques learned in gymnastics classes in elementary school in St. Louis before he ever started playing football.

OU coach Barry Switzer grounded Sims after six games this season—that is, told him to stay on the ground because his flying act was too dangerous.

Sims combines speed and a darting running technique with the power to break tackles, although he is only 6'0" and weighs 205 pounds.

Sims is Oklahoma's first back to rush for 1,000 yards in one season since Washington did it in 1974, and he broke the Sooners one-season rushing record of 1,665 yards, set by Greg Pruitt in 1971. His total for eight games this year is 1,176 yards.

Oklahoma even installed the I formation last spring to supplement its wishbone attack. Often in the wishbone, the play of the defense will determine which Oklahoma back carries the ball. But with Sims at tailback in the I formation, Oklahoma can be sure to get him the ball when it wants.

However, the I has been used sparingly this season.

But the most valuable player in Oklahoma's attack is Lott, a powerful 5'11", 205-pounder who makes the wishbone work.

Lott is the first Oklahoma quarterback to read the wishbone since Jack Mildren left in 1971. That means the quarterback reads what the defensive reaction is on the option play. He has the option of handing off to the fullback or keeping the ball himself. If he keeps the ball, the quarterback then has the option of pitching to a trailing halfback or keeping the ball.

Switzer calls Lott the best wishbone quarterback in Oklahoma history.

And Lott's value was painfully evident in two games this season. He missed the Kansas game because of a sprained ankle suffered in Oklahoma's victory over Texas, and the Sooners escaped with a 17–16 win over the Jayhawks. That was far below their average of 40 points a game.

Then Lott was hurt in the second half of the Iowa State game the next week. After Lott left the game, Oklahoma got ball possession in Iowa State territory four times and came away with only one touchdown.

But being hurt is one of the disadvantages faced by wishbone quarterbacks because they carry the ball so much. And Lott is convinced he will have to play the rest of the season with a tender ankle.

Oklahoma has tried to improve its image as a passing team this season. The Sooners attempted only 68 passes during the entire 1977 season. But Switzer maintains it's not the number of pass attempts but the number of completions that counts.

And Oklahoma led the Big Eight Conference in touchdown passes in 1977 with eight.

But Oklahoma is passing more often this season in order to open up its running game.

Lott has completed only about one-third of his passes this season, but he already has equaled his touchdown pass total of 1977 with five.

Lott was the center of a minor controversy following Oklahoma's surprising loss to Arkansas in the Orange Bowl last season.

He wears a bandana to protect his short Afro hairstyle when he wears his football helmet. In fact Lott has a collection of 200 bandanas, many sent to him by admiring fans. But a few not-so-admiring fans criticized Lott for the practice after the bowl loss.

He didn't wear the bandanas in practice last spring but decided during the summer that anyone who thought wearing a bandana could determine the outcome of a football game wasn't much of a fan anyway.

So Lott wears his colorful bandanas this year, usually selecting the colors of the opposing team for use in games.

Sims, Lott, fullback Kenny King, and halfbacks David Overstreet and Jimmy Rogers make up what Switzer calls Oklahoma's best backfield ever.

King, who at 205 pounds is light for a fullback, provides the quickness and potential long gain Switzer wants at the position. In fact King was a halfback in high school. That's where the offensive staff wanted to play King. But Switzer insisted King be tried at fullback.

As a sophomore he led the Sooners in rushing with 791 yards and 5.6 yards a carry in 1976. But he has been in and out of the lineup because of injuries the last two years.

Senior guard Greg Roberts, who made the Football News All-America team in 1977, is the leader of a big offensive line. Switzer claims Roberts will be the first offensive lineman selected in the National Football League draft next year.

And the Oklahoma coach said Roberts's play against Texas this year was the best by an offensive lineman in Switzer's 13 years as a Sooners coach.

Ironically, a freak accident during the summer in which Paul Tabor, the starting center in 1977, suffered a badly cut hand was turned to Oklahoma's advantage.

Tabor, who had taken over the starting assignment when 1976 starter Jody Farthing was injured, wasn't expected to be able to center the ball until midseason. And Farthing had decided that he would not play this year.

But following Tabor's accident, Farthing, who had remained in school, asked Switzer to take him back on the team. Now Farthing is starting at center and Tabor at guard and the offensive line is stronger than anticipated.

Three Oklahoma defensive players were first-team All-America selections in 1977: linebacker Daryl Hunt, nose guard Reggie Kinlaw, and linebacker George Cumby as a sophomore.

Following the 1977 Orange Bowl victory over Michigan, Switzer predicted Kinlaw, who was a sophomore reserve at the time, would be Oklahoma's next All-American lineman.

The 220-pound Hunt is a punishing tackler who has started since the third game of his freshman year in 1975.

"Daryl Hunt wants anyone who even sees him in practice to go away knowing they have seen the best linebacker in the country," said defensive coordinator Rex Norris of the intent senior.

Cumby was moved from fullback to linebacker last year when it was obvious Oklahoma needed more speed at the position. And Oklahoma's coaches were uncertain whether Hunt would recover from knee surgery.

Hunt did recover and Cumby's performances surpassed even the most optimistic expectations of Oklahoma's coaches. Thus, the Sooners had the rare situation of having two All-American linebackers in the same season.

But Cumby's change from the offensive backfield to defense is far from unusual with this team. For one thing, Switzer likes to recruit as many offensive backs as he can. He claims you can't have too many of them. However, Oklahoma's opponents probably figure the Sooners do.

Safety Darrol Ray, cornerback Jay Jimerson, and end Bruce Taton, all starters, played quarterback as freshmen at Oklahoma. Starting end Reggie Mathis was a tight end on offense for two years. And starting tackle John Goodman and end Barry Burget, who started some games at end last season, were running backs in high school.

Thus, it is not surprising that one of the major strengths of Oklahoma's defense is its speed.

For example, Goodman is 6'5" and weighs 240 pounds, but he ran the 40-yard dash in 4.6 seconds—backfield speed—as a freshman. He has gained 40 pounds since then, but claims he has retained his speed.

And Cumby, who was named the Big Eight Defensive Player of the Year last season, once was described as making tackles on the field in places most linebackers never see.

The Sooners defense has been impressive in crucial games this season. But Switzer believes the Sooners aren't physically strong enough to be a great defensive team. And Oklahoma has lost both its starting safeties for the season.

Bud Hebert had not recovered enough from knee surgery to play this season. And Sherwood Taylor suffered a neck injury in practice the week of the Texas game.

That meant Ray and Mike Babb had to be moved from cornerbacks to safeties because the second-team safeties were freshmen.

Oklahoma coaches call the 6'2", 210-pound Ray the best athlete on the defensive team and he responded to his position change by intercepting five passes in Oklahoma's first five games.

Even so, by the end of the season the Sooners may prove to have as good a defensive team as there is in the Big Eight Conference this year. But the conference has not had an overwhelming defensive unit in the last couple of seasons.

Place-kicker Uwe von Schamann is a boost to both the Oklahoma offense and defense.

Switzer likes Oklahoma to kick off to open games because von Schamann can kick the ball into the end zone, forcing the opponent to start on its own 20-yard line. The idea is to stop the opposition there and get the ball near midfield.

The theory has been successful, as Oklahoma scored on its first offensive series in its first five games this season.

Von Schamann, who kicked a 41-yard field goal in the closing seconds of Oklahoma's 29–28 victory over Ohio State last season, holds most of the Sooners kick scoring records. And he already is among the top 10 scorers in Oklahoma history, with all his points coming from field goals or extra points.

Through the Kansas State game, von Schamann had kicked 111 extra points in a row, an NCAA record.

The Sooners also establish another NCAA record each time they score in a game. They have scored in 139 straight games through the Kansas State contest.

And even though Lott can't pass like Slingin' Sammy Baugh and Sims may be grounded in a way, the Sooners seem likely to extend that record.

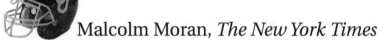

Malcolm Moran, *The New York Times*

BOSWORTH: GETTING BETTER MEANS GETTING TOUGHER

A two-time consensus All-American, Brian Bosworth set the OU record for tackles in a game with the staggering total of 22 against Miami in 1986. The only player ever to win the Butkus Award (presented to the nation's top linebacker) twice, the Boz was eventually kicked off the team for steroid use. This profile of the brash, sometimes outrageous linebacker ran in The New York Times *in 1999, before his final season at Oklahoma.*

He had quickly become a leader of a defensive unit at the University of Oklahoma that had pushed, shoved, bullied, talked, fought, and, above all, played its way to a ranking atop the national college football polls. As a sophomore last season, Brian Bosworth won the Butkus Award as the outstanding linebacker in the nation. He forged a hairstyling statement rarely seen under football helmets: flat (and yellow) on top, close-cropped on the sides, tail in the back: the Boz.

He helped defeat the University of Texas, an achievement that gave Brian Bosworth even more pleasure than disclosing, in advance, how he would help defeat the University of Texas. Yet some time after the convincing Orange Bowl victory over Penn State that permitted the Sooners to claim a sixth national championship, Bosworth felt a sense of imperfection. He discovered that feeling as he watched films of the games.

"Last year I didn't think I tackled hard enough," he said. "I didn't think I hit people hard enough. I wanted to be more agile, more flexible. I was looking for something that would give me an edge."

Members of the Big Eight Conference, plus those who play with the eyes of Texas upon them, plus others from Miami to UCLA, might be interested in knowing that the Boz studied karate. He became a green belt. He worked two hours a day, three times a week, in a karate

78

studio here, in addition to his weight lifting, his summer-school schedule, and his running routine. His regimen would go for much of the day and last until after 9:00 PM.

Can there be a ball carrier alive who would suggest that Brian Bosworth did not use maximum force last season?

"He's just giving you conversation," said Barry Switzer, the Oklahoma head coach, about Bosworth's perceived imperfection. "He's a machine. He's the ultimate machine."

If his coach is right, Bosworth is seeking to improve upon the ultimate. He remains 6'2", but at first glance, even in T-shirt and shorts, he appears larger than he did on New Year's night. Bosworth's weight, which dropped slightly under 230 at the end of last season, increased to 248 before the start of practice.

He worked to find greater power in his legs and with the movement of his hips. "We have to learn how to break stuff," he said. "Cinder blocks and boards and stuff like that. In order to do that, you have to do it in a quick and precise manner."

Throughout Bosworth's two seasons he has developed a reputation for quickly correcting something he thinks has gone wrong. If a game has started and Bosworth decides he or his teammates are listless, his manner is very quick.

"Whatever gets the motor started," Bosworth said quietly. "Whatever picks you up. If it's a fight the first play of the game, if you have to instigate it to get it going, that's what it takes. I've had to do that several times. I'll walk on the field, and just don't feel right. If I need something to get me going, I'll get in somebody's face and start a fight with them. All of a sudden, I guess I'm in a good mood."

At the highest levels of the college game, some survive with the use of a fury manufactured by blind rage, while others call upon an ability to make clinical observations amid the madness. Bosworth has excelled by combining the two seemingly contradictory processes.

He can use a powerful body to produce the necessary level of violence to impose his will and yet retain the control needed to make intelligent decisions. He can keep his balance on that line that separates crazed aggression and rational thought. "It's his intensity level," Switzer said. "His emotional level. His ability to psych himself up to play with such a violent attitude."

Bosworth's words and his actions have made him the focal point since his first game against Texas, a week when players—especially young players—are expected to keep their lips zipped. Bosworth, who grew up in suburban Dallas, was eager to offer his feelings about the University of Texas, its fans, Coach Fred Akers, and anyone who had ever worn burnt orange. His maturity has left Bosworth with a hint of diplomacy, but his feelings have not changed.

"When you sign that letter, you sign that letter to play Texas," Bosworth said before the start of practice recently. "When you sign that letter of intent to play here, your first obligation is to play and beat Texas. That's your first goal." "Of anything?" he was asked. "Of anything," he said.

"I've never liked the way they play, the way they come out with those bells, thinking they're God's gift to college football. It's a feeling I get. And it's not necessarily the players. The players are going to do what's asked of them. It's the coach. I just didn't like the way Coach Akers approached me, like this is it. This is Texas football and you've got to like it. It's God given. If you don't like it, you're a Communist."

Bosworth seemed to know what he was doing. "People love to hate Oklahoma," he said. "I guess that falls in the same category of people love to hate me, especially in Texas. That kind of lights my fire a little bit. That's fine. I'd rather have people hate me. You don't keep an angry dog down. You better keep away from him before he bites you. I played the same way in high school."

In the 1982 season, Bosworth's senior year, the football team at MacArthur High School in Irving lost eight of its 10 games. "But I still talked," he said. "We normally got beat up, but I always got a few good shots in there on somebody."

The experience shaped his outlook. After enduring that much losing, he just wanted to win. After missing out on individual honors that usually go to those on successful teams, he was more interested in just getting a chance.

"I didn't know a whole lot about the coaching staff," Bosworth said. "Didn't know anything about it when I signed. I just wanted to play for a mystique, somebody, something who knew they were good year in and year out. Texas can never say that. They were always close but they were never there. Oklahoma was always there."

At the same time, however, he wondered if he belonged. Now that the linebacker has developed his own mystique, with the hair, the "44" earring in his left earlobe, the Butkus Award, and the Heisman Trophy candidacy the school has chosen to promote; now that he weighs nearly 250 pounds and can still consistently run 40 yards in 4.5 seconds, according to Switzer, it is difficult to imagine a time when Brian Bosworth was not sure if he was good enough.

"I knew he would be a good player," Switzer said. "I didn't know he'd be 250 pounds and run 4.5. You couldn't envision that."

"Anybody that could sit here and say they knew he was going to be a great player is crazy," said Gary Gibbs, the defensive coordinator. "They're telling you that after the fact."

Bosworth remembered the uncertainty when he entered Switzer's office during his recruiting visit. "I questioned myself at the end of my senior year," he said. "I questioned my ability. I sat down and asked him: 'Now, Coach, why do you want me here? Why recruit me so hard when you can get another linebacker that's more well known?' He just said: 'I want you here. I think you're a good player. I want you to help me out somewhere down the line.'"

It was hard for Bosworth to believe what he was hearing.

"Who was I to question the greatest college football coach?" he said. "I can't say: 'Coach, I don't believe you. You're cracked.' He must know what he's doing."

"The only thing he promised me when I came for my recruiting trip was the publicity," Bosworth said. "He said: 'If you deserve the publicity, I'll make sure you get it. If you don't deserve it, then you won't get it. You'll get everything you deserve playing here, and I'll always be here for you.' I took that as a promise from him. He's always done me good."

Bosworth weighed 210 pounds when he arrived. His light brown hair was parted on the right. His eyes were wide. His freshman picture showed a face any parent would welcome at the front door. He ran 40 yards in 4.6 seconds, sometimes more. He did not play that first year.

At the end of the 1983 season, the year Bosworth was redshirted, the Sooners played their last game, at Hawaii. They had lost to Ohio State, Texas, and Nebraska. They had been shut out by Missouri. There had been discipline problems. They had lost Marcus Dupree, their most talented running back, who had suddenly decided to go home to Philadelphia, Mississippi. One morning at breakfast in Hawaii, Bosworth was sitting by himself when he saw Switzer approach. Recalled Bosworth: "He sat down and he said, 'Brian, next year I'm going to need you to play like a senior. Not a freshman. A senior.'"

By the next year, his second at Oklahoma but his freshman season, Bosworth's public feelings about Texas made him the most outspoken member of the team. The attention overshadowed his play—which included an important fourth-down tackle in the 15–15 tie with the Longhorns—and the adjustment to his new life.

"When I came up here, I was thrust into this society of fast life, fast pace, do it at your own risk but do it anyway because peer pressure makes you do it," Bosworth said. "You've got to make new friends, and you find out your new friends do things you're not used to.

"The last year, I just got into the wrong crowd. I always had a strong opinion about drugs. I said, thanks, no. I'll go out and have a good time on my own, but I don't need to spend $200 just to have a good time. I can sit right here and still remember tomorrow what I did last night.

"As time went on, the people I hung around with said: 'Is he really like that? Is he a phony? What's up?' That was actually said to me. I said, 'That's it.'"

In his second year in college, Bosworth was old enough to go to clubs. Suddenly he was an eyewitness. "All of a sudden, I'm right next to it. The guy right here is doing it," he said, and looked down at his right elbow. "The guy in the backseat's doing it. Knowing about it is one thing, but close is different."

He ended friendships. He had seen what drug problems had done to Stanley Wilson, the former Oklahoma running back now trying to begin again with the Cincinnati Bengals. "It's really weird, and scary, how athletes can work so hard to establish something, and then they're willing to throw it all away," he said. As a 21-year-old who expects to complete work for his marketing degree next spring, Bosworth has spoken against drug use with the same force that the teenager once used to taunt the University of Texas.

Within the borders of the state of Oklahoma, there is the realization that Bosworth could be a better player this year, and yet a less imposing figure. Tony Casillas, the overpowering nose guard who won the Lombardi Award last season as the most outstanding lineman in the nation, will no longer be the object of an opponent's attention. The replacement for Casillas, Curtice Williams, is a sophomore with chronic knee problems. The replacement for Williams in preseason workouts, Tony Woods, is a sophomore who made three tackles last year.

The longer-range concern is that if Bosworth earns his degree next spring, he will be eligible to go to the National Football League. He said he is not yet prepared to talk about that possibility. There is the defense of a championship, and the possibility of a "triple-double," an unprecedented third time that a team has won a number one ranking in consecutive seasons. Notre Dame, with its record total of seven championships, is within reach. And there is always Texas. "I want to make sure I never lose to Texas when I'm here," Bosworth said.

There are many opponents to be broken in a quick and precise manner.

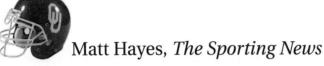 Matt Hayes, *The Sporting News*

BETTER SOONER THAN NEVER

The Sooners' fourth Heisman Trophy winner, Jason White put together the best season a Sooners quarterback had ever had, tossing for 3,846 yards and 40 touchdowns in 2003. Matt Hayes wrote this story on White for The Sporting News *midway through his Heisman-winning year.*

Two ACL injuries—one on each knee—cost Oklahoma quarterback Jason White most of two seasons. Now healthy and at the helm of a surprisingly potent offense, he's making up for lost time.

In the dorm of destitution, Jason White was number three on the pity list.

At the top of the list was roommate Michael Thompson, the onetime rising star cornerback for Oklahoma who was battling back from a horrific car accident that left him nearly dead with a broken leg, a broken jaw, two broken ankles, and bruised lungs on a barren country road. Roommate number two was Dan Cody, the Sooners' onetime star defensive end whose life had gone from batting 300-pound offensive tackles on the field to fighting the frightening enormity of clinical depression.

Then there was White, the onetime future star at quarterback recovering from a measly ACL surgery on each knee, operations in which they open your knee like a helpless frog in a high school biology experiment, then say, good luck, kid. Ten months of rehab for each knee, nearly two years of lonely, soul searching nights and monotonous, isolated days. Still …

"How was I supposed to feel sorry for myself?" White says.

To know Jason White is to know he wouldn't have, anyway—no matter the circumstances. So when he took a helmet to the chin from Texas defensive tackle Marcus Tubbs last weekend, when he was split open and bleeding and staggering to his feet in the middle of yet another Sooners blowout in the Red River Rivalry, when no one would've blinked had he sat for the remainder of the game, he shook it off and led OU to its zillionth touchdown in what has become a one-sided series.

It's just the way he's wired. His dad busted his hump for years pouring cement in the tiny town of Tuttle, Oklahoma, where young Jason spent many days doing the same thing. There is no questioning why; you just do it because, frankly, life is tough, and the lessons learned from the highs and lows eventually will pay off. Who could've imagined the lows would include suffering the worst injury in sports on each knee, one right after the other healed, both occurring without contact and away from plays?

Never

So, don't read so much into Jason White's subdued, sensible tone after he threw for 290 yards and four touchdowns and missed just four of 21 pass attempts in a 65–13 rout of Texas. Two years of painful purgatory have left him with a perspective few can grasp. That's why he avoids conversations about a Heisman Trophy race he has suddenly seized control of. And it's why folks say his play has him—hushed tones, please—closing in on Josh Heupel status. In 2000, the last time OU won it all, Heupel became a folk hero with his gutty, determined play as the Sooners' star quarterback.

If this season finishes the way it could—with a win at the Sugar Bowl in January—they'll canonize White in Norman.

"It's more than the game itself," says Sooners defensive tackle Dusty Dvoracek. "It's a life story."

This story began, fittingly, two years ago in the creaky old Cotton Bowl against the hated Longhorns. A year after OU did the unthinkable and scored 63 points against Texas, the Sooners were fighting against turning momentum and losing grip of a close game before White replaced Nate Hybl and steadied the ship in a 14–3 victory. Three weeks later at Nebraska, after the player many schools recruited as a safety had won the starting quarterback job, two years of second-guessing and second chances began. White was rolling out and throwing on the run; one awkward step later, his left knee snapped like one of those fried Twinkies at the Texas State Fair.

The normal recovery time for an ACL injury is nine to 12 months; many take longer. Any player at any level will tell you the toughest part of competition is not competing at all. It's hours of painful rehab with no tangible reward, just the hope that things will get better while your teammates celebrate yet another big win.

By the time fall 2002 rolled around, White was completely healthy and again had won the job from Hybl. The season began with a laugher over Tulsa, followed by a big nonconference game against Alabama. White's season was over before the first quarter ran out. Another ACL injury, this time to the right knee.

"I never really thought, 'Why me?' White says. "It was more like, 'What the hell is going on?'"

It's understandable, then, that there were more than a few skeptics when White returned this fall. Oklahoma coach Bob Stoops declared all summer that this could be his best team yet, which is sort of like saying this Beatles song is better than that one. The only question mark, it seemed, was White—specifically, his knees.

But here we are in October, with White playing better than anyone in the country and the top-ranked Sooners as close to unbeatable as any team can be in this season of upsets.

Through six games White has thrown for 1,762 yards, 20 touchdowns, and just three interceptions. He has hit 69.0 percent of his passes, and with him at the helm, the offense simply doesn't misfire. The Sooners have scored 52 or more points in their last four games; against Texas, it could've been 80. Is there such a thing as a 10-run rule in the Big 12? Stoops actually showed mercy on the Shorties in the second half, with White throwing just four times before leaving early in the fourth quarter.

In Stoops's five seasons in Norman, OU has been known mostly for its nasty, game-wrecking defenses. His coaching history is defense, his attitude is defense. But this season's team is all about the offense, which is playing so well it's overshadowing a unit that can be tossed into the argument about the best Sooners defense ever. More than anything, this team is all about White, whose inspirational comeback and nearly flawless play has coaches and players at a loss for suitable praise.

"One knee injury, maybe," says offensive tackle Wes Sims. "But *two* knee injuries? I don't know if I could do that. I mean, that's asking a lot."

Here's the scary part: with just 10 career starts under his belt, White is still getting better. He is playing so well that he has forced OU to rethink its short and controlled passing philosophy. The Sooners' scheme includes five to seven deep throws a game because he throws the deep ball so well. White has stretched the field for an offense with the most underrated receiving corps in the country, led by Mark Clayton—who looks more like, well, *Mark Clayton* with every game.

The offense is playing so well that, coordinator Chuck Long has had to scale back in practice for fear of overusing White's arm. In 2000 Heupel threw so much in practice and took so many hits in games that his left (throwing) elbow was the size of a grapefruit by the end of the regular season. He had no zip on the ball by late November and later led OU past Kansas State in the Big 12 championship game and Florida State in the national title game on will alone.

Think about that. For two years Jason White's knees were the coaching staff's biggest concern. Suddenly, it's his right arm.

Maybe that will win him a couple sympathy points with his former roommates.

Show Stoppers?

So, Oklahoma looks unbeatable, huh? We're not disagreeing, but we'll just show you who *can* beat them—and who really doesn't have a chance despite what you might think.

Can Do

In the regular season: Oklahoma State. The 'Pokes, who have won the last two in the series, match up well with OU. OSU goes to maximum protection and forces the Sooners to cover physical receivers and light ends with a reduced rush. When successful—see last year's blowout—OU's front seven slows and the running game opens.

In the Big 12 title game: Missouri. OU struggled to beat Kansas State in a rematch in the 2000 title game, and the 'Cats didn't have a dynamic quarterback like Missouri's Brad Smith. Mizzou's game plan for Round 2: Smith breaks containment and picks up big gains to keep OU guessing, and the Tigers don't implode with turnovers.

In the Sugar Bowl: Virginia Tech. The Hokies are a miniversion of OU, with a zone-blitzing, risk-taking defense and a balanced offense run by a quarterback who can dictate tempo. Plus, Tech running back Kevin Jones has the strength to make OU defenders miss and the speed to run away from them.

Can't Do

In the regular season: Texas Tech. The Red Raiders can keep it close early, but their protection is spotty and eventually will wear down. In other words, Tech quarterback B.J. Symons can do only so much before the OU rush takes control.

In the Big 12 title game: Nebraska. Forget about the rivalry aspect; the Sooners are more talented and better coached, and the front seven would dictate the game by stopping Nebraska's running game and forcing turnovers.

In the Sugar Bowl: Miami. Even if the 'Canes reach New Orleans—and they won't—quarterback Brock Berlin doesn't play well under pressure, and the running game, now led by Jarrett Payton, lacks dynamic ability. What do you think the Sooners defense will do to these guys?

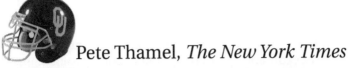

Pete Thamel, *The New York Times*

RISING STAR FROM TEXAS PLAYS FOR THE OTHER GUY

He finished second in the Heisman Trophy voting in 2004, but then again he was just a freshman. Adrian Peterson blazed across the college football horizon with a fresh, powerful running force that hadn't been seen in many years. The New York Times ran this profile on the Sooner back in the middle of his incredible first season in Oklahoma.

Judge Bascom W. Bentley III's office at the 369ᵗʰ District Court is so cluttered with sports memorabilia that there are two burnt-orange autographed game jerseys from Texas stars Cedric Benson and Derrick Johnson balled up on his desk like dirty laundry.

In this gritty town of 17,598, Judge Bentley reigns as the supreme Longhorns fan. His collection is vast and diverse; it includes a football signed by the 1968 Texas team and pictures of him in the Oval Office with President George W. Bush, an ardent Texas fan.

This week, as number two Oklahoma prepared for its attempt at a fifth consecutive victory over number five Texas, Bentley was bracing for the cruel twist to what has become his annual heartache.

Oklahoma's newest star, the true freshman tailback Adrian Peterson, hails from Bentley's native Palestine (pronounced Pal-is-TEEN). Peterson, considered the nation's most talented recruit last season, has already blossomed into a star, running for over 100 yards in each of Oklahoma's four victories.

At one point during an interview in his office on Thursday, Bentley got so worked up talking about Peterson's defection over the Red River to play at Oklahoma that he accidentally drank out of a soda can into which he had been flicking his cigarette ashes.

"It'd be like your wife running off with Brad Pitt," Bentley said, shaking his head. "You understand it, but it still hurts."

Considering that Oklahoma has won the past four games, including last year's 65–13 blowout, it is understandable that the Sooners have been able to poach top recruits from talent-rich Texas.

Last year the nation's top high school quarterback and tailback were in Texas. Peterson and quarterback Rhett Bomar each signed with Oklahoma. In all, 21 of the 51 players on Oklahoma's two-deep roster are from Texas.

Still, few players went through a recruitment as intense as Peterson's. NCAA Division I coaches argued in the Palestine football office over who would talk to him first. A hostess from UCLA called a family friend's cell phone for updates. The process proved overwhelming.

"It was insane," said Jeff Harrell, the Palestine coach last season, who is now an assistant athletics director and assistant coach in Texarkana.

College coaches tend to be coy about recruiting, a fickle game of pandering to talented teenagers. But even the Oklahoma recruiting coordinator, Bobby Jack Wright, could not stifle his laughter when asked if OU's four consecutive victories and the blowout last season helped in the recruitment of Peterson.

"That might or might not have had anything to do with it," he said, chuckling. "I don't know."

The game between Oklahoma and Texas is played every year in Dallas, located roughly halfway between the universities.

Each year, the universities exchange home games, which is significant because that team can play host to recruits. Last year, Texas played host to Peterson, and he got a firsthand view of the 65–13 loss.

Steve Eudey, who was Peterson's legal guardian for 14 months and shepherded his recruitment, said the game affected the process.

When Texas recruiting coordinator Michael Haywood called Peterson after the game, Eudey said that Peterson said to him, "Coach, y'all got beat baaaaaad."

Oklahoma did not make Peterson available for interviews this week.

For Texas fans, it would hurt even more to walk into Peterson's house on North Sycamore Street in Palestine and see his bedroom.

The walls are barely visible, covered with letters from virtually every college in America, from UCLA to Iowa to Harvard. One handwritten letter from Texas reads: "That's the most impressive tape I've ever seen as a high school junior running back."

Still hanging on the wall is a signed picture of former Longhorns star and Heisman Trophy winner Ricky Williams. Also on the wall are posters of Texas A&M and handmade signs that were hung in Peterson's hotel room when he visited Southern Cal.

Even his mother, Bonita Jackson, said he grew up loving Texas. "He always wanted to be a Longhorn," she said.

In recruiting, things are never that simple, especially when the nation's top player is involved. In Peterson's case the recruitment took on a life of its own. Harrell said he spent two hours a day fielding calls from Internet recruiting services; they would pester him for every detail.

Oklahoma won with persistence, a strong pitch, and a smart strategy.

Their starting tailback, Renaldo Works, graduated last season, allowing the Sooners to offer Peterson a chance to play immediately. Oklahoma backed that up with visits so frequent from assistant coach Darrell Wyatt that Eudey said, "He practically had an apartment here."

While head coaches poured into Palestine, Oklahoma coach Bob Stoops never did. Stoops and Wyatt visited Peterson's father, Nelson Peterson, at the Texarkana Federal Correctional Institution. Nelson Peterson is serving a 10-year sentence for laundering drug money.

"That was very important to Adrian," Jackson said. "Him and his daddy have a close bond. That meant a lot to him to make him a part of the process."

After Stoops visited the prison the warden barred all other coaches from visiting.

Right around when Stoops visited Nelson Peterson in December, Eudey said that Adrian Peterson made up his mind. Texas's coach, Mack Brown, did not visit until the final day of the recruiting period, January 31. Peterson was not even in town, and he had already decided.

Now the whole state gets to see if Peterson can help Oklahoma continue its run against the Longhorns.

Quarterback Josh Heupel was one of the leaders of the 2000 Sooners' 13–0 squad, which earned Oklahoma its seventh overall national championship.

Section III
THE TEAMS

Harold Keith, *Sooner Magazine*

SOONERLAND'S UNDEFEATED ELEVENS

The first few decades of Oklahoma football produced a handful of undefeated teams. This article on OU's early undefeated teams ran in Sooner Magazine in 1928.

Three of Them Made Glorious History for Bennie Owen

Take out the war year 1918, a year that saw the University of Oklahoma sweep clean its short schedule of six games, and Bennie Owen and all Soonerland for that matter can bask in the glory of three particularly successful seasons: 1911, 1915, and 1920.

Seventeen years ago Owen developed a small, fast 11, which he dressed in quilt pants and moleskin jackets and sent out to win every one of its eight games that campaign, including a 6–0 defeat of the University of Kansas, which marked the first time a Sooners 11 ever licked a Jayhawker one. That Sooners team was the team of 1911.

The small student body of that season idolized its team. The night before every home game saw gallons of "pep" unbottled and poured all over the campus. Bonfires were built, speeches made, parades staged, holidays declared, and whenever the team returned from a road trip, hundreds of students walked down to the little frame depot to welcome it home.

To start the season off, the Sooners annihilated Kingfisher college, 104 to 0, beat the Oklahoma Aggies 22 to 0, and slashed through Washburn for five touchdowns and a field goal for a 37–0 triumph. Then the team trekked northward to meet Missouri and Kansas, ancient and bitter foes.

Compared to the beefy Missouri 11, the light Sooners, dressed poorly and wearing little protective armor, looked distressingly weak. They seemed slow in signal drill, confused plays, and fumbled frequently. They appeared awed by their husky Tiger opponents and the vociferously hostile Mizzou crowd. "Ho, ho!" laughed the spectators at Columbia that crisp November afternoon. "This bunch of hayseeds won't see our 40-yard line. Another feast for the Tiger."

But the whole thing was a clever Sooners plot engineered by Owen. And the ruse worked. Missouri, richly deceived, failed to recognize it in time and as a result the game was taken away from it in the first 15 minutes of play before the Tiger recognized it was up against the speediest 11 in the Southwest. A 15-yard sprint by little Fred Capshaw brought the first Oklahoma touchdown, and five minutes later Raymond Courtright got off a stupefying 35-yard dash around end for six more points. Oklahoma coasted in on that lead to win the game, 14 to 6.

In a blinding snowstorm on old McCook field at Lawrence, Kansas, the Sooners defeated Kansas, 6 to 0, Capshaw warming his frozen right foot by twice bisecting the crossbar with field goals. Neither team tallied a touchdown.

Capshaw also won the Texas game for Oklahoma that year with an eight-yard drive through the bulky Longhorn line.

Capshaw was the demon of the 1911 team and is still regarded by many as the greatest halfback Owen ever produced. On nearly every other down this little 145-pound chunk of dynamite would rip off a 25-yard or 35-yard gain. Several times he ran back punts and kickoffs for touchdowns, dodging and sidestepping with spellbinding facility. He was a marvel in a broken field, being wonderfully quick to take an opening.

Besides Capshaw, other outstanding players of the 1911 team were Billie Clark of Comanche, Oklahoma; James Rogers of Ozark, Missouri; Jimmy Nairn, the peppy tackle from Nowata; Sabert Hott of Wakita, the first of the famous "Terrible Hotts"; Bill "Six-Shooter" Moss of Fairfax; Roger Berry of Pond Creek; Roy Spears, the rangy center from Granite; Claude Reeds, the hard-hitting but youthful fullback; and Courtright, about as good a halfback as Capshaw, but not quite, perhaps.

Owen's 1911 team's chief scoring weapon was lightning speed and its individual "ace," little Fred Capshaw.

The record of the 1911 crew is as follows:

Oklahoma	104	Kingfisher	0
Oklahoma	62	Epworth	0
Oklahoma	22	Oklahoma Aggies	0
Oklahoma	37	Washburn	0
Oklahoma	14	Missouri	6
Oklahoma	6	Kansas	0
Oklahoma	34	Alva Normal	6
Oklahoma	6	Texas	3
Totals	285		15

Four years later, in 1915, Owen coached another all-victorious 11 that was more nearly an ideal Owen 11 than any other the little one-armed man ever produced, for it was declared to be the most wonderful employer of the forward pass in the nation.

Where Owen's 1911 squad placed its main reliance upon speed and had for Capshaw, its greatest player, the 1915 Oklahoma team used the pass for most of its points and built its attack around Park "Spot" Geyer, who could drive nails with a football at 30 yards and take buttons off a man's pants at 40. Missouri, bewildered, was overwhelmed by the pass, 24 to 0. Geyer rained long throws to Homer Montgomery and Jess Fields and also to the two sets of halfbacks Owen used. With Texas leading 13 to 7, Geyer crossed them up by firing a short pass when the Longhorns were looking for something else and then kicked goal to give Oklahoma a 14–13 victory. Three thousand students were at the station to greet the team upon its return home from the Texas victory.

At Lawrence the Sooners whipped Kansas 23 to 14 and then waded through the remainder of their schedule to make a season's sweep of the nine games. In the Kansas game Geyer set a record when he threw the spinning ball 55 yards to McCasland for a score. Geyer was named All-American fullback by one critic and kicked 50 out of 54 place-kicks to rank first in the country in this regard. His toss to McCasland was the record aerial flip in the nation for 1915.

Montgomery and Fields, the former from Muskogee and the latter from Dewey, were perhaps the best pair of ends Oklahoma ever had in a single season. Both were ball hawks who could catch a football with one or both hands, running, crawling, or standing still. Willis Hott of Medford, the last of the terrible trio, was a mighty tackle. Other deserving players of that year were Elmer Capshaw, Montford Johnston, George Anderson of Ardmore, Leon Phillips of Arapaho, and Curry Bell of Granite.

This great team, described by many as Owen's very greatest, never scored less than 14 points in each game.

The 1915 team's record:

Oklahoma	67	Kingfisher	0
Oklahoma	55	SW Oklahoma	0
Oklahoma	102	Northwest Oklahoma	0
Oklahoma	24	Missouri	0
Oklahoma	14	Texas at Dallas	13
Oklahoma	23	Kansas	14
Oklahoma	14	Tulsa	13
Oklahoma	23	Arkansas	0
Oklahoma	21	Kansas Aggies	7
Oklahoma	26	Oklahoma Aggies	7
Totals	369		54

Speed had been the vital factor in 1911 and the forward pass brought fame in 1915; Owen's 1920 11, which won a Missouri Valley championship in its first year, was not only both speedy and dangerous with the pass but had the power and drive to win by straight football when the occasion for it arose.

Owen had several big rugged backs in 1920, backs like Phil White, Harry "Dutch" Hill, and Sol Swatek. He also turned out three wonderful ends in Captain Dewey "Snorter" Luster, Lawrence "Jap" Haskell, and Howard "Tarzan" Marsh and had four giant linesmen in Erl Deacon, Bill McKinley, Roy "Soupy" Smoot, and Dow Hamm, the latter a center who played through four seasons without a substitution.

Oklahoma that season lampooned Missouri 28 to 7, overwhelmed Drake 44 to 7, whipped Washington 24 to 14, and then took the championship by smashing through Kansas for a 20 to 9 triumph. A 7 to 7 tie with the Kansas Aggies was the only time during the season the team wasn't driving aggressively. Against the Oklahoma Aggies the Sooners scored 35 points and then let the subs finish the job.

Marsh, Smoot, Swatek, McKinley, and Hill made the first All–Missouri Valley 11. Smoot was chosen on the All-Western and made one critic's second All-America selection. Phil White made the All-Western and also one critic's All-America.

The 1920 team's record:

Oklahoma	16	Central	7
Oklahoma	35	Boomers	7
Oklahoma	24	Washington	14
Oklahoma	28	Missouri	7
Oklahoma	21	Kansas	9
Oklahoma	36	Oklahoma Aggies	0
Oklahoma	7	Kansas Aggies	7
Oklahoma	44	Drake	7
Totals	211		58

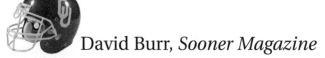

David Burr, *Sooner Magazine*

THE CHAMPS

The first is always the sweetest. It didn't matter that the Sooners dropped a close contest to Kentucky in the Sugar Bowl—they won the mythical national title for the 1950 season. David Burr authored this piece on the '50 Sooners before the season ended.

With the season half over and two tough Texas teams behind them, the Sooners are proving themselves.

Does the University of Oklahoma have the nation's number one football team?

That question will be haunting coaches and football writers until the season ends, but for Oklahomans it was decided beyond question October 7 and 14. On those weekends OU defeated Texas A&M 34–28 and Texas U. 14–13.

Behind, and seemingly on the thoroughfare to destruction, the Sooners fought both Texas teams to a standstill and then managed to come up with an uppercut that floored the south-of-the-border opponents. In both instances they did it the hard way with only seconds standing between national prominence and Landonism.

John Cronley, *Daily Oklahoman* sports editor, accredited the wins over the two tremendous teams to poise. Whitney Martin, Associated Press sports writer, mentioned heart. Heart or poise or both ... that's what champions are made of.

A few plays in the two games will be remembered again and again when Sooners alumni gather. One of these was a conversion attempt by All-American tackle Jim Weatherall in the Texas A&M game that would have tied the score 28–28. He missed, and Big Red came charging down the field with less than two minutes remaining in the game to clip the Aggies. Most observers agree that the missed point was the fuel that fired the team to the king-sized effort.

At the Texas gabfest, the goal-line stand of the Sooners near the end of the first half proved the local lads' class. Again the clock was running out—this time on the Texans. When the last series of plays began, Texas was on the 1-yard line. The Sooners were penalized for being offsides halfway to the goal line. For three consecutive plays the Texans tried to move the ball 18 inches but failed. Not bad work for a line that was playing without benefit of even one first stringer from last year's team.

If the two Texas encounters were hard on the nerves of the fans, they were most assuredly chillers for Bud Wilkinson. In his first football letter appraising the 1950 Sooners chance for survival, he said, "I think we will have a hustling, interesting aggregation that should get better as we go along. We could lose all of our early games—one or two of them by big scores—but we are hoping that our improvement each week will enable us to play a close game with all our late-season opponents."

Bud has been chastised in print as a poor prophet for those remarks, but a diagnosis of the statement would seem to indicate that King Charles knew what he was talking about. True, Boston College didn't measure up in a 28–0 rout, but both Texas A&M and Texas should run many a team off the field before the season ends. That OU didn't get such a treatment can be attributed to the aforementioned hustle, poise, and heart, with a good deal of coaching generously sprinkled in.

The classic portion of the quote would seem to be "a hustling, interesting aggregation." You can't get much more interesting and survive in the gridiron wars.

As to the "close game with all our late-season opponents," Wilkinson had his work cut out for him to provide an explanation that would not be chucklesome. He also had words that should strike a certain amount of fear into Big Seven opponents.

"We are improving each week," he told 400 guests at the Oklahoma City Sportswriters and Sportscasters weekly luncheon in Oklahoma City. "We will be all right if we continue to show improvement as we go along," Bud continued. Referring to the Kansas State Homecoming game, he said, "We can't afford a letdown this week; the morale factor in football can't be underestimated—I wish the season were over, right now."

Nobody was much worried by the word of warning. For most fans the season was over the rough spots. Of course, it was exactly this attitude that Wilkinson was warning against. And there are definitely several threats remaining from in-conference foes. By the time this magazine is off the press, the Colorado Buffs, playing their first full conference slate, will have tried to make their season complete by kicking the Sooners out of the throne room.

The conditions for an upset will be pregnant with possibilities as OU goes to Boulder to play. The game is November 4. On the following Saturday dangerous Kansas will tackle the Oklahomans at Lawrence (November 11). Then comes Missouri November 18 at Norman, followed by a rebuilt Nebraska team November 25 at Owen Field. The season will be over officially December 2 in Stillwater with the traditional Aggie-OU game.

Some achievements in addition to the Texas and Texas A&M victories have been made. With the Texas win the Sooners stretched their win streak to 24 (count 'em) games—the highest such victory skein going in the nation. It is also the longest ever built up at OU. The Sooners victories over Texas the past three years tied another OU record. Only once before, in 1910–11–12, were the Sooners able to beat Texas in three consecutive tries. And that's not all. There's a new record in the making. It should be written into the books when and if Colorado is defeated. With that game the Sooners should own a 27-game consecutive-win record. If they do, they will have beaten the record set by Cornell in the '20s of 26 consecutive wins without ties. (Notre Dame's recently snapped winning streak was longer than the Sooners but contained two ties. The present Army team is working on a streak that is one short of Oklahoma but that also includes ties.)

In all of the preseason guessing, only one Oklahoman was seriously mentioned for All-America honors—Leon Heath. There was much lamenting concerning the loss of backfield stars George Thomas, Darrell Royal, and Lindell Pearson. Graduation managed to make a shambles of the 1949 line—something no opponent was able to do. So what happens? A new group of pigskin personalities make their pitch. And what a pitch it is. Names on the tongues of fans after three games would probably read something like this: Heath, Weatherall, Vessels, Arnold, Jones, and Anderson. If the fans can handle tongue twisters, other names, like Clark, Catlin, Keller, Mayes, Janes, et al., would be bandied about.

The first two names on the list will undoubtedly be on one or more All-America rosters. Leon Heath, the mule train from Hollis, is proving himself every bit as good as the dopesters figured. His running game has been nothing short of spectacular and his precision blocking is a marvel to behold as well. He catches passes like an end. In short, in a season where good fullbacks are throwing their weight around—two of the best seen hereabouts in a long time were Smith of Texas A&M and Townsend of Texas—Heath will do to take along.

Then there's a boy by the name of Jim Weatherall. He's played as many dramatic roles as John Barrymore. To begin with, Jim boots the conversions. And he's been right successful in his first three encounters. He's kicked 10 extra points and missed one. But the one he missed was a lulu, as mentioned earlier in the story. Again in the Texas game a win depended upon his toe in circumstances quite like the A&M brush. This time he didn't miss. He was named Lineman of the Week by the Associated Press following his brutal line play in the Texas A&M game. Following his selection he said, "Gosh, am I surprised. But I don't think I really deserve it." The Texans have reason to rue the loss of the White Deer, Texas, high school graduate.

If Billy Vessels doesn't make the grade from an unknown freshman to All-American sophomore halfback this year, he must certainly be considered a top candidate for Sophomore of the Year. "Curly" is from Cleveland, Oklahoma. He came of age as a member of the Big Red in Dallas when he scored two touchdowns and ripped off 76 yards rushing against a fine Texas line. He caught two passes for 22 additional yards. He looked good against Texas A&M and Boston College and must be one of the players Bud meant when he spoke of his team improving each week.

The hero of the Texas A&M get-together may have been Weatherall but he certainly shared honors with Claude Arnold, senior quarterback from Okmulgee. Arnold appeared as fit a replacement as anyone could hope for to fill the Mitchell and Darrell Royal title roles. With less than two minutes to go and trailing 27–28, Arnold moved his team down the field with as pretty a flurry of passing as you would care to see. With the clock running out, he took his time and generaled the team to a spot four yards away from a touchdown. That was all Heath needed.

The line offers more greats in the image of Burris, Walker, West, Dowell, etc. Dean Smith, senior tackle from Tulsa, was a standout defensive performer against Texas. Clair Mayes, senior guard from Muskogee; Frankie Anderson, senior end from Oklahoma City; and Bert Clark, junior guard from Wichita Falls, Texas, add something extra to their work. Yes, the Wilkinsons sport many individual standouts, but it is the team play that has paid such large and beautiful dividends.

As this is being written, the Sooners are riding in the exact spot in national rankings as they did when they completed the 1949 season— number two. Whether they can bypass Army or Southern Methodist for the top rung remains to be seen. This reporter has already had ample demonstration of what the Big Red can do. In the September issue of *Sooner Magazine* he wrote that if OU defeated Texas, he would believe in miracles. Well, he does. And just to show that one error in guessing has not dimmed the editor's ardor for soothsaying, check the following:

1. Leon Heath and Jim Weatherall will be selected for more than one All-America squad. Heath should be on the AP first string and Weatherall on the second.
2. Heath, Weatherall, Vessels, Anderson, and Mayes will make All–Big Seven. Bert Clark is a good candidate also. Arnold will probably miss because of a quarterback at Iowa State named Bill Weeks.
3. Wilkinson will not be Coach of the Year. He'll be at the top of the balloting and might repeat except for the notable reluctance of

the experts to let a coach keep the honor two years and running. For the Sooner's money, Bud deserves the title even more this year than last.

4.   A bowl game is certainly in the offing if the team wants it. What bowl they'll play in probably depends on who the opposition will be. If SMU should make it to the Cotton Bowl, sentiment would undoubtedly favor a match to see which is the best in the Southwest.

But enough speculation. In a sports season already spiced by the Whiz Kids of Philadelphia, the Sooners are writing their own ticket. And they're doing it in much the same way as the youthful baseball team. With poise and heart—the stuff that champs are made of.

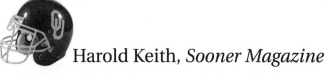 Harold Keith, *Sooner Magazine*

THE SOONERS OF '56

Probably Bud Wilkinson's best team, the 1956 Sooners never had a close game and shut out six of 10 opponents. The no-repeat rule kept the team from competing in a bowl game. Harold Keith wrote this retrospective look at the mighty '56 Sooners.

Slimmed by summer running and dieting, Oklahoma's defending national champions scrimmaged on the second morning of fall practice as they began drills for the opening game of 1956 against Coach Jim Tatum's North Carolina Tar Heels at Norman. Tatum had switched from Maryland back to Carolina, where he had coached in 1942.

Led by cocaptains Jerry Tubbs and Ed Gray, the Sooners reported for duty nearly six pounds lighter per man than they had been in spring practice. Oklahoma kept most of its 1955 talent and drew a fair number of sophomores besides.

"I hope everybody tries as hard this year as last," Wilkinson said. "Last year we had great effort. We went after everybody hard. However, very few people try as hard to stay good as they do to get good."

The Sooners assimilated that challenge just as they did their daily training routine. They were awakened in three waves, at 5:30, 5:40, and 5:50 AM. Clad in pajamas and jeans and yawning, they walked across the street to the stadium and drank a juice consisting of two parts of frozen grape to one of lime. Trainer Ken Rawlinson said that concoction stayed down better than anything else.

Scheduled early to avoid the 90-degree heat, the morning workout lasted from 6:30 to 8:30, after which the Sooners showered and trooped back to Jeff dining room for breakfast, a two-hour nap, and group instruction meetings with various coaches in the field house. After lunch was served, with sherbet for dessert, came the afternoon nap, more meetings, and the afternoon workout from 4:00 to 6:00.

Midway in both morning and afternoon practices all activity was halted while student managers distributed cartons of frosted orange quarters that had lain all night in the deep freeze. The hot players went for those. There was no water on the field. If it was dusty, an astringent was brought out and practice halted while the players gargled.

After dinner the men had free time. If the night was hot, they sometimes went to a movie theater and dozed in the air-conditioning. There was an inflexible rule that they must be in bed with the lights out at 10:30 PM, but the coaches made no bed check. They didn't have to. "We disciplined ourselves," says guard Buddy Oujesky. "A strong closeness existed among us."

Would Oklahoma fast-break again in 1956, the press asked Wilkinson? "Very probably," Bud replied. "It's a system that succeeds because it creates a tempo the defense isn't accustomed to. To combat it, the defense must learn to use fewer defenses and call them faster. Any time you can play a game at your own tempo, it's to your advantage."

As the Burris brothers had proved, farm work was excellent for developing football players. One of the sophomores that fall was Bob Harrison of Stamford, Texas, whose father lived in town but farmed 1,000 acres, chiefly row crops like cotton and maize. Harrison drove a tractor, chopped cotton, and pulled bolls. Stamford always had a good team.

"During my last three years they finished 14–1, 12–1, and 9–1. After they got rid of me, they won 35 straight," Harrison chuckles.

The sophomore who got kidded the most was swarthy little Jefferson Davis Sandefer III of Breckenridge, Texas. "Lots of 'yes, sirs,' in a name like that," he remembers. "Always had a lot of nicknames," he went on. "Don't want to repeat some of them."

The Sooners called him Jakie. His dad was J.D. Sandefer Jr., a wealthy Breckenridge oil operator. The only trouble with that was the Sooners never let Jakie forget it. The first thing he did as a sophomore was sprain his ankle. "They said I fell off my purse and hurt it," he recalls. They made a great show of urging him to persuade his father "to buy the university so we can all pass."

Young Sandefer took all the well-meant jesting in stride. Usually he just grinned and went along with the gag. Occasionally he would originate some of it. Like the recession. Everyone was talking about it. "If it doesn't slacken off, I'm gonna have to let my old man go," he told the team. He was highly respected by the Oklahoma players.

Brewster Hobby, a freshman from Midwest City, had his mind set on becoming a major league baseball player. With his father he was planning a visit to a professional club when Wilkinson and Sam Lyle, Bud's assistant, showed up at the Hobby residence to have breakfast with the family.

"Bud sold me, strongly and sincerely, on the importance of getting a good education," Hobby recalls. "He said I could play baseball at OU, and I did."

Hobby recalls his first contact with Port Robertson. "When he walked up behind you and cleared his throat, a gentle little scratchy sound, you knew you were in trouble," says Hobby.

When Hobby missed a week of classes while recuperating in an Oklahoma City hospital after surgery for removal of a calcium deposit, he forgot to get a dismissal slip from the surgeon. Robertson made him go back to Oklahoma City for the slip. When you missed a week of classes, you had to give Port a reason.

The 1956 backfield had one change. Robert Burris had graduated at right half. Clendon Thomas, who had played left half for the alternates, was moved into Burris's spot. "At first it was awkward trying to run and throw going to my left," Thomas says. "Also learning the corner position on defense. But it got a little easier with each game."

Thomas and Tommy McDonald made a great pair of halfbacks. Let's let quarterback Jimmy Harris describe each. "Clendon ran with a long stride. He'd be going full speed after the first two steps. He kept his head up and hit the open hole as well as anybody I ever saw. He was easy to hand off to. I always knew exactly where he'd be. He was a fine defensive back, too.

"Tommy's strong point was enthusiasm. He had more desire than anybody I ever saw. He was a bit of a showman, and the people loved it. He could jump and catch the ball, and he could throw it. He was smart, and he could hit. He could have played defensive back with the pros. He was an excellent player."

After the Orange Bowl game Billy Pricer again had surgery on both knees and then rejoined the team. He is believed to have submitted to more knee operations—seven—than any other Sooners player in history. His powers of recuperation were remarkable.

Joe Rector, a Muskogee sophomore, learned right off about Wilkinson's meticulous preparation for each game. "He was so organized," Rector remembers, "that we'd play the game back and forth 10 times before the actual kickoff. Once it started, we could have played it blindfolded. This gave us lots of confidence. I always knew exactly what I was supposed to do on every situation. It was automatic."

The North Carolina opener was notable because the Sooners were aiming for a new record of 31 straight victories, tying that of Bud's 1948–50 teams. How many schools have had coaches who twice directed their teams to 31-game winning skeins?

Oklahoma's problem was casualties at left halfback (McDonald, hyperextended knee; Sandefer, ankle twist). Otherwise the Sooners were ready.

Tatum's Tar Heels, like nearly every opponent Oklahoma met, came after the Sooners hard. But the Sooners quickly put the game away. Pricer's 78-yard quick kick set up the first touchdown. Thomas's deft handling of an intercepted pass, which he lateraled to McDonald for 40 more yards, introduced the second. With only 44 seconds left in the first half, Harris saw McDonald streaking for the end zone with the Tar Heels in hot pursuit. Like a smooth roper whose hemp flows freely through the loop, Harris shot the pass in a long beeline, and McDonald snared it. Pricer kicked goal. Wilkinson used 59 players. Oklahoma won 36–0.

In the most unusual double injury in Sooners football history, both tackle Wayne Greenlee and guard Ken Northcutt broke small bones in their legs and were lost for the season. Both were hurt in the first half while playing side by side in the Sooners starting line. Each broke his leg about three inches above the ankle. They shared a room at the university infirmary. The scheduling of the operations put an end to the parallel. They couldn't both be operated on simultaneously. They tossed a coin. Northcutt won the flip. He decided to go second so that Doctors Don O'Donoghue, the surgeon, and Mike Willard, team physician, could "practice on Greenlee and be ready for me." That's the way it was done.

Wilkinson played his starters only 18 minutes during the 66–0 romp over Kansas State at Norman, but the Sooners seconds and thirds performed so impressively that they got most of the praise dished out by the Wildcats when reporters interviewed them after the game. Center Kerry Clifford praised the Sooners middle guards, "especially that 70 [Dick Gwinn]." The entire Kansas State squad acclaimed the Sooners hustle.

A classic illustration of the burning Sooners hustle was contributed by McDonald while the starters were on the field. Once when McDonald was roughly upended across the sideline and lost his shoe, he left it lying on the turf and, hurrying back to the huddle, worked his fake into the line while wearing only the sock on his left foot.

The Texas-Oklahoma series had reached an odd milestone. Although Longhorn outfits had thrashed Sooners clubs 30 times while losing 18 and tying two, Oklahoma teams coached by Wilkinson held a 7–2 margin over the Orange, and all Oklahoma gloried in it.

"When we flew into Fort Worth the day before the game," recalls Pricer, Sooners fullback, "we were kidding and cutting up. Bud called off our Friday practice. Then he called a team meeting. To our surprise, he was quiet, subdued, resigned to defeat.

"You haven't practiced at all well this week," he said, "but then it's no disgrace to be beaten by a team as strong as Texas. Even when they beat you tomorrow, remember, you're still Oklahoma. So be sure to hold your heads up high."

"That got us to thinking," said Pricer. "We had a team meeting and voted not to go to the movie that night. Instead, we chose to stay in our hotel and study our game assignments. But at breakfast next morning, the coach was still gloomy. During our pregame meal he let us have it again. 'Keep your heads high,' he told us. 'It's no disgrace to get beat by as strong a team as Texas.' By that time we weren't about to let Texas beat us. We had too much pride, speed, and togetherness."

In the Sooners dressing room before the game, the Oklahoma squad was suited, ready to play. But Wilkinson hadn't come in to lead them out. It was almost kickoff time, and the tension was as thick as low country fog.

Gray, lying on the floor, raised up on one elbow. "Wish the old man would come on in and tell us that bird story so we can go out and kick the hell out of 'em," he growled. The Sooners roared. That crack by their cocaptain loosened them up beautifully for the fray.

The Sooners showed their enthusiasm from the opening kickoff. McDonald ran it back 54 yards to the Texas 44. Oklahoma scored in seven plays. Thomas knifed across from two yards out, riding the shirt-tails of blockers John Bell, Tom Emerson, Bill Krisher, and Tubbs.

Coach Ed Price and his staff had Texas ready to play. Once Texas rushed so hard on a pass that Oklahoma lost 29 yards. Then Harris called a fooler. Pricer backed up a step, faking a quick kick. He swung his leg but instead of booting the ball handed it off behind him to Thomas on a Statue of Liberty play. Picking up downfield support by Tubbs and Oujesky, Thomas ran 44 yards to the Texas 20. Two minutes later McDonald zipped between two tacklers to score.

Just before the half Harris rocked back on his heel and sent the ball winging on a long cross-country ride that suggested a squadron of wild geese cruising in regal splendor toward some distant feeding ground. Down on the Texas 20, McDonald leaped for it, speared it on his fingertips, and, helped by Bell's block and also Oujesky's, raced across the goal with only 27 seconds left on the clock. Elated, McDonald turned around, ran back up the gridiron, and grinning joyfully, jumped astride Harris, yoking his legs around the quarterback's middle and his arms around Harris's neck.

"McDonald's enthusiasm ... the obvious thrill he got out of doing something well, certainly was impressive," wrote Homer Norton, former Texas Aggie coach who covered the game for the *Houston Post.* Norton's 1939 Texas Aggies had won the national championship. Anything he wrote about football was read with attention.

Oklahoma's starters began the last half by driving 80 yards from kickoff to score. Thomas took it over with an eight-yard shot. McDonald helped with an incredible catch of a Harris pass while lying almost on his side.

Blackie Sherrod, *Fort Worth Press* sports editor, described the game as follows: "The rampaging citizens from up country did everything with a tremendous display of energy. They ran furiously, blocked and tackled like they were angry with the universe. They passed, and yes, even fumbled, in a high-handed manner."

Once in the last half, the Sooners came out in a Swinging Gate formation, in which all their linemen were strung out 15 yards to the right of Tubbs with Thomas stationed behind them. Tubbs, the center, got over the ball. Harris, Pricer, and McDonald lined up in tandem behind him. With Tubbs blocking, Harris ran down the left sideline to the Texas 39. There he lateraled to Pricer, who ran 10 yards farther. The Sooners soon scored.

"They are an exceptionally interesting club to watch," Norton wrote of this maneuver. "They used everything in the book.... I was impressed with their ability to come up with a surprise play when they needed big yardage for a first down.... Oklahoma has now put the pressure back on the defense.... Bud Wilkinson has done an outstanding job. I sincerely believe that he is the smoothest and cleverest coach in football today." The final score was 45–0.

In the Kansas game Oklahoma yielded two touchdowns while winning 34–12. Those Jayhawker touchdowns were the first scored against Gomer Jones's defense in eight straight regular-season games.

The most astonished person in the stadium was probably Oujesky. "Some Jayhawker 'chinned' me when I rushed through trying to block a punt," Oujesky remembers. "I was knocked colder than a wedge. When I came to on the bench and saw that '12' under 'Kansas' on the scoreboard, I couldn't understand it. I got scared. I jumped up and started to go back into the game, but Gomer wouldn't let me."

The Sooners started well. Thomas ran back the kickoff 40 yards and six plays later scored on the handoff. With McDonald holding, Harris kicked goal. Then the militant mood of the Jayhawkers asserted itself. Homer Floyd, their speedy fullback, ran the kickoff back 36 yards to McDonald, last Sooners tackler. Tommy nailed him, but Kansas drove 45 yards to score. Dennit Morris got a hand on their extra-point try. Oklahoma led 7–6.

Then the Sooners scored three times. McDonald used a block by Pricer to skirt the strong side for 12 yards and the first score. After Harrison, Morris, and Doyle Jennings stopped Kansas runs, forcing a punt, the alternates trekked 61 yards to pay dirt, Bob Timberlake making a diving catch of David Baker's pass to score. Baker kicked goal.

The starters came in and scored on a dash by McDonald, and Oklahoma led 27–6 at the half and apparently was cruising. With the Notre Dame game next on the slate, there seemed no purpose in trying to annihilate one's northern neighbor. But Oklahoma won the last half only 7 to 6. Kansas fought magnificently.

"After the game," McDonald remembers, "the Kansas fans swarmed the field like they'd beaten us." "We had our feelings hurt," remembers Pricer. "Bud and Gomer were busy cheering us up. We didn't think anybody could even score on us, let alone score 12."

Oklahoma destroyed Notre Dame 40–0 at South Bend, the first time the Irish had been shut out in 47 straight games going back to Michigan State in 1951. The Sooners defense held the Irish rushing to

1.9 net yards a play; intercepted four passes, two of them for touch-downs; blocked an Irish punt; and held Paul Hornung, the big Irish quarterback who later won the Heisman Trophy, to a total of seven yards rushing in 13 carries, knocking the ball loose from him three times. The game was broadcast to millions on national television. The South Bend crowd of 60,128 constituted an all-time record.

"We were all emotional and tight," remembers Harris. "We wore our game faces. Although they'd been beaten by Michigan State, all we heard was how tough Notre Dame would be at South Bend.

"Jay O'Neal and Dale Sherrod and I went into Bud's room for a quarterback meeting," Harris went on. "Bud had a funny little fighting grin on his face that we'd never seen before. 'Just relax,' he told us. 'We're going to kick the hell out of these guys.'" The quarterbacks stared at him in awe.

Harris remembers that against the Irish the Sooners used for the first time a new formation with the left end widened and the right half flankered. "This was new to Oklahoma," Harris points out. "We could option either way. This opened us up, got us out around the ends, gave us a lot of versatility for the type of team we were—lean, quick, super-fast." In this game the Sooners abandoned their fast break, staying mainly with the double flankers, who needed time to return to the huddle after each play.

The Sooners came out first for their calisthenics. "Notre Dame's squad appeared, ran through the Sooners circle, then came back through it again, stopped, and started taking their calisthenics, growling like dogs," recalls Pricer. Wilkinson moved the Sooners off a little and soon sent them to the dressing room. The afternoon was bright and sunny, 64 degrees at kickoff. A slight east wind was blowing.

The Sooners got off to a great start, marching 69 yards in 10 plays to score. Oklahoma's blockers cut McDonald around right end for 18. Then they broke Thomas around the opposite flank for nine more. Harris kept moving Oklahoma with ground plays until they reached the Irish 14. Then he rolled out to his right and hit Bell with a running pass for the first touchdown. "Jimmy was a fine thrower," recalls Thomas. "He was more accurate than Billy Wade."

On Notre Dame's first scrimmage play the 205-pound Hornung swung the Sooners left flank at full speed. Tubbs, Sooners center, flashed in fast from his linebacker post and hit Hornung a solid crack, flattening him and driving him back deep into his own backfield.

"Tubbs was the nicest guy in the world until he put on his helmet," remembers Thomas.

"We had an X-stunt on for the play," recalls Oujesky. "I slanted to the inside. Notre Dame's right guard and right tackle both went for me.

This left Tubbs an open avenue. I'd grown up wanting to go to Notre Dame. I'm sure my size didn't impress them, so I was delighted to be a small part of beating them." The only Catholic on the Oklahoma team, Oujesky would have no difficulty making the All-America Catholic team.

Wilkinson sent in the alternates. Baker quick-kicked 60 yards to give Oklahoma field position. On fourth down from their 22, Notre Dame tried a punt by Dean Studor. A faulty snapback made him kick late. Steve Jennings blocked the ball. Timberlake caught it in midair and ran to the Irish 3. Two plays later O'Neal scored on a quarterback sneak behind blocks by Harrison, and Steve and Doyle Jennings. Carl Dodd kicked goal. Oklahoma led 13–0 at the first quarter.

Early in the second quarter the Sooners starters entered and wheeled 64 yards to the end zone in eight plays. Harris's 17-yard pass to McDonald to the Irish 18 was the long gainer. Thomas hit very fast on the handoff and was scarcely touched after his blockers burst the Irish line. Thomas still remembers Krisher's block. "As we ran up to the scrimmage line, Bill widened out to within a foot of Tom Emerson, our right tackle. His Notre Dame opponent widened out with him. When the ball was snapped, Bill drove straight through his man. The hole was so wide that after Tubbs came across to get their linebacker, all I had to do was run."

Just before the half ended, Morse, of Notre Dame, tried a forward pass. Rushed by Pricer, he threw hurriedly. McDonald snatched the ball from an Irish receiver's hands and, using open-field blocks by Pricer, Emerson, and Thomas, ran the interception back 55 yards to score. When Harris kicked goal, Oklahoma led 26–0 at intermission.

Boyd Gunning, OU alumni secretary, related an amusing sidelight to that play at a later alumni breakfast in Chicago. A big Irish rooter, weighing about 260 pounds and wearing a little green derby over one eye, was making himself obnoxious in the stadium. When on an Irish punt McDonald signaled for a fair catch, this big guy stood and yelled, "Chicken! Chicken!"

Later, when little Tommy picked off Morse's pass and, hitting the ground in high leaps, ran 55 yards to a touchdown, an Oklahoma woman who was wearing a white dress and sitting four rows down from Green Derby stood and faced him.

"Sir," she said, "that's chicken, Southern style!"

Notre Dame came back hard in the last half, driving from kickoff to the Sooners 35 before McDonald intercepted a Hornung pass. Here Oklahoma drove 83 yards to a touchdown. Tubbs, Krisher, and Oujesky blocked Harris over on a sneak.

Early in the fourth period Thomas intercepted Hornung's pass and ran down the right sideline 36 yards to another touchdown, with Bell taking out the one tackler who might have stopped the play. Pricer remembers, "I hit Hornung just as he released the ball. I rolled over on one knee. I heard the crowd roaring, and I thought Hornung had completed the pass. I looked up and here came a wave of green jerseys chasing Thomas, who had the ball."

Bell, who had fielded a pass to score Oklahoma's first touchdown and had thrown a smashing block to set up the last one, was living proof that you don't have to have exceptional ability to be a good football player. His hustle and aggressiveness were the talk of the Oklahoma squad. They called him everything from "Mad John" to "Herman the German." "He's the tiredest and hustlingest guy out there," said Emerson. "He and Tommy McDonald set the pace." "A full-speed guy. Can't do it any other way," laughed assistant coach Lyle. "He hits like a horse and a half," said McDonald, who played behind Bell on defense.

A quiet, droll, mature fellow, Bell could sit down with you and talk about crops, farm parity, or politics. He subscribed to five magazines. He could sleep like a log with the radio or television turned on full blast. Although he was the most immaculate dresser on the squad, in a football game he tried to undress every opponent he tackled.

The Sooners were lighthearted, almost festive and gay, on the night before the Colorado game as they watched a Bud Wilkinson Quaker Oats commercial on national television while having dinner in a Denver hotel. In the commercial Wilkinson was holding a small boy on his lap.

"I don't like Quaker Oats. It's sissy food," fussed the boy. Bud said, "If it's sissy food, then I have 60 sissies who eat it every morning as part of their training schedule."

Next morning the Sooners were having their pregame breakfast. Harris, McDonald, and Pricer were sitting together. Wilkinson and Gomer Jones were dining at a small table in a corner. There was no oatmeal anywhere.

Harris asked the waitress to go to Wilkinson's table and ask "the white-haired gentleman" when his boys could have their oatmeal. She approached the two coaches just as Gomer was picking up his cup of hot coffee.

"Your boys want to know when they can have their oatmeal," the waitress told Bud.

Gomer, strangling with mirth, began spitting his coffee all over Wilkinson. "Bud always blamed me afterward, but I had nothing to do with it," Pricer insists. "I was too busy eating. When there's food around, I don't talk. I eat."

That afternoon Oklahoma kicked off before a sellout crowd of 46,563 that packed Colorado's new stadium at mile-high Folsom Field. The mercury stood at 27 degrees, and it was tooth-chilling cold.

Business manager Ken Farris remembers that he had purchased 36 sets of long underwear for the Sooners to wear beneath their uniforms. The sky was overcast. Although it had snowed five inches, the Colorado people had done a thorough job of cleaning the field. The footing was excellent, considering the circumstances.

After Ward Dowler, the Buff quarterback, punted out on the Oklahoma 10, the Sooners tried a quick kick, but Colorado was ready for it. John Wooten, their guard, blocked it, and John Bayuk, their fullback, had only to field the bounding ball in the end zone for a touchdown. The sellout crowd stood and roared its pleasure.

After the Sooners alternates came in and fought evenly with the Buffs, Wilkinson sent his starters back into the game, and they scored when quarterback Harris drilled a forward pass down the middle to McDonald, who caught the ball on the run and sped across the goal. The 6,240 Oklahomans who had traveled nearly 700 miles, mostly by auto, part of it through a blizzard, cheered, but the Sooners missed the conversion. Colorado led 7–6.

Then came a tragic play. Late in the first quarter Colorado quick-kicked. McDonald ran back and swept up the ball. "I had a bad cold," McDonald says today, "but I didn't tell anybody because I wanted to play so badly. I kept asking Ken Rawlinson for throat lozenges to suck on. I looked around and saw that Colorado was all spread out. Picking a path, I ran the punt back 75 yards to a touchdown when Billy Pricer, our fullback, rolled the last Colorado tackler with a beautiful downfield block.

"In the end zone I turned around and saw a red flag lying on the grass back up the field. To myself I said, 'Who in God's world could pull a red flag out of his pocket under circumstances like these? If he only knew how sore my throat was, how hard it had been to sprint 75 yards in that altitude, and how difficult it was for me to breathe, he would never have dropped that flag.'"

Colorado's ground game tore Oklahoma to shreds in the second quarter. Harris postponed touchdowns by tackling Dove and later halfback Howard Cook in the Sooners secondary. Dove double-reversed for a touchdown. Later, on a pitchout off Coach Ward's T formation, Stransky crossed the goal standing with only 36 seconds left in the half.

McDonald shot through to block Stransky's conversion. This proved to be an important play. However, the Sooners trailed 19–6 and appeared doomed to defeat.

In the Sooners dressing room at the half, Wilkinson hadn't come in. "Everybody was getting antsy," Rector recalls. "Then Jerry Tubbs yelled 'Sit down!' and we all sat down. Nobody panicked. Finally Bud walked in. His face was white.

"'Men, take off those OU jerseys,' he told us. 'You don't deserve to wear the colors that the people who played ahead of you wore while building that fine Oklahoma tradition.' He'd warned us all week that we weren't practicing well after the Notre Dame victory."

President Cross, who frequently visited the Sooners' halftime sessions, recalls that Wilkinson, gradually becoming calmer, told his team to put the first half out of their minds and start a new ballgame when play resumed. They were not to try to catch up. The second half would be a new game that they were capable of winning by three touchdowns if they put their minds to it. He finished his commentary with the remark, "Here's one man who thinks you can still win."

"He left the dressing room to let us think about it," remembers Oujesky. "Our senior leaders took over." Tubbs and Gray arose. "Okay," they said, "Let's go out and get it done."

"And when our guys decided they could do it, we went down on the field," Thomas remembers. "I don't mean to sound cocky, but we knew we could do anything we wanted to do. Nobody could beat us. Nobody could handle us. Get out of our way!"

The battle's turning point came on only the fourth play of the last half. Colorado had kicked off over the Oklahoma goal. Oklahoma had the ball on its own 28, fourth down, two to go. Harris decided to gamble, going for the first down. "Let's block," Harris warned his huddle. "This might be the ballgame."

Thomas got it on a slashing three-yard buck behind blockers Krisher, Emerson, and Bell. "I knew that Clendon could hit the hole and cut fast," Harris explains his choice. "He was big and fast and easy to hand off to. He and Bob Herndon were the best I ever played with at taking a handoff at full speed."

With the line blocking magnificently, the Sooners drive lengthened. McDonald's 11-yard burst with a pitchout put them over the center stripe. McDonald's 22-yard cutback earned a first down on the Colorado 15. Soon the Sooners were on the Buffalo 6, fourth down and one to go.

Tubbs brought word back that Colorado was loaded in a goal-line defense. Harris called the option run or pass. McDonald threw to Thomas in the end zone for the touchdown.

"Jimmy pitched it to me," McDonald remembers. "The Colorado players were in my face. Clendon was so wide open. I said to myself, 'Okay, boys, come and get me. Here goes the ball.' I was elated. Nobody was within three yards of Clendon!" Harris kicked goal. Now the Buffalo lead had been cut to 19–13.

"I was never so tired in my life," remembers Tubbs. "A winning tradition gives you so much pride. You reach down and get a little bit more." Thomas added, "That pride was started by the guys way back. Then it rubbed off on us. We played to win. None of us wanted to be on the team that ended the winning streak."

In the third period Harris skipped back 18 yards with Dowler's punt. The Sooners line began blocking with purpose and savagery. From the Buffalo 11, Harris pitched the ball to McDonald running wide to the right. Tommy faked a pass and with a surge of speed dove past a tackler into the end zone. That tied the game, 19–19.

On the extra point Tubbs snapped the ball perfectly to the kneeling McDonald. The Sooners line protected stoutly. Tommy fielded the ball and set it up. Harris booted it squarely between the posts to give Oklahoma a 20–19 lead.

Pricer said, "Dennit Morris was hurt, and I had to play three quarters. And after our third touchdown I had to kick off. Bud had told me, 'If you're tired, tell us and we'll get somebody else in.' I walked to the sideline. 'Coach,' I said, 'I'm pooped.'

"Bud grinned. He reached over and patted me on the rump. 'Go ahead and kick off and go down and get the tackle,' he said. Damn! That pat on the rump lifted me sky-high. I did kick off and go down and get the tackle. I could have played another full quarter."

The fourth period began. Tubbs and Pricer contained the Buff attack with smashing linebacking. Harris rolled to his left and spied Thomas running laterally across the end zone. Harris hit Thomas in the corner with a perfect pass good for 16 yards and the game-clinching touchdown. Harris kicked goal. Oklahoma 27, Colorado 19.

"That Colorado crowd was a wild one," remembers Doyle Jennings. "They kept shelling us with snowballs and Coke-bottle tops. We were glad we wore helmets. Colorado had cleaned the snow off the field good, but after the game the field was so snowy from those snowballs that it looked like fresh snow had fallen."

After the game Wilkinson had high praise for Ward's Coloradans. He said, "Their offense is by far the most potent we have encountered this season. They are a sound, poised, courageous team." The Buffaloes proved it that season by finishing 8–2 and defeating Clemson in the Orange Bowl.

At Ames, Iowa, the weather was good and the field dry, and the Sooners laced the Cardinal and Gold 44–0. Oklahoma started the fracas by twice crisscrossing its halfbacks, with pleasing results. First Harris pitched to McDonald, who ran wide to the right, then handed off to Thomas coming back wide to the left to the Cyclone 22. Five plays later McDonald bucked it over.

Three minutes later Harris reversed the strategy. This time he pitched to Thomas going wide to his left. Thomas handed off to McDonald coming back wide to the right. Emerson blocked the end and Tubbs flattened the defensive halfback so neatly that Tommy ran the distance without being touched. Oklahoma led 13–0.

With only 28 seconds left in the half, the Sooners starters came into possession on the Iowa State 45. It didn't seem possible to score in such a short time. But Harris somehow fit four plays into 26 seconds. On the first, his screen pass was slapped down by Chuck Latting of the Cyclones. Then Harris passed to Don Stiller for 14 yards, and Stiller rolled across the sideline to stop the clock. Harris pitched to McDonald, who skirted the Cyclone left flank for 15 more and was tackled out of bounds with only eight seconds left.

On the fourth and final play Harris flicked a pass to Stiller for 16 yards and a touchdown with McDonald blocking out an opponent on the goal.

Rector, sophomore right end, was the surprised recipient of a battlefield promotion that left him unnerved. "I was playing behind John Bell and Timberlake," recalls the rookie. "It was my first road trip, and I thought I was going to sit on the bench and watch the whole ballgame. But in the last three minutes Bell was ejected by the officials, and Timberlake sprained an ankle, and before I knew it I was in there, and I wasn't ready.

"I played lousy. Going down on a punt, I ran into Tubbs, fell, and lay there, resting. I thought of something Vince Lombardi once said, 'Fatigue makes cowards of us all.' It was a great lesson for me. After that I always heeded Bud's insistence that everybody should be ready mentally."

As the last half started, Tubbs made a play that sparkled like a new silver dollar. Iowa State had reached the Sooners 30 after completing a pass. Quarterback Charley Martin tried another. Tubbs intercepted it and headed up the field. He ran the first 15 yards like a fullback, bowling over two tacklers. Then he adopted the tactics of a halfback, outsprinting all his pursuers, cutting away from one tackler on the 10 and diving into the end zone to evade the last one. The play illustrated the great determination with which the rangy Sooners pivot played.

Stung by a curious AP poll that dropped them into second place in the nation, though they drew 92 first-place votes to 58 for top-rated Tennessee, the red-jerseyed Sooners were in an exasperated mood when they spread across the field to receive the opening kickoff against Missouri. It was the first time in six weeks that Oklahoma had been forted up at home.

Oklahoma promptly fumbled that opening kickoff back to the Tigers on the Sooners 30. However, Pricer and Tubbs wrecked the Tigers plays. Gray rushed the passer so hard that he threw wildly. On fourth down Missouri went for it, but Bell rocketed through and tackled quarterback Jimmy Hunter for a 13-yard loss, giving the Sooners possession on their own 43.

Then the game went down its logical groove. Wanting the victory badly along with restoration of their leadership in the national polls, the Sooners struck off touchdown after touchdown. As so often happened, they did it largely with defense. Four times they intercepted

Tigers forward passes (McDonald two, Harris one, Coyle one), and each time these led to touchdowns.

Once Missouri came storming back with a 36-yard run by Hank Kuhlmann around the Sooners left flank. Kuhlmann seemed loose for a touchdown until McDonald sprinted across and knocked him over the sideline, turning him a complete flip. When only 12 seconds remained in the first half and the Sooners had the ball on the Missouri 41, Harris, as usual, laughed off the odds and spiraled a long touchdown pass to Stiller to beat the gun. At that point of the campaign Harris's seasonal record was 20 completions in 28 throws for .714 percent, though many of his pegs were running throws delivered while going to his left.

Early in the second half the stadium public-address man announced that, back East, Tennessee had beaten Mississippi 27–7. Goaded by the information, the Sooners turned it on and scored five more touchdowns, though Wilkinson used five full teams.

The final score, 67–14, distressed Wilkinson. "I've been thinking all night about the size of the score," he told me Sunday morning. "We were all fired up. You can't ask your boys to turn it off." An unusual coach, Wilkinson spent all day molding those slick Sooners powerhouses and then worried all night because they had done so brilliantly what he had taught them to do.

McDonald had another dashing day. Although he played less than half the battle, he rushed 136 net yards, averaging 12.3 a carry, and twice trod just inside the white chalk of the sideline for thrilling 58- and 23-yard touchdowns. He also pegged a touchdown pass to Thomas, intercepted two Missouri passes, and prevented a Tigers touchdown when he capsized Kuhlmann with the sideline tackle.

Concluding Wilkinson's first decade as head coach undefeated in conference play, the Sooners subdued Nebraska 54–6 at Norman, rushing 506 net yards and passing 150. With Tennessee extended a bit while conquering Kentucky 20–7, Oklahoma pulled further ahead in the AP and UP polls to determine the national champion.

With 1:43 left in the half, Oklahoma fans had the thrilling situation they so enjoyed: Harris versus the stadium time clock. Could Jimmy take the Sooners across the goal, 43 yards away, in 1:43? Jimmy did it so quickly that he punched out the stadium timepiece with one blow. Rocking back on his heel, he fired the ball down the fairway to McDonald, who made a leaping grab and scored. Bud suited 55 men and played them all.

New goals awaited Oklahoma every week they played, yet the biggest of all confronted the Sooners at Stillwater. Gilmour Dobie, like Wilkinson a former Minnesota quarterback, had coached University of Washington teams that from 1908 through half of 1914 won 39 straight games, the all-time national record, Stone Age or modern, in college football. The Sooners had tied it with their Nebraska victory. Could they break it in the last game of the season?

Ineligible for bowl play, the Sooners closed their year against Oklahoma A&M at Stillwater. A few days before that game Vernon Snell, longtime sports editor of the *Oklahoma City Times*, asked Sooners seniors how they felt about their final tilt against the Aggies.

Pride came into Tubbs's face when the question came to him. "I only hope I'm able in life to be in an organization with as much unity and spirit as this team. I'm taking away so much more than I can ever repay," he said.

Byron Searcy, Oklahoma's rangy, part-Indian tackle, who scaled a slim 203 and wore a burr haircut, likened the Oklahoma team's flaming spirit to a biblical passage in Matthew: "And whosoever shall compel thee to go a mile, go with him twain." "It's that second effort you learn at Norman that's so important," he said. "In high school I think I made a real good first effort. But at Oklahoma it's the second effort they're most interested in. They go on the theory that everybody will make a good first effort."

Emerson, the 6'4" tackle from Wilson, a serious, studious zoology major, grew taut for a moment when reminded that the Aggies game was the last of his life for the Sooners. "I truly hate to see it come," Emerson said slowly. "Somehow I foresee emptiness after it's over. These years have passed by so fast. It's a shame we couldn't bow out at home."

But the Sooners didn't bow out badly at Stillwater. They drove the opening kickoff back to a touchdown. Pricer burst through, cut back, and ran 37 yards to score. The Aggies tried a pass, but O'Neal leaped for it, scooped it off his shoestrings, and ran 63 yards down the sideline for another touchdown.

In the final moments Wilkinson inserted an all-senior team that marched 77 yards to the Aggies 2-yard mark. Gray, the tackle and cocaptain, faced Harris in the huddle with a challenging grin. "I've never scored," he said. "It's my time."

Adjustments were made, and Harris called the play. Gray and Thomas traded positions, Gray going to right half and Thomas into the line. "If you think I didn't block for him after all those times he'd blocked for me, you're crazy," Thomas said later. McDonald leaped into one of the guard spots.

"On Gray's play, I was the center," says Pricer. "The ball was snapped. Old Beaky came over the top. He was carrying the ball like a girl, with both points exposed, front to back. His whole arm was wrapped around the center of the ball. After he scored, he wouldn't give the ball to the referee. On the sideline Wilkinson was laughing his head off."

"You've been playing me at the wrong position for four years," Gray told Bud when the coach sent in another unit. The Sooners seniors wanted Bill Harris, senior end from Ardmore, to try the extra point, but somebody erred on the snap, and Bill didn't have a chance to get the ball off the ground. But he was in there with his group at the end. Final score, 53–0.

Thus the Sooners won their third national championship in six years under Wilkinson. They measured Tennessee 104 first-team votes to 48 in the AP poll and outdid the Vols 26–5 in firsts in the UP coaches poll. Wilkinson's career record with Oklahoma was 90 wins, seven defeats, and three ties in regular-season play for .927 percent. His bowl record was 4–1.

Oklahoma's statistical feats in 1956 were almost endless. In offense, the Sooners led the country in total yards with 481.7 net a game, in rushing with 391 a game (a national record), and in scoring with 46.6 points a game. They were second in kickoff returns with 24.5 yards average per runback; second in own fumbles lost with 32; third in most yards penalized, 76.3 a game; and ninth in punt-return defense, holding opponents to six yards each runback. They averaged seven touchdowns a game, garnering a total of 70 in the 10 contests.

The Sooners submitted their finest national defensive showing of all time. They placed second in team defense with 193.8 yards a game yielded, second in pass interceptions with 26 for 423 yards, fourth in interception avoidance, yielding only five interceptions in 100 throws, fifth in punting with 40.7 yards averaged, eighth in rushing defense with 138.3 yards yielded, and eleventh in pass defense with 55.5 yards yielded a game.

Thomas led the nation in scoring with 18 touchdowns and 108 points; McDonald was second with 17 and 102. McDonald placed fourth in interception returns with six for 136 yards. Pricer punted 11 times for an average of 48.6, but the Sooners didn't kick enough to qualify him for the national minimum. Only one other man in the country had a better average.

Oklahoma won the foremost-player prize of the times when the nation's coaches voted center Tubbs the Walter Camp Award as the outstanding player in the nation. No interior lineman had ever won it before. McDonald won the Robert W. Maxwell Memorial Award and also the *Sporting News* Award. McDonald and Tubbs knocked each other out of the balloting for the Heisman Trophy, Tommy finishing second, Tubbs fourth. Four Sooners players were selected on All-America first teams: Tubbs, Krisher, McDonald, and Gray.

McDonald's admiration for Tubbs still runs high today. "He was a coach's dream," the halfback praised, "smart, great competitor, great attitude, great agility, excellent speed. He'd do anything the coaches asked. He was just plain old Jerry. He wasn't cocky. He was everything that typified an Oklahoma player—humble, compassionate, unselfish, ready to lay his life on the line for that football team. We all liked him so well that we wanted him to be our captain. Later he and I spent a week together with the College All-Stars, and he was everybody's choice there for captain."

Wilkinson's football lettermen were then graduating at a 90.6 percent pace, with his powerful 1949 team having graduated every one of its 19 senior lettermen, his 1951 team having graduated all seven of its seniors, and his 1954 team having graduated 12 of 13. The 13th man on that squad, Tom Carroll, lifted his outfit to a perfect rating three years later when he took two degrees simultaneously, one in petroleum engineering, the other in geological engineering.

Of his 1956 team Wilkinson said in his alumni letter, "I hope Gomer and I will be coaching for a fair number of years, but I doubt if we will ever be associated with a group of seniors, or a squad, with a finer balance of personalities or a more wholesome attitude towards the game than those who played for Oklahoma in 1956. These are the basic reasons why our team has played well."

Sooner Magazine

PROUD TEAM, PROUD SEASON

They didn't win the national championship—they finished number two in the polls—but the 1967 Sooners returned Oklahoma football to a highly prestigious level, as well as capturing the hearts of Oklahoma fans across the country.

Second in the Nation but First in the Hearts of Their Emotionally Wrung Aficionados

Now that we've all this time on our hands—something like two months—before spring football practice, a pleasant way to pass the hours, so empty without the voices of Curt Gowdy and Paul Christman to fill them, is to savor the season just past. So while all the Stillwater grads are polishing those gauche orange-and-black state auto tags, why not curl up with some old Chuck Fairbanks Football Letters and drift into reverie?

The Sooners of 1967 are a team to revel in. They won 10 of 11 games, often with drama, more often with devastation; they captured the Big Eight title; they were voted the second best team in the country; and they beat Tennessee in the Orange Bowl. We should have known. Fairbanks was quoted by Bill Connors as saying before the season began that he had "always been lucky and a winner," which has to be either the most creditable statement by a public figure in 1967 or the most massive understatement since a recent Playmate was described as "a typical American girl."

In building such a gleaming season, the Sooners drew heavily on two of their most conspicuous resources, heart and desire—terms worn smooth through endless and tiresome usage by coaches and sportswriters but still laden with meaning and importance. It was these two immeasurable intangibles that, blended with skill, brought OU from behind to win against Kansas (14–10) and Nebraska (21–14) and held off surging Missouri (7–0) and Tennessee (26–24). The Sooners usually dominated their opponents, however, with chilling execution as demonstrated in scourges against Washington State

(21–0), Maryland (35–0), Kansas State (46–7), Colorado (23–0), Iowa State (52–14), and Oklahoma State (38–14). The lone loss to Texas (7–9) was even valuable, for it was in the Cotton Bowl that the team became aware of its potential strength. The team gained coherence against the Longhorns, and it played consistently, formidably, and sometimes awesomely the rest of the season.

The causes for concern in August became causes for celebration by December. Each of the pivotal points—the offensive and defensive lines, the punting, the sophomores, injuries—turned into strong suits, none more spectacularly than the offensive line, coached by Buck Nystrom, one of the stars of an outstanding staff. Nystrom is an emotional giant of a man who imbues his charges with courage, determination, and pride. His line, green with sophomores, performed with brilliance. The Sooners led the country in rushing much of the season and finished first in the conference. Vince Gibson of Kansas State called it the "best coached offensive line I've ever seen." It was at least a miracle.

The defense was equally impressive. Under the direction of another master coach, assistant head man Pat James, it led the nation in point prevention, built around magnificent Granville Liggins, best nose guard in the nation.

The Player of the Year was quarterback Bob Warmack. One of the nation's most underrated quarterback, a kid who went through almost two full seasons without a nickname (it's "Wicked Worm" now) and who is so skinny, Frank Boggs points out, that he has to wear the No. 11 jersey, Warmack was undeniable in 1967.

OU's avoidance of injuries was crucial. As it turned out, not one starter was ever injured. The Sooners were solid all year. This would be remarkable for a marching band; for a football team, it's incredible.

The season ahead is another matter. There's Notre Dame, North Carolina State, and Texas for openers, but it is unnecessary to burden oneself with such thoughts now. This is the time to reflect on the 1967 team and to envision the recruiting fruits it is certain to bring. The '67 Sooners—they were among the best of OU's great teams.

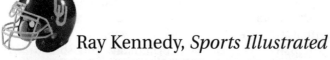

Ray Kennedy, *Sports Illustrated*

THE BEST TEAM YOU'LL NEVER SEE

The Sooners were on probation—no television and no bowl games for three seasons. What OU fans saw—very little of the rest of the country did—was one of the best college football teams ever. The Sooners were undefeated in 1973 and 1974, and after coming off probation at the end of the 1975 season, they won the Orange Bowl and the national championship. Sports Illustrated *ran this profile of the outlaw Sooners in 1974.*

You can spin the dial all fall but you will not find the powerful Oklahoma Sooners. On NCAA probation, they cannot be televised, play bowl games, or even be ranked, according to one poll.

It is as if the redoubtable Fay Wray, rescued from atop the Empire State Building while King Kong was batting down bi-wing fighter planes, went before a news conference, brushed back her frazzled locks, and exclaimed, "What giant gorilla?"

That or something outrageously close to it is the position that United Press International finds itself taking these days after agreeing to ban teams on probation from its weekly college football poll. UPI's new policy might have gone unnoticed except for the fact that one of the censured teams is a big grinning monster that just will not go away. In fact, the Oklahoma Sooners have been going ape all season and, while not exactly swinging from a skyscraper, they are very conspicuously holding forth right up there in the number two spot in the other major poll, run by the Associated Press.

All of which introduces paradoxes wrapped inside rule books. Because of the stance taken by the NCAA, ABC, and UPI and their various awards, rankings, TV shows, and statistical lists, plus the fact that Oklahoma is barred from bowl games and network TV this season, the formula for the Sooners' exposure is: UPI can cover but never rank, ABC can mention but never show, and the NCAA can list but never recognize.

The situation would be even more outlandish if number one Ohio State were to lose one of these Saturdays. That would give the rival AP the unique opportunity of awarding a mythical national championship to a team that is by and large unseen and nonexistent.

But shed no tears for Oklahoma. The Sooners are making their presence felt this season the same compelling way that Red China did when it was barred from the United Nations. They keep menacing people. With a smile, of course. Once penitent, the Sooners have even gone so far as to trade their pious faces for an attitude that borders on the carefree.

"They can keep us off TV and ban us from the bowls," says Coach Barry Switzer, "but nobody said that we couldn't win and have some fun."

Against Colorado two weeks ago, the merriment began with cries of "Let's win this one for the UPI!" After roughing up the Buffaloes for a quarter or two, the regulars sprawled on the sideline like so many young gods taking their leisure. One Adonis donned his celebrity sunglasses. Center Kyle Davis flirted with a blonde in the third row. Halfback Joe Washington, taking off the hand-painted silver shoes that carried him for 200 yards, four touchdowns, and perhaps a step closer to the Heisman Trophy, strolled to the stands to cadge a Coke.

Indeed, if the team continues to mangle opponents, Sooners fans will not see much more of the starters than the rest of blacked-out America. In last week's 63–0 win over Kansas State, for example, the regular defense played only long enough to leave one lasting impression. Led by All-American Rod Shoate, a swift and punishing linebacker, and the double-trouble brothers, LeRoy and Dewey Selmon, up front, Oklahoma did not exactly tackle runners. They avalanched them.

Quarterback Steve Davis, a licensed Baptist minister, showed no mercy in the ruthlessly efficient way he ran the wishbone. And Washington, the nation's leading all-purpose runner, displayed his wiggly, flip-flop moves as he ran for another 100-plus yards. "Anybody who tries to cut with him," says Switzer, "who tries to go east, west, and north at the same time with him, will break both knees and ankles." Another Washington trademark is soaring over tacklers with a grand vaulting leap that would do Nureyev proud. A former hurdler, Joe says, "When you can't go around somebody or through them, the best way is to fly over them."

Last week's victory over Kansas State also kept Oklahoma's unbeaten streak flying along at 24, the longest in the country. "I'll tell you one thing," says Switzer. "We gotta be the nation's number one unranked team."

For all his whimsy, Switzer deeply resents "our alleged nonexistence" in the UPI poll. Being snubbed, he says, is the least of it. "There are enough other polls around to make up for UPI. Heck, I'd just as soon be ranked in *Playboy*. Besides, the one great criterion is winning and as long as we keep doing that, people will recognize us."

What rankles Switzer is the fact that the UPI poll, the votes of a panel of 35 coaches, is governed by his peers—or "biased rivals" as he calls some of them. That is why he views the ruling, which was passed by the American Football Coaches Association in January by a near unanimous vote, as a direct attempt to get Oklahoma. "If it wasn't, then why impose it now?" he asks. "We're the only team that it really hurts. Do you reckon they'd have come up with the rule if we had gone 6–5 last year? No way. It's probably a good rule. I just object to the timing of it. Lord knows we've already suffered enough penalties."

Oklahoma's woes began in the spring of 1973 when the Big Eight, backed later by the NCAA, put the Sooners on a two-year probation for recruiting violations committed during the tenure of Chuck Fairbanks, who resigned after the 1972 season to coach the New England Patriots. The most serious charge was leveled at an assistant coach, since departed, for knowingly accepting a forged high school grade transcript for quarterback Kerry Jackson.

Switzer, hit with the sentence shortly after he replaced Fairbanks last year, complains that as meted out, it is in effect a four-year penalty. Along with the ban on postseason play in 1973 and 1974, the eight winning games in which Jackson appeared in 1972 were forfeited and, to accommodate ABC's contract with the NCAA, the TV blackout was pushed ahead to cover 1974 and 1975.

Nonetheless, Switzer believes that in some perversely wonderful way the crisis inspired his young, unsure Sooners "to play far above their capabilities. How else can you explain the fact that a team that was picked for no better than fourth in the conference went 10–0–1 and ended up number three in the country last year? Something else besides talent and coaching snuck in there."

Now Switzer sees his fellow coaches sneaking up on him and, he says, that kind of "additional punishment of the innocent we can do without." Notre Dame's Ara Parseghian professes some sympathy. "It's possible that a coach may be totally guiltless," he says. "But if the problem is severe enough to warrant NCAA sanctions, it's possible he can be playing and winning with recruits who normally wouldn't be there. It's unfortunate that the guy stepping in has to be victimized."

Darrell Royal, whose Texas team has lost four straight years to Oklahoma, takes a harder line. "I resent even playing them when they develop a monster team with illegal tactics," he says. Adds another coach, "I'm darn sick of Oklahoma. One more violation and they can bar them from football permanently as far as I'm concerned."

Without pointing fingers, Switzer says that ranked teams coached by men like Parseghian and Royal, both of whom happen to be on the 12-member AFCA board that drew up the poll proposal, automatically moved up a notch in the ranking when Oklahoma was banished.

Even so, Switzer appreciates AFCA executive director Bill Murray's argument that football demands special rules because "it is the only NCAA sport that depends on polls instead of playoffs to settle a national championship. The NCAA does not allow teams on probation in other sports to compete for the title, so we feel that the same restrictions should apply in the polls."

What Switzer does not buy is Murray's insistence that "the vote was not aimed at Oklahoma because, for one thing, there are four other teams on probation." Just how crucial to the standings those probations are was demonstrated recently when UPI listed California in a tie for 19th place. Trouble was, California was also on probation and a hasty correction had to be made.

As Penn State coach Joe Paterno contends, the polls have imperfections built into them. "I don't believe in them," he says. "It's a publicity gimmick. No one really knows from week to week which is the best team." In fact, how can one coach on the East Coast evaluate a team on the West Coast that he has never seen? Also, beyond the inclination to vote for your friends, some coaches vote for upcoming opponents to make them look more formidable.

Like their voting patterns, the reactions of other coaches tend to follow regional and conference ties. Bill Mallory of Colorado, a Big Eight member along with Oklahoma, says, "I feel Oklahoma should be rated in the polls. They are considered eligible for the Big Eight Conference race and they are not required to forfeit any games. The penalty of ineligibility for bowl games and exclusion from TV is enough."

North Carolina's Bill Dooley, conversely, believes that "if we voted for Oklahoma or any other team, it would mean an endorsement for everybody to go out and cheat, get on probation, and win a national championship."

The Associated Press, whose poll is made up of votes by 63 sportswriters, takes the view that "we're not in the business of policing college football. As long as Oklahoma continues to field a deserving team, we'll rank it." Nonetheless, several AP voters agree with Bob Roesler of *The* (New Orleans) *Times–Picayune* when he says, "I have very strong feelings that a school on probation should not be in the polls. But I vote for Oklahoma, since I'm playing by the AP rules."

Though Royal may "resent" having to play the Sooners, he is wed to them economically for better or worse. Right now it is worse, for as Switzer points out, "People like Texas and Nebraska are on a form of probation, too. If ABC doesn't televise our games with them, then they're left out in the cold." The Big Eight is also feeling the squeeze. By Switzer's estimate, the conference stands to lose more than $2 million because of the TV ban.

Has the probation had any effect on recruiting? "None," says Switzer, "because a lot of schools we recruit against are on permanent probation. They're never going to any bowls."

Switzer knows exactly where he is going in the immediate future: into a $5.3-million stadium expansion program and, possibly, independence from the Big Eight. Anyone showing interest in these and other subjects will find it hard to resist the *Barry & Larry Show,* a rapid-fire talkathon in which Switzer shouts into one ear and assistant coach Larry Lacewell into the other while sitting in front of a flamenco guitarist in the wee hours:

> Barry: "If dropping us from the poll was such a good idea, then why didn't they think of it way back in 1957 when Auburn won the national championship while on probation?"
>
> Larry: "I'll tell you one thing, they ganged us."
>
> Barry: "When they put us on probation, I said, 'I'm a fighter! I'm a competitor! I'm a winner! And nothing is going to stop us!'"
>
> Larry: "Ol' Barry may be snakebit, but he could hire out as a cheerleader."
>
> Barry: "Whup! Whup! Whup! We could have beaten Notre Dame or Alabama just like that last year."
>
> Larry: "There's an old Arkansas saying: It ain't bragging when it's a fact."

Another fact is that all three of the Switzer's children were conceived about the time of a bowl game. Greg is their 1967 Orange Bowl son. Kathy is their 1968 Astro–Bluebonnet Bowl daughter. And Doug is their 1971 Sugar Bowl baby. "My wife," says Switzer, "is the only one who is happy that we can't go to a bowl this year." She and Woody Hayes, that is.

Jay C. Upchurch, *Sooner Magazine*

THE MAGNIFICENT SEVENTH

The Sooners team that could, the 2000 squad just kept winning and winning and winning. Their dominating play against Florida State in the Orange Bowl left little doubt that they were the best college team in the nation. Jay Upchurch profiled Bob Stoops's first national championship squad.

Sooners Magic is back with a vengeance as Bob Stoops's troops bring home national championship number seven with an unprecedented 13–0 season.

In the end, the outcome was normal. Expected. Routine, even. These Sooners had done exactly what they were supposed to do. Still, it was quite unbelievable.

Torrance Marshall, providing the epicenter for a mass of adoring fans, celebrating teammates, and quote-hungry media types, had to do one more double take at the Pro Player Stadium scoreboard just to make sure his eyes weren't deceiving him—that it wasn't all one big dream.

It wasn't.

Marshall, an imposing 6'2", 255-pound linebacker, just moments earlier had delivered the performance of his career in helping number one Oklahoma complete one of the most amazing stories in college football history via a 13–2 Orange Bowl victory over number two Florida State. The Sooners senior, in front of his hometown fans in Miami, Florida, earned Most Valuable Player honors while spearheading a defensive assault that shut down the Seminoles' previously unstoppable offense.

The reality of a magical 13–0 run that culminated with a national championship title left Marshall in a state of euphoria.

"It was a storybook ending for me to have it play out like it did. I've come such a long way in my lifetime, and ever since I got to Oklahoma, everyone around me has been so supportive—like family," said

Marshall, who arrived in Norman prior to the 1999 season after stints at Miami-Dade Community College and Kemper Military College in Missouri. "A lot of people really didn't believe we were for real, but ... honestly, every player on this team believed we could do this, and that says a lot about our coaches."

That is where this success story begins—with second-year coach Stoops and his young staff preparing for another late-night, midsummer study session in one of the film rooms. Maybe it was June or maybe July, but during one of those sessions the blueprint for the 2000 football season was devised, tweaked, and put into motion.

Positive energy, confidence, discipline, work ethic—ingredients lacking under the previous regime—were a crucial part of the Stoops plan that had been launched upon his arrival at Oklahoma. Each element took root during his first season, then blossomed this past fall.

Sure, Stoops had promised success and delivered some encouraging results during that first season, producing a 7–5 record and the program's first bowl appearance in five years. But few outside the program believed it possible for the 40-year-old Ohio native to completely turn things around in such dramatic fashion.

Sooners fans had heard the talk—and the promises—before, and the threads of faith and patience had become fragile over a 10-year period that saw the once-proud, tradition-rich program decline into the depths of obscurity.

But Stoops never wavered. He stressed tradition, welcoming back past heroes like Barry Switzer, Brian Bosworth, and Joe Washington. While his public speeches were filled with words like *improvement, pride,* and *contender,* they barely scratched the surface when it came to the inspirational psyche he instilled at practice every day. Stoops, along with every member of his staff, brought raw, unbridled passion, energy, and toughness back to OU, and it was evidenced in every corner of the program.

A good blend of new recruits and leftover untapped talent provided the makings of something special. But getting the job done on the field against opponents from one of the toughest conferences in the country would be the ultimate test.

Stoops was the first to admit the '99 Sooners fell short of their expectations despite dramatic improvements from the previous three seasons' all-time low of 12–22. The Sooners had a chance to finish that first campaign on a high note with a victory over Mississippi at the Independence Bowl. But a valiant comeback was thwarted by a late Rebels field goal, leaving OU to ponder what might have been during a painfully long off-season.

"A year ago in the Independence Bowl, we were down [21–3] in the first half against Ole Miss," answered Stoops when asked to pinpoint a crucial moment in taking OU to the next level. "Our players have a great comeback and take the lead with about a minute and a half left in the game, and we're not capable of finishing. Our players ... that made them hungrier."

That appetite did nothing but grow during spring practice and on into summer workouts and finally initial fall drills. There wasn't so much a feeling of urgency in the Sooners' preseason preparation as there was a sense of deep purpose and conviction.

More experienced, deeper in talent, and better prepared, the Sooners charged into the 2000 season expecting success from the opening kickoff. Leaders emerged at every juncture—quarterback Josh Heupel and linebacker Rocky Calmus were obvious, followed by Marshall, Bubba Burcham, Roy Williams, and Seth Littrell. The list grew with every practice and every game.

Two wins. Then four, six, seven, eight ... This unbelievable ride shocked the college football world and pleased Sooners fans to no end. Stoops originally had asked only his players to believe; then, each step the Sooners took throughout the fall helped spread that faith to the masses.

"You don't just say you expect to win. You earn the right to expect to win by the way you've prepared, by what you've invested, by the way you've played," said Stoops, describing his team's confidence level and overall mind-set going into the Orange Bowl. "We believe we've done what's necessary to hold that confidence and not just talk about it.... I believe our players have earned the right to play that way."

By the time top-ranked Oklahoma had beaten Florida State on January 3, 2001, every opponent had been slain and all doubters silenced.

The Road to the Title
Game One: Oklahoma Number 20
Fast Start Versus UTEP

The season started innocently enough on the first weekend of September with an old acquaintance making his first return to Norman as coach of the opposing team, Texas–El Paso. Head coach Gary Nord had served as offensive coordinator during the tumultuous and short-lived regime of Howard Schnellenberger, losing his job after a disappointing 5–5–1 season in 1995.

Much was made of Nord's return visit, but the actual game failed to live up to the pre-battle hype. UTEP was a 27-point underdog and played like one in the 106-degree heat, wilting early after several failed gambles, then totally collapsing under the strain of seven turnovers.

The much-ballyhooed Sooners offense started slowly but managed to turn the myriad of UTEP miscues into a 55–14 season-opening romp.

Heupel, the 1999 Big 12 Conference Offensive Newcomer of the Year, settled in to throw for 274 yards and two touchdowns, while freshman running back Renaldo Works stole the show late by running over, around, and through the UTEP defense for three fourth-quarter touchdowns.

The Sooners defense applied the bend-but-don't-break principle against the Miners, surrendering 342 yards of offense, most of it meaningless.

Game Two: Oklahoma Number 19
Chalking Up Another Big Win
Arkansas State came to Norman for what was expected to be a non-conference clash of anticlimactic proportions. And that's exactly what it was.

Heupel led the Sooners on a 15-play, 80-yard scoring drive to open the game. The senior signal caller capped the march with a one-yard touchdown run that opened the floodgates on a 45–14 blowout.

The game also marked the emergence of Norman senior J.T. Thatcher, as he scored on a 66-yard punt return to put the Sooners on top early, 14–0. Thatcher, who had not started a game since his freshman season, finished the evening with a school-record 160 yards on five punt returns.

Heupel tallied 301 yards through the air and three TD passes, while Works continued to be the biggest surprise of the young season, rushing for 109 yards and one touchdown on only 12 carries.

"We were sharper than we were a week ago," noted Stoops, "but we still need to improve on the penalties, and we need to play smarter. J.T. Thatcher had a great game on both special teams and defense [safety]. He's only going to get better as the season goes on."

Prophetic words from the man in charge, as Thatcher would indeed become a key piece to the puzzle the Sooners were set on solving.

Game Three: Oklahoma Number 16
The Little Man Comes Up Big
Entering the season as the Sooners' number one running back, Quentin Griffin had taken a backseat to freshman teammate Works during the first two OU victories. Undaunted, the 5'6" Griffin proved he had plenty to contribute during the Sooners' 42–14 romp over Rice.

In helping OU improve to 3–0 after a week off, Griffin rushed for 117 yards and three touchdowns. The speedy sophomore also caught three passes and was the perfect decoy in sparking the OU passing game to its best performance of the season so far.

"I had been a little disappointed, but I learned that you can't get discouraged when things don't always go your way," offered Griffin, reflecting the sentiments instilled by Stoops and his staff. "I prepared myself the same as I did the two previous weeks, and today I was able to come up with some big plays. It feels pretty nice."

It looked even better. Suddenly, the Sooners had two legitimate threats in the backfield, and one of the best blocking fullbacks in the league in Littrell. That was great news for assistant Mark Mangino, who took over as offensive coordinator when Mike Leach departed for Texas Tech in the off-season.

Known more for its wide-open passing attack in 1999, the Sooners displayed an offensive balance that turns ordinary teams into something extraordinary.

The Rice victory also exhibited the first signs of a potentially great defense. The Sooners held the Owls' offense to 108 second-half yards and used a pair of late turnovers to slam the door shut.

Game Four: Oklahoma Number 14
The Sooners Get Defensive
The Sooners took their fans on a roller-coaster ride in their Big 12 Conference opener against the Jayhawks, a team that had beaten OU five straight times coming in.

Despite being a 24-point underdog, Kansas threw the ball against a porous Sooners defense plagued by busted coverages and an inability to pressure KU quarterback Dylen Smith. Smith maneuvered the Jayhawks offense for 284 yards and 16 points through the first 23 minutes of action.

The Sooners defense was shell-shocked.

"We gave up some big plays off of mental errors early," said OU defensive back Ontei Jones. "It just seemed we were able to make some adjustments and correct those mistakes, especially in the second half."

Defensive coordinators Mike Stoops and Brent Venables were ready with the corrections, beginning in the second quarter when defensive tackle Ramon Richardson sacked Smith and forced a fumble recovered by Corey Callens, thwarting a golden KU scoring opportunity. The Sooners capitalized by marching 82 yards in eight plays to take the lead for good at 17–16.

From that point on Smith and the Jayhawks didn't have a prayer. The previously shoddy secondary play improved dramatically and the Sooners applied pressure Smith simply couldn't escape. By the end of the day the OU defense had sacked the KU quarterback six times and forced seven turnovers, including five interceptions.

Safety Williams stepped squarely into the spotlight with a game-high 13 tackles, and Thatcher added three interceptions. As a side note, Heupel threw for 346 yards and was beginning to earn some Heisman Trophy consideration.

OU had won 11 straight home games, but things were about to get interesting with their first "road trip" to Dallas to meet archrival Texas.

Game Five: Oklahoma Number 11
Red River Blowout

Red River Showdown time was the Sooners' first real test of the 2000 season. After all, Texas came into the much-anticipated battle as a five-point favorite, ranked number 10 in the land.

With Kansas State and Nebraska next up for Stoops's troops, many were calling this stretch "Black October." The wisdom was that if the Sooners could emerge from this abyss with a 5–2 mark, it would be a positive springboard into the rest of the season.

Oklahoma wasn't buying any of it. Stoops's "all for one, one for all" outlook seemed like a cliché, but try telling the Longhorns that after they suffered a 63–14 loss at the hands of their rivals.

Incredibly, the Sooners stalked into the Cotton Bowl and, in one fell swoop, erased years of misery and mediocrity by running, passing, and defending their way to one of the most lopsided wins in the series' storied history.

The Sooners, who improved to 5–0 for the first time since 1993, scored the first 42 points of the game. Much of the talk focused on Heupel and the OU passing attack, but Griffin made headlines as well with his six-touchdown performance.

Led by some brilliant secondary play, the Oklahoma defense was too good as it held the high-powered Horns to only 154 total yards, including minus-seven on the ground. Calmus scored on a 41-yard interception return in the second quarter, and overall the Sooners forced three Texas turnovers.

Cornerback Michael Thompson provided the perfect microcosm of the game. While much of the pregame talk centered around Thompson as a potential weakness against Texas quarterback Major Applewhite, the sophomore answered any and all questions with four tackles, a forced fumble, and a fumble recovery.

The Horns never knew what hit them.

Game Six: Oklahoma Number 8
K-State's Winning Streak Is Over

After rolling over Texas in such unbelievable fashion, a road victory over second-ranked Kansas State seemed almost too much to ask the following Saturday. But the Sooners were only just beginning their climb back to national prominence, and the Wildcats stood in the way.

Not for long.

Even the confidence behind a 25-game home winning streak and 50,000 purple-clad fans were not enough to detour the Sooners' suddenly unstoppable Heupel-led juggernaut. The OU quarterback threw his name into the Heisman hat for good with a 29-for-37, 374-yard, two-touchdown performance that propelled his team to a 41–31 triumph.

The victory came against the number-one-ranked defense in the country and was representative of just how far the Sooners had come since Stoops took over at the controls.

"I'm going to say we're on a mission," offered OU receiver Curtis Fagan, who caught a 12-yard touchdown pass from Heupel in the opening quarter at Manhattan. "We're on a mission to put OU back on the map. We're not back yet, as far as winning a Big 12 title or a national championship, but this win was a step in that direction."

While Heupel continued to break just about every OU passing record in the books, receivers like Fagan, Antwone Savage, and Josh Norman made sizable contributions, and the running game was still doing its part to keep the team moving in the right direction.

The Sooners hit the Wildcats with a 17-point first-quarter barrage and never really looked back as they built a 38–14 advantage. When the Sooners finally spoiled a late K-State rally, it was time to turn their attention to number one Nebraska.

Game Seven: Oklahoma Number Three
Will the Real Big Red Please Stand Up?
In their previous seven meetings with Nebraska, all losses, the Sooners had been outscored 263–61. In 1997 the Cornhuskers demolished OU 69–7. Thatcher and Littrell played in that game as freshmen and were left with the bitter taste of one of the worst losses in school history.

This game presented a chance not only to avenge that loss, but also to replace Nebraska as the best football team in the Big 12 Conference—and in the country. The Sooners would not let this opportunity slip through their collective fingers.

But it didn't look promising after the visiting Huskers jumped out to a 14–0 lead in the first quarter.

While some of the 76,000 fans may have sunk into their seats with expectations crushed, Memorial Stadium still rocked, and the OU football team wasn't about to back off or back down. Confidence burned brightly in Stoops's eyes, and his team fed off of that faith.

The OU defense stiffened, holding Nebraska to nine first downs, 136 total yards, and zero points over the final three quarters. Meanwhile, the Sooners offense scored 31 unanswered points.

"The fans were great, the atmosphere was great," said Stoops. "You want the fans to try to influence the game—make the opposing team feel like it's up against not only us, but something bigger."

Defense helped get the momentum turned back in OU's favor, and no one group played a bigger role than that of Calmus, Marshall, Roger Steffen, Williams, Thompson, Derrick Strait, and Brandon Everage. Those seven players combined for 60 tackles, two sacks, a forced fumble, and an interception return for a touchdown.

A national television audience watched as a one-yard run by Griffin cut the deficit to 14–7 and a 34-yard pass from Heupel to Fagan put things back on even terms. A Tim Duncan field goal put the hosts on top to stay, and an eight-yard run by Norman sent OU fans into a halftime frenzy.

Strait provided the clincher when he picked off an Eric Crouch pass and returned it 32 yards for a touchdown and a 31–14 lead.

"It wasn't exactly a great situation [down 14–0], but no one panicked," said Stoops, whose team improved to 7–0 overall and 4–0 in league play. "We settled down, got our reads down, and got used to the pace and the speed. And once we did that, we were in good shape. That shows character, and it shows we're not a fragile team."

The Sooners were anything but fragile, bolting to the number one spot in the national polls, including the all-important Bowl Championship Series rankings.

Game Eight: Oklahoma Number One
Sooners Bomb the Bears

Baylor was next on the Sooners' list of victims, and the Bears barely put up a fight. Heupel continued to produce Heisman-like numbers in this laugher even though he played only the first half.

Thatcher got things off and running for OU with a 60-yard punt return for a touchdown. And the Sooners added three more scores in the opening quarter. Heupel scored on a four-yard run and then delivered two scoring strikes to Fagan to make it 28–0.

"Looking at all the teams and all the players that are involved with the Heisman hype, I think Josh has added the most value to his team," said OU receiver Damian Mackey. "[Josh] is very valuable to our team, and there is no telling where we would be if we didn't have him."

According to many Heisman voters, Heupel had moved to the top of the ballot by the time the Sooners exited Waco with a 56–7 victory. His numbers were comparable to any in the country, but his leadership skills seemed to give him that extra edge.

The win improved the Sooners to 8–0 and put them in the driver's seat for the Big 12 Championship Game in Kansas City.

Game Nine: Oklahoma Number One
Surviving the 12th Man

Very few places are tougher to play than Kyle Field in the heart of Aggieland in south Texas.

Texas A&M is usually ranked and always a worthy opponent. But the Aggies, when tucked inside the mass of humanity at their home stadium—well, they are practically unbeatable. On this day 87,188 fanatics, also known as "the 12th man," stuffed themselves into the joint and sat back hoping for a big upset.

And for the longest time, it looked like 23rd-ranked A&M just might pull it off.

But Oklahoma reached back to borrow a little Sooners Magic from the past, and Marshall delivered it with a fourth-quarter interception return for the go-ahead touchdown. The momentum-turning play helped OU rally from a 24–10 deficit and eventually pull out a 35–31 victory.

"During the course of a season, a lot of football teams find themselves in a game where they are not playing their best football, and you've got to find a way to win," said Heupel, who threw for 263 yards and a touchdown, but also was picked off twice. "This football team found a way to win."

The Sooners ultimately outscored their hosts 22–7 in the final quarter, keeping their expectations intact: to run the table in the Big 12 South, win the conference title game, and win a national championship. Yes, now the Sooners were actually thinking very seriously about winning it all.

Heupel played a key role in the come-from-behind win, completing 10 of 13 passes for 81 yards and scrambling for 28 more during the final 16 minutes. But the OU defense kept the perfect season alive with two crucial goal-line stands in the closing three minutes.

Jones batted away one fourth-down pass at the Sooner 1-yard line and then teamed up with Strait to make the clinching tackle on another fourth-down play moments later.

"We all wanted to be in the fire. There wasn't anybody who shied away from it," said Marshall, who had seven tackles to go along with his clutch interception. "We look forward to situations like this—to proving ourselves."

Nine wins, no losses. Another monumental win in what was fast becoming a season of monumental wins.

Game 10: Oklahoma Number One
Familiar Face, Familiar Results
The Sooners came out of the A&M game battered but ready to meet their next challenge—Texas Tech. The Red Raiders, with Leach at the helm, were familiar with OU's offense, and it showed during a sluggishly played game won by the Sooners, 27–13.

Oklahoma improved to 10–0, but suddenly looked vulnerable—on offense, no less. An elbow injury Heupel suffered in the Texas game flared up, and he was intercepted twice for the second game in a row.

He threw for a season-low 248 yards and was unable to generate much in the way of big plays or big drives.

Fortunately, the Sooners defense picked up the slack again. Calmus and Williams had huge games, combining for 23 tackles, and Thatcher's 85-yard interception return for a touchdown was the big play of the first half. A six-yard pass from Heupel to Trent Smith and touchdown runs from Works and Griffin accounted for the other OU points.

"The kids have set high standards for themselves, and they know they didn't perform to their potential today," said Mangino, whose offense rolled up 384 total yards, but hurt its own cause with four turnovers.

Game 11: Oklahoma Number One
Getting Out of Stillwater Alive

All that stood in the way of Oklahoma and its first undefeated regular season since 1987 was an Oklahoma State defense ranked 75th in the country. That and a lot of orange and black.

On their opening possession, the Sooners marched 99 yards in 11 plays to take a 7–0 lead. Heupel hit Fagan with a three-yard scoring toss to start what looked like a blowout victory.

Final score: OU 12, OSU 7.

Obviously, the blowout never came, and victory almost slipped away altogether in the closing moments. However, defensive back Strait saved the day and the season when he batted away the potential game-winning pass on a fourth-and-goal situation with 3:15 remaining.

The Sooners offense simply never got going against the Pokes, who had dedicated the game to recently fired coach Bob Simmons. It was like a bowl game for the hosts, and they played very inspired football.

OU didn't, as Heupel admitted afterward.

"It's disappointing because we know we're better than that," he said after passing for a career-low 154 yards. "Lack of execution.... The difference between being successful and not successful is a very thin line, and we were on the wrong side of it today. We need to get things corrected and get ready to go next week. The defense is playing great football—can't say enough about what they've done. They've been carrying this football team the last couple of weeks."

True, the OU defense was the only thing in sync for the Sooners late in the regular season. Calmus, Marshall, and Williams were outstanding, and Thatcher picked off his eighth pass at OSU.

The offense needed to rev up before the 11–0 Sooners headed to Kansas City for the Big 12 title game.

Game 12: Oklahoma Number One

The Wildcats Run Out of Lives

For the first time in two months, the Sooners were actually facing more than a few skeptics as they prepared for a rematch against K-State in the conference championship game. The biggest question was the health of Heupel's throwing arm.

Could he deliver one more win to earn the Sooners a shot at the national title in Miami?

Anyone who doubted simply didn't know Heupel. As far as he and the rest of the Sooners were concerned, there was never any doubt.

On a frigid December night at Kansas City's Arrowhead Stadium, Heupel, while far from perfect, was at his best with the game on the line in the fourth quarter. And the OU defense was, again, its usual dominating self. Together they produced a 27–24 victory that clinched Oklahoma's first shot at a national title since 1987.

"It really was a total team effort. That's the way it's been pretty much all season. This is a magical time for OU football—I really believe that."

A win over Florida State in the Orange Bowl would be title number seven for the Sooners, but they weren't looking that far ahead on this night.

"It's been a long season, and it's been a great ride so far," said Heupel, whose fourth-quarter heroics included a 17-yard touchdown pass to Andre Woolfolk. "To win the Big 12 championship, to beat a great Kansas State team twice, is something special, and you should enjoy it. There is a certain chemistry on this team."

The Sooners trailed 10–3 early, but Heupel led the comeback by repeatedly hooking up with go-to guy Smith, who established career highs with eight catches for 96 yards. He also scored a second-quarter touchdown that tied the game at 10–10.

Heupel, who would finish second to Florida State quarterback Chris Weinke a few days later in the Heisman balloting, scored on a seven-yard run in the third quarter, then put the Sooners on top to stay with a strike to Woolfolk. Then late in the game, Heupel and Griffin led OU into field-goal position, where Duncan booted a 46-yarder that proved to be the difference.

The defense did the rest, holding the Wildcats to 239 total yards and 14 first downs.

"It really was a total team effort. That's the way it's been pretty much all season," said Jones. "This is a magical time for OU football—I really believe that."

The Finale: Oklahoma Number One
Bringing Number Seven Home in Style
Entering the 67th FedEx Orange Bowl as a double-digit underdog only served to further inspire top-ranked and undefeated Oklahoma. But who could have imagined that a 26-yard Duncan field goal in the opening quarter would be all the scoring the Sooners would need?

After all, number two Florida State, owner of the number one offense in the country, averaged 42 points and 549 yards a game during the regular season. On this night, however, OU's defense provided the biggest statement of the season by holding the defending champion Seminoles to zero points and 14 first downs in a historic 13–2 Sooners victory.

"We were mad. We didn't get much respect from many people around the country, and we felt we had something to prove," explained Jones, who had five tackles, forced a fumble, and sealed the victory with an interception.

And prove it they did.

For all the pre-bowl buzz, Florida State's speed and talent never surfaced during the course of this one-sided battle. Weinke and the FSU offense never built any momentum, finishing the evening a telling 1 of 15 on third-down conversion attempts.

The Sooners carried a 3–0 lead into the second half, and Duncan added a 42-yard field goal to make it 6–0. With just over nine minutes to go, Calmus stripped the ball from Weinke, and Williams recovered for OU deep in Seminole territory. Two plays later, Griffin sprinted 10 yards to pay dirt, making it 13–0.

Only a botched snap on an OU punt attempt spoiled the shutout—but certainly didn't take any of the luster off the crowning achievement in the Sooners' fantastic season.

"I'm really proud of our football team for the toughness they showed and the way they have gone about this entire year and the way they approached this bowl game and the way they played this game," said Stoops, who was the defensive coordinator for Florida's 1996 national championship team.

"I said it all along: we came into this game fully expecting to win. Our players prepared the entire month with that in mind. It was never enough just to be in this game. Our players prepared for one thing and one thing only, and that was to win. That would be the only way this season would be complete."

Mission accomplished. The headlines read: "Oklahoma Sooners: National Champions."

In the wake of the national title, Marshall took one more look through the misty rain at the Pro Player scoreboard before making his final walk to the locker room. He and fellow Miami native Jones truly had given the home folks something to cheer about.

"We knew we were number one all along, but the media kept doubting us," said Marshall. "The key was we believed in ourselves all season, and to be number one is incredible."

Stoops and his staff instilled that belief, that cornerstone of this team's success. After running the gauntlet of Black October and winning 12 straight in the regular season, how could anyone have doubted this Oklahoma team in the end?

The answer is, they shouldn't have.

Bud Wilkinson was the winningest college football coach of his era and perhaps the most revered figure in Oklahoma football history.

Section IV
THE COACHES

JUST SAY "BENNIE"

...And you've summed up Sooner spirit.

The man who started the Sooners tradition of winning football, Bennie Owen, notched 122 wins as Oklahoma's head man. This profile of the legendary Sooners coach ran in Sooner Magazine *in 1930.*

It is not given to anyone to comprehend *all* that Bennie Owen has done for the University of Oklahoma. It's not likely that even Bennie realizes all he has meant to the school. And it is certain he would never claim the credit that is his merited due.

No man west of the Father of Waters has served any school longer in an athletic capacity than Bennie has served the Sooners. That in itself tells a story of vital significance to anyone blessed with a lifelong enthusiasm for athletics, mostly of the school and university variety.

It places Bennie's name alongside that of Yost of Michigan, whose pupil he was, Stagg of Chicago, and Dan McGuggin, of Vanderbilt. That, I believe, composes the list of men who, either as football coaches or as athletics directors, have seen 25 years or more of consecutive service in the same American college.

Thus has come to Oklahoma, through Bennie, national fame, well deserved and thoroughly appreciated in Soonerland. Because of Bennie, an Oklahoma alumni can speak up in any company of college men anywhere in the land and be sure of striking a spark of interest.

This much I can pledge every Oklahoman I know to be true from my personal experiences as a newspaperman that have ranged from the Yale club in New York to the University club in Seattle and from the broad expanses of Texas to the press box at Stagg Field in Chicago.

Never have I injected myself into football fanning bees anywhere in the land without letting it be known that the game is known in Oklahoma. And never has some such assertion failed to provoke questions about Owen. Mostly the comments run something like this: "That man Owen must be a whiz. How did it happen that Oklahoma got him? And how has Oklahoma been able to keep him?"

Since Sooners are celebrating, all too informally to some of us, the rounding out of 25 years of service to the school by Bennie, it may not be amiss to answer those questions somewhat at length.

The answer may be of some benefit to those long out of school who have been too busy making a living, getting married, and raising children to realize how time has passed and how much Bennie has done for their alma mater.

Certainly the story, inadequately as I may tell it, should, because of the facts and not their manner of presentation, be nothing short of an inspiration to the younger Sooners who may be seeking the best of guidance for their careers yet to crown their efforts.

Bennie Owen was a whiz of a football coach before he came to Norman in the fall of 1905. He had coached sensationally winning teams at Washburn and Bethany College after assisting Yost at Michigan the first year "Hurry Up" startled the Middle West with a championship 11 at Ann Arbor.

Oklahoma, with fewer male students enrolled in both preparatory school and the university proper than now have football suits issued to them each fall, had games scheduled with the Haskell Indians, Kansas, and Texas. The "Terrible Swedes," who had beaten Oklahoma under Owen much as they pleased, had no such attractive schedule.

My recollection is that it was Bennie's desire to coach a team that was to meet Kansas, as well as Oklahoma's desire to acquire the services of the best coach in the Southwest, that caused a union of a coach and a school that has meant 25 years of unbroken progress for both.

At any rate it would be hard to imagine any new coach being received with more genuine enthusiasm per capita than was Bennie when he reached Norman early in September 1905. And enthusiasm was almost all he found.

There were very few football players. Mostly the suits were old, unwashed, and rotted with the sweat and blood of former battles that all too often had found the Sooners on the small end of lopsided scores.

The contrast between the size of the new coach and the enormous confidence in him was startling. Those who attended the decidedly damp homecoming game last November saw more than 11 of Bennie's first varsity. It was my privilege to know them all as a fellow student. I lived in the same house with many of them. I massaged their bruises and knew their most intimate thoughts connected with football as well as other student activities.

I risked and escaped expulsion by a narrow margin to write of their heroic efforts and the indifference of some few faculty members for their physical welfare. So I think I am qualified to speak authoritatively of the travail of both coach and players in giving birth to the successful, long, and strictly honorable Owen system that has become Oklahoma's most cherished tradition.

In a month's time Bennie had made good beyond all question. This came about through an 18 to 12 victory over the best team the Haskell Indians ever had. It was achieved on a Monday afternoon after 60 minutes of the fiercest fighting—and I mean exactly that—that I have ever witnessed on any gridiron anywhere.

Those Indians were big, fast, tough, mean, and clever as the deuce about slugging their opponents when the referee and umpire weren't looking. After acquiring a number of black eyes and bruised jaws, there was enough retaliation to put an end to that phase of play.

The school went wild over the victory. Students saved the faculty the trouble of suspending classes the next day. Norman saw more shirttails the night after the game than McCall ever had in stock at one time. And the next day was given up to whole-souled celebration by students and faculty alike.

The team was too badly bruised to do more than take a sound licking from a giant Kansas team the following Saturday at Lawrence. But for the first time in the history of the school a real crowd of fans had gone outside the state with a Sooners football team. That constitutes Bennie's second big contribution to the school.

In four weeks he'd shown the school a winning team. In another week his success had been responsible for crystallizing Sooners spirit to a greater extent than ever before.

A week later Oklahoma's first victory over the Texas Longhorns had put football and school spirit permanently on a higher plane than it had occupied before.

Bennie not only made good football teams. He made men of players and students alike. He did this by example, not by preaching.

As a college reporter that first fall of Bennie's presence in Norman, I dogged his footsteps night after night as he followed his players up and down Boyd Field. I listened to his talks before games. I never heard him use profanity on or off the field. I never heard him abuse a player for boneheaded playing. And yet he seldom failed to make his men feel their failures and learn valuable lessons from them.

"Murder, murder, murder," was his favorite and most repeated exclamation when a pet play failed to work or a player missed a wide-open tackle.

When players lagged, Bennie often injected himself into the scrimmage. Then the fur flew. It seemed every man of the opposition became animated with the desire to stop Bennie and even undress him in the bargain. They used to throw him pretty hard and pile up on him. But all he did was grin.

Bennie capped his first season with a triumph over his former team, the "Terrible Swedes" from Bethany.

There were many students that rainy Thanksgiving night in Oklahoma City who wanted to make much of what is now called *whoopee*. Saloons were as open, as warm, and almost as well lighted as the modern picture palaces. Most of us had some extra change in our pockets as a result of the game.

Everyone wanted Bennie to join a rollicking parade that proposed to tour brass-railed emporiums. But Bennie knew better than to get out of character that way. His refusal didn't offend. It simply increased the respect of the student body for their new coach.

"Boys, I feel just great the way I am about the victory this afternoon," said Bennie as he was surrounded in the old Lee hotel lobby. "I don't drink. You don't want me with you. I don't blame you for feeling as you do. If you must celebrate, try to remember that your conduct tonight will reflect on your school just as the team's conduct reflected on it this afternoon."

The celebration didn't last so long as it might have. There was much yelling. Sooners yells were given on the streets and many other college yells were roared out stumblingly from before the long mirrors behind the mahogany bars. None missed the midnight Santa Fe to Norman because of the celebration. Yet all were very, very happy.

Through the next 24 years, in season and out, Owen has continued to shape the destiny of Oklahoma athletics and mold by fine example the character and manhood of Oklahoma. What the school has achieved in athletics is due primarily to him and his rare ability to lead the youth of his chosen state.

Owen Field and the stadium are a magnificent physical tribute to Bennie and the university's growth. But best of all is the Owen spirit that has been imparted to thousands.

He has overcome physical disaster met in a hunting accident and gone on undaunted to greater victories. Because of his character and charm he was privileged to marry a lovely daughter of Oklahoma. Because of that and the nearly always proper appreciation of his ability by Sooners, other schools were unable to lure him away by offers of gold.

Bennie has worked from the first for Oklahoma because he loved his business and knew how to play the game as it has been played by few other men anywhere in the land.

He wasn't a Sooner born but he's truly a Sooner through the highest order of sacrificial services to the school, and thousands of Oklahomans hope that when he dies, he'll be a Sooner dead.

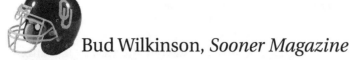

Bud Wilkinson, *Sooner Magazine*

BUD WILKINSON'S FOOTBALL LETTER—1952 SEASON FORECAST

In the early 1950s Sooner Magazine *had an exclusive agreement with Bud Wilkinson to publish a season forecast letter written by the legendary coach. These were Wilkinson's thoughts on his team before the 1952 season.*

Dear Sooner:

Boyd Gunning, our alumni secretary, has asked me to write you a letter about football at OU this fall. I think our team will compare favorably with the team we had last season.

How many games we will win is something else. Because of our more difficult schedule and the tough caliber of our competition, it is difficult to estimate this. If the ball bounces well for us, we could be a poor team and win eight. Yet if we don't get the bounces, we could be a good team and still win only three or four.

I can be definite about one thing—the schedule presents the greatest challenge we've been up against since I became coach at Oklahoma. Pitt and Notre Dame have come on our schedule at a time when each will be very rugged. Texas always gives us a terrific test and will again this fall. The Big Seven is growing progressively better every year. Colorado, our opening opponent, will be very hard to beat. They've lost only one game at Boulder the last two years, by four touchdowns to three to our national championship club of 1950. And they return a solid front of lettermen.

Kansas will probably be the toughest of all. I honestly believe they have the best offense in America. Their 1951 backfield—Jerry Robertson, Charley Hoag, Bob Brandeberry, and Bud Laughlin—returns intact and in Gil Reich, the West Point transfer who will be their new quarterback, they have a wonderful player. He looked so good in practice that two former quarterbacks, Chet Strehlow and Jerry Bogue, have been changed in position to end. Kansas retains the core of its fine offensive line, headed by tackle Oliver Spencer. The Jayhawkers expect to have their best defensive team in years. On top of all this, we play them on their home field at Lawrence.

Nearly all our toughest opponents must be met away from home this year, which poses a terrific obstacle. Colorado, Texas, Kansas, and Notre Dame, all of them powerhouses, will be encountered away from our home soil. Last year we found out how hard it is to defeat a team forted up on its own field when we met and lost to Texas A&M at College Station. We'll face that situation at least four times this coming season.

Our main problem in spring practice was to develop enough overall line strength—reserves as well as starters—to play the schedule. We spent a lot of time with our linesmen in the spring practice and were happy to see some improvement. Several new boys you haven't heard of much—Kurt Burris, Wray Littlejohn, Ross Ausburn, Jerry Wilkes, Don Brown, Steve Champlin, and Milt Simmons—looked improved. We're counting on them to come through this fall and give us the reserve strength we'll need so badly.

Max Boydston's shift from fullback to end will help us. Our end situation was very discouraging before spring practice. I don't mean to be critical of the boys we have there, but they're just not as good yet as they need to be, and our end situation remains critical.

Our problem of locating a linebacker to replace Bert Clark, our hard-hitting cocaptain of last year, remains unsolved. Sam Allen of Chickasha will be one of our linebackers. Lester Lane, sophomore from Purcell, looked very promising at defensive halfback and may win a berth there. He has a pair of basketball hands that should come in handy when the opposition throws passes in our secondary. Lester tackles well, too. He may become the first OU athlete since Tom Rousey in 1942 to win both a football and basketball letter.

What we need most is to build up our speed in all 11 positions. We're not a slow team but we're not fast, either. Our 1952 schedule is so rough that we've got someway to have every player running a step or two faster this fall. As an example of how important speed is, take our 20–27 defeat in the spring game with our alumni here last April 5.

Jack Jacobs of the alumni threw a forward pass to George Thomas. One of our boys almost knocked Thomas out of bounds. If he had reached him, we would have led 14–7 at the half. But he didn't quite reach him and Thomas scored, tying the game 14–14 at the half. Multiply that step through an entire football game and you see how disastrous it can be. If every man on our squad would run a step faster next fall than he ran this spring, we'd be a 20 percent better football team.

This is roughly the way we will line up on offense when our autumnal practice begins late in August:

LE—Max Boydston, Kay Keller, Dick Ellis, Merle Owens, Reece McGee, Jenings Nelson.

LT—Roger Nelson, Jim Davis, Steve Champlin, Kurt Burris, Jerry Wilkes.

LG—Dick Bowman, Doc Hearon, George Cornelius, Don Brown, Chet Bynum.

C—Cocaptain Tom Catlin, Sam Allen, Gene Mears, David Shelton, Jim Acree, John Washington.

RG—J.D. Roberts, Bobby Gaut, Milton Simmons, Jerry Ingram, Ray Powell.

RT—Ed Rowland, Melvin Brown, Ross Ausburn, Wray Littlejohn, Ron Thompson.

RE—Carl Allison, John Reddell, Bob Berendzen, Mickey Imel, Bill Coffman.

QB—Cocaptain Eddie Crowder, Gene Calame, Billy Ballard, Lester Lane, Jack Van Pool.

LH—Billy Vessels, Buddy Leake, Larry Grigg, Bob Herndon, Juel Sweatte.

RH—Tom Carroll, Merrill Green, Jack Santee, Jack Ging, Dale Lawyer, Bob Pyle.

FB—Buck McPhail, Joe Gaynor, Jerry Donaghey, Chuck Baker, Bob Santee, Pat O'Neal.

Our losses include ends Jack Lockett and Hugh Ballard, tackles Jim Weatherall and Art Janes, guards Fred Smith and Bert Clark, center Bill Covin, and backs Dick Heatley, Frank Silva, and Billy Bookout.

We will have to develop new punters and PAT kickers for the first time in three years in order to replace Heatley and Weatherall.

Buck McPhail and Buddy Leake will probably do most of both varieties for us.

The designation of special days on our home schedule is as follows: the Kansas State game at Norman on October 25 will be Band Day, the Missouri game at Norman on November 15 will be Dad's Day, the Nebraska game at Norman on November 22 will be Homecoming. We hope to see you at all of our games and we are very grateful to you for your support.

Booton Herndon, *SPORT Magazine*

BUD WILKINSON: THE WINNINGEST COACH IN FOOTBALL

In November 1956, at the height of Bud Wilkinson's winning ways at OU, SPORT *magazine ran this article on the legendary coach.*

The cynics will tell you he wins because he has enough oil money behind him to buy all the talent in the Southwest and doesn't mind working his horses until they drop. But the real reasons for Bud's success are much more complicated.

One of the big drawbacks of the hazardous business of writing about sports is the remarkable ease with which you can make a fool of yourself. People who read sports stories aren't shy; when they think you're wrong, they tell you about it. This is why sports columns are so full of hedging. In predicting a Notre Dame victory over Muskingum Teachers, for example, any sportswriter with all of his buttons will manage to throw in a phrase or two on which he can fall back later. "You have to remember that a football takes funny bounces," he will write, or, "Muskingum has always played its best against Notre Dame, and you never can tell."

But there is one thing worse than making an honest mistake, and that is to be taken for a sucker. Call somebody a bum, for example, and although you may run the risk of losing a few teeth the next time you encounter him or his big brother, at least nobody is going to give you a horse laugh. But call him a nice guy, a stickler for sportsmanship and clean play, and an honest-to-God gentleman, and, sure enough, the next time you walk into Toots Shor's, somebody at the bar is going to die laughing at you.

And so it is that when you start to tell the true story of Charles Burnham Wilkinson, head football coach and athletics director at the University of Oklahoma, you've got to be ready to take a razzing. Because Bud Wilkinson is just too good to be true.

First of all, just take a look at the record: Wilkinson has been head coach at Oklahoma for nine years. He has never lost a game in the Big Seven Conference. His teams have finished in the Associated Press' list of the top 10 football teams in the country for eight straight years and have won the national championship twice. Oklahoma went into the 1956 season possessing an all-time national record of having scored in 106 consecutive games and boasting a string of 30 consecutive wins, needing just one more to tie its own modern record. The Sooners have placed 20 players on various All-America teams during Wilkinson's tenure. In short, Oklahoma has become a football tradition, taking its place with the great teams of Notre Dame under Rockne and Leahy, Michigan under Yost, Tennessee under Neyland, and Minnesota under Bierman.

Now, all that is fact and it is easy to report. There can be no doubt that Wilkinson is the most successful coach in football today. It's explaining how he does it that becomes difficult. The easy way out would be to say, as many already have said, that Bud has gobs of Oklahoma oil money at his disposal and can buy up all the players he needs. Another suggestion, heard less frequently but still expressed on occasion, is that he will stop at nothing to win, that he's victory crazy.

For selfish reasons, I wish those answers were true. Then I could advance them fearlessly and run no risk whatsoever of making a fool of myself. The trouble is, they aren't true.

The real reasons for Wilkinson's success are much more difficult to explain. They embody such concepts as philosophy and faith, conviction, intelligence, devotion on the part of his assistants and players, and hard work. There are many coaches in this country who say that such talk is hogwash. The only answer I can give them is a question: Would they, or would they not, like to trade records with Wilkinson, here and now?

Wilkinson is tall (6'2") and comparatively slender (190 pounds). He's 40 years old but looks younger. His hair is prematurely gray but looks blond, and he has light blue-gray eyes. He has an eye-crinkling, shy smile, and he makes expressive gestures with his big, graceful hands. He likes to dress in blue—light blue suit, blue shirt, dark blue and red striped tie, for example—and he always looks neat and well-groomed. Women have been known to comment favorably on his appearance.

Wilkinson attends his church—he's an Episcopalian—regularly and occasionally sings in the choir. His two boys are acolytes. He encourages his players to attend both Sunday School and church.

Wilkinson doesn't give his football players any training rules whatsoever; that would be too easy. He expects them to meet and master temptation on their own, without guidance from the coaching staff. He expects them—husky young men from Oklahoma and Texas, turned loose at a training table—to eat sparingly, turn away seconds, and keep their weight down.

He doesn't scrimmage his team at all once the season starts, and he maintains a surprisingly light practice schedule. (No practice Monday, a half hour Friday, and an hour and a half other days.) He believes he can teach more football conversationally than he can by having his men knock their heads together.

Despite the fact that Oklahoma has always finished in the top 10 in yards gained rushing, proof of a mighty offense, Wilkinson picks his boys for their *defensive* ability, then teaches them what they need to know about offense. One year his first team was composed of 10 high school linebackers. A standout offensive player like Alan Ameche of Wisconsin and the Baltimore Colts, who ruefully admits he's a poor defensive player, would not have made the Oklahoma third team.

Bud isn't as interested in making and breaking records as he is in helping his boys develop character and moral toughness. His players are excellent citizens of the college community; they graduate at a 90 percent rate. Three Oklahoma players made the All-Scholastic last year (no other team placed more than one). Bud really doesn't have too much trouble selling such boys on Oklahoma, and he doesn't have to pay them under the table. As it says in a sound and thorough 56-page handbook for high school boys put out as a labor of love by Oklahoma's passionate publicist, Harold Keith, Oklahoma is just naturally the right place for the top boys of the area to go. If some of the other publicists I know who spend their time griping about Wilkinson's success would put in half the time and thought Wilkinson's boy Keith does, they might have a better understanding of the Oklahoma story.

Wilkinson does indeed have some alumni money for scholarships, but it is far less than is available at many other institutions and he says flatly that he wishes he didn't have to have any at all. He welcomed the National Collegiate Athletic Association investigation that found Oklahoma guilty of breaking certain regulations during 1954–55. (Extending a scholarship to five years for a boy making good progress toward his degree was one of the sins.) "I think the NCAA and its executive director, Walter Byers, are doing a great job," he told me enthusiastically. "I hope they keep right on doing it, too."

By now, probably, some of the cynics are convulsed with laughter. One of them, undoubtedly, is the coach who told me: "Bud Wilkinson is a complete and utter hypocrite. There's not a sincere bone in his body. But he'll give you that big smile with those pearly teeth, and crinkle up those baby blue eyes, and you'll walk out of there in a daze thinking Bud Wilkinson is the greatest man alive."

So, before going any further, here are what some pretty tough individuals have to say, candidly and frankly, about Wilkinson.

About his character: Witness: Leon Heath, Oklahoma All-American, 1950; fullback, Washington Redskins. "He's a saint."

About recruiting high school players: Witness: Jim Weatherall, Oklahoma All-American, 1951; tackle, Philadelphia Eagles. "Why should you give any boy anything extra to come to Oklahoma? What finer privilege could any kid want than to play under Bud Wilkinson? Even if you didn't play football and never even saw him, you'd still be better off just spending four years in the same town with Bud Wilkinson."

On the subject of dirty play: Witness: Jerry Tubbs, this year's cocaptain, who, barring injury, has All-America made in the shade, and who is a good Baptist boy who turned down a scholarship to one big university because he saw some students drinking beer. "We don't play dirty. Bud doesn't want us to."

About hypocrisy: Witness: Sam Lyle, one of Bud's assistant coaches. Lyle was captain of the 1949 LSU team that was trampled, 35–0, by Oklahoma in the Sugar Bowl. He coached a year at LSU and three at Georgia Tech before coming to Oklahoma. "I'll admit I couldn't figure Bud out," Lyle said. "He wasn't like any coach I'd seen before. He never raised his voice, on or off the field, no matter what kind of a boner was made. He would sit and talk quietly to players, talking about things like moral firmness, instead of running another rough scrimmage. At Georgia Tech, Bobby Dodd, who's also an intellectual on the subject of football, would get all enthusiastic and say, 'This is the play that's going to win the ballgame for us!' But Bud, under the same circumstances, will duck his head modestly and say, 'I hope this play will help us a little.'

"He comes out with a piece of philosophy from time to time that floors you. Take this one: 'Perfection is not attained at that point at which nothing else can be added, but at that point at which nothing else can be taken away.' I used to lie awake nights analyzing that statement. I finally decided there just isn't any way anybody could say it any better.

"But anyway, I finally got to where I couldn't stand it any longer. *Nobody* could be that good. He *had* to be a phony. I went to Gomer Jones, who's been here with Bud for eight years, and who played in a pretty tough league himself, and I put it up to Gomer."

Sam grinned. "I guess I'm lucky Gomer didn't deck me right then and there. He just looked at me, and he said, 'Bud Wilkinson is a gentleman, and the finest gentleman you will ever meet in you life.'

"I haven't questioned Bud Wilkinson's sincerity and integrity since. Take my word for it: He's everything he appears to be. He's the guy you wish you had for a father."

To one boy, as a matter of fact, Bud was like a father. That was Billy Vessels, a homeless kid bordering on delinquency who, after one conversation with his coach, went on to become an All-American and a college graduate. Said Billy of that conversation: "It was like a message from God."

Had enough? The evidence is overwhelming; Wilkinson is, impossible as it may seem, just what he seems to be.

But how does this win football games? For the fact remains that, no matter how saintly the coach may be, in the game of football you've got to dig in and move the other guy out of there. Well, first of all, as a player himself, Bud was not unaccustomed to this maneuver. A Minneapolis boy, he played for Minnesota during those glorious years when Bernie Bierman was head coach. Wilkinson was a running guard in 1934 and 1935 and quarterback in 1936. Bud says the switch wasn't too difficult; Minnesota ran from a single wing and the quarterback was the blocking back.

Even so, with just one season under his belt, he was named to the College All-Star team and he quarterbacked the squad to victory over the Green Bay Packers in the All-Star Game of 1937.

Bud says he acquired most of his technical knowledge of football from Bierman. He also learned the importance of physical fitness in this ultraphysical game. One of the things about Oklahoma's 20–6 victory over Maryland in the Orange Bowl last New Year's Day was the amazing rapidity with which the Sooners ran off their plays. In the third quarter, particularly, playing in the Florida heat, they picked themselves up off the ground, charged into and out of the huddle, and ran off another play before Maryland could get its defenses formed. Frequently Oklahoma players even knocked officials out of the way getting back to the huddle. If every single player had not been at the extreme peak of physical condition, this maneuver could never have worked. As it was, sportswriters covering the game counted off such miraculous performances as three plays in 37 seconds on one occasion, and three plays in 38 seconds on another. During the entire game, Oklahoma ran 73 plays from scrimmage. (During the regular season, in a couple of games they actually ran off more.)

How can you attain this superb physical condition? Wilkinson says it comes only from punishing yourself in practice after you are already dead tired. In other words, run those wind sprints, hit that dummy, again and again and again. This is not a brand-new Wilkinson concept. He learned it himself, the hard way, at Minnesota. "I'll never forget it as long as I live," he says. "It was a cold, raw day and we were practicing in the field house. Coach Bierman had us running wind sprints. We'd run, then stop, then he'd have us run again and again and again. It was torture. But I have another clear memory, too. It was of the game on the very next Saturday. We beat Iowa, 52–6."

Wilkinson's father, a prosperous mortgage loan broker in Minneapolis, wanted his boy to come into the business with him, but

Bud chose coaching. He was backfield coach at Syracuse when World War II came. He was commissioned in the navy and assigned to the navy's preflight training center at the University of Iowa. There he met head coach Don Faurot, the originator of the split-T formation. Wilkinson, along with the other assistant coach, Jim Tatum, was fascinated by the new formation. The two, both ardent students of football, would get together and discuss it by the hour.

The split-T formation is, apparently, all things to all men. Faurot, Tatum, and Wilkinson all have written books on the split-T and all of the books stress entirely different features of the formation. Bud hammers home the point that a split-T team can strike with swiftness over a broad front. The halfbacks line up behind their respective tackles; either can go straight forward, and the pitchout can go wide to either side.

Another feature of the split-T formation, particularly as practiced by Oklahoma, is the importance of holding on to that ball. Oklahoma maintains possession of the ball by making first downs. Instead of going out for the touchdown on every play, they try to punch through for three or four yards, looking for the first down. As long as they keep making first downs, they not only have a chance of making a touchdown, but their opponent has no chance at all. Oklahoma rarely throws a pass.

In addition to helping coach winning football teams in the navy, Bud also served as deck officer on the aircraft carrier *Enterprise* and saw plenty of action in the Pacific. He came to Oklahoma just as the 1946 season opened. Tatum had landed the head coaching job there and held a spot open for him.

That first postwar season is something the folks in Oklahoma would just as soon forget. Big Jim Tatum, the Carolina bulldozer, who has never been caught listening, was a little too much for them. Football players—nearly all service stars—poured in from all points of the compass. Jim had a good year, all right, winning seven games, losing three, and beating North Carolina State in the Gator Bowl. But some of the heads of the university got to asking themselves if it was worth it. After the season ended, Jim began traversing the three legs of the triangle between Oklahoma, Maryland, and North Carolina, issuing conflicting statements en route. The Oklahoma regents learned they had lost their football coach to Maryland with somewhat the same feeling that they might watch a tornado disappear over the horizon.

The first reaction was to throw out everybody who had had any connection with Tatum. Wilkinson, however, had made his customary terrific impression on everyone, and when the dust settled, the man who had hired Tatum was out, and the man Tatum had hired was in. Wilkinson became both head football coach and athletics director.

There was a question there for a while whether this was a compliment. People who were there say that Wilkinson turned gray in just a few months that year, picking up after Tatum. He was then 31 years old.

Even at that he won seven, lost two, and tied one in 1947, his first year as head coach. In 1948 Oklahoma lost the opener to Santa Clara but went on from there to 31 consecutive victories, losing to Kentucky, 13–7, in the Sugar Bowl at the end of the 1950 season. The next winning streak started in 1953, following a defeat by Notre Dame and a tie with Pittsburgh, and was up to 30 straight when this season opened.

How does Wilkinson do it? Well, here we go again. It's true that he has great intelligence and an executive ability that would net him many times his present income for a fraction of the hours spent on the job if he had gone into industry. It is true that he operates in a part of the country where football comes naturally. People work together in Oklahoma and Texas, enjoy community enterprise, and are proud to cheer for their team. Bud says his job would be much more difficult at a school like Harvard, say, where the emphasis is on the individual and on sophistication rather than on teamwork and unashamed enthusiasm. But then again, of course, Oklahoma plays, and beats, teams from other unsophisticated sections of the country.

Most of his All-Americans, in fact most of his players, have come from Oklahoma, and Oklahoma is far from a populous state. You could lose its population in a corner of New York or Pennsylvania. Three years ago Oklahoma placed two men on most All-America teams. Both—Max Boydston, end, and Kurt Burris, center—were from Muskogee, Oklahoma, population 30,000. By contrast, not one All-American came from greater New York, with a population of 9 million. Does this mean that the citizenry of Muskogee is of such astronomical superiority over that of New York? Or does it mean that two Muskogee boys had the good luck to play for a coach who would bring their natural ability to superb heights and give them a top-ranking team as a showcase for their talents?

The truth of the matter is that the one reason Oklahoma wins football games is Wilkinson. He does it with such intangibles as philosophical attitudes, inner faith and conviction, and unswerving moral determination. If you want to laugh at that, go ahead. All I can do is tell you what kind of company you're in. One guy who laughed real hard, for instance, is an ex-coach who once lost nine games in a row and is this year clerking in a haberdashery. Wilkinson emphasizes morale, condition, and toughness—both mental and physical. Football, he says, is a hard, rough, driving game. It demands the willingness to hit harder than the other fellow, to go all out for something you want, something you believe in, and something that's good and honest and clean. This willingness, more than size or physique, is the mark of the

Wilkinson player. It manifests itself in several ways. Oklahoma has, for example, no training regulations whatsoever. There is no written code, no list of forbidden fruit. It's up to each player to curb his own desires and to maintain his own physical condition, not just in season but the year round. And not just physically, but mentally as well. As Bud has often said, the boy who stays up late in the middle of the summer, who takes one drag off a cigarette after the season is over, probably hasn't hurt himself at all physically. But he has permitted a small crack to form in his own mental armor.

Bud says he isn't primarily interested in the one narrow phase of human accomplishment marked by victory, but rather in the whole overall development of the human character. Yet look at how this development—particularly in toughness, both physical and moral— pays off. Tatum, who ought to know, says that Oklahoma is the greatest second-half ballclub in history. Oklahoma has frequently been outplayed by teams for three quarters but has come back in the fourth quarter to win. Two notable examples of that are the back-to-back games again California and Texas Christian in 1954. Both pushed Oklahoma all over the field, but they couldn't put a dent in the boys' mental armor or superb physical condition. And Oklahoma beat them both in the fourth quarter.

Everyone knows that Oklahoma beat Maryland, 20–6, in the Orange Bowl; that looks like a terrific victory. Let's look at the game more closely, however. Oklahoma trailed, 6–0, at the end of the half. It was in the third quarter that the boys unleashed that trip-hammer attack. Yet, in their first drive downfield, the officials had to measure for first down on six consecutive sequences. A bunch of boys with less physical stamina, less moral determination, would never have been able to put on such a drive. Oklahoma, however, put on two of them, each for a touchdown. The fourth-quarter touchdown, an 82-yard run with an intercepted pass, was anticlimax, for Maryland had no recourse but to throw passes in the fourth quarter.

One individual play points up the whole foundation of Oklahoma football. It also, just incidentally, happened to win the game.

It was in the second quarter. Ed Vereb, Maryland's outstanding offensive star, had already scored once on a 15-yard run around end. Later in the first half he broke loose over his own right tackle on the far side of the field, then cut back, eluded several Oklahoma tacklers, and barreled down the left sideline with no one between him and the goal, 50 yards away. A runback of the movies shows what happened. You see Jay O'Neal, the second-string quarterback, playing left halfback on defense, come in swiftly. You see him meet Vereb after the Maryland speedster has already crossed the scrimmage line. Vereb, flashy and fast, sidesteps, swivels his hips, and eludes the tackle. O'Neal, carried on by his own momentum, runs completely out of camera range. Note now that O'Neal is going full speed toward the Maryland goal at this moment, while Vereb is heading downfield toward the Oklahoma goal. Naturally, of course, O'Neal is now out of the play entirely. The camera follows Vereb as he runs laterally toward the left sidelines, gets in the clear, then cuts on the burst of speed. Ten yards, 30, 50. Now, all of a sudden, into the field of vision, running diagonally on a carefully plotted line of intersection, giving it all the desperate determination his heart can hold, comes O'Neal. Somehow back there he stopped, turned around, and set out on pursuit. The whole thing is ridiculous, of course. O'Neal isn't particularly fast; Vereb is. But it is now obvious that the thought of *not* pursuing never entered O'Neal's head. If he had spent a 10th of a second more thinking about it, he wouldn't be in the picture, much less closing the gap. But close it he does. He knocks Vereb out of bounds 10 yards from the goal. O'Neal ran 66 yards to make that tackle, after having been completely out of the play.

Oklahoma then took the ball away from Maryland and Maryland's poise was seriously cracked. You can make all sorts of conjectures about whether Maryland would have gone on to score again if Vereb had made it that time. But one thing is certain. Even if the rest of the game had gone on as it did, and Oklahoma had scored its two touchdowns in the third quarter, Maryland would never have thrown the ball away and given a sophomore back named Carl Dodd an opportunity to run 82 yards with an intercepted pass.

There is just one more small item about that Orange Bowl game that might be of interest. Some of the players, during the days before the game, asked Bud if they could go swimming. "Of course you can," Bud said, with some surprise. "However, it's my personal opinion that swimming might tend to have some weakening effect. I don't think I'd do it myself."

Nobody went swimming.

Wilkinson disclaims much of the credit he gets for molding character. He points out with some asperity that the regulations that curtail the amount of time for practice cut down on the amount of teaching and training he would like to impart to his boys. This strange rule makes it necessary for Wilkinson to go out and recruit players who have proved themselves already, rather than work with boys who have developed more slowly, or who haven't had the benefit of excellent high school coaching.

One of the boys who came ready-made in both moral courage and physical ability is this year's cocaptain, Tubbs, of Breckinridge, Texas. All-State center in Texas and star of the high school East-West game played in Memphis each August, Tubbs was certainly sought after. Breckinridge is almost equidistant from the University of Texas and the University of Oklahoma, and Jerry visited both schools. It was Baylor, however, that came closest to landing him. Baylor is a Baptist school, and Jerry is a deeply religious boy. His family wanted him to go to Baylor. Other people in the town leaned toward the University of Texas. But no one at all wanted a Texas boy to go to Oklahoma. In one regard, that is the reason he went. "You see," Jerry says, "if I had gone to Baylor and it hadn't worked out just right, I could always have said it was somebody else's fault. 'Well, they talked me into it,' I could always have told myself. But if I came to Oklahoma, and something went wrong, the responsibility would be on my own shoulders. I couldn't blame my family, I couldn't blame my friends. And that's the way I'd rather have it, so I came to Oklahoma. I haven't regretted it for a minute. Baylor's a fine Baptist school with a good coach, I'm sure. But Coach Wilkinson is more than a coach. He'll be an inspiration to me as long as I live."

Bud didn't know all of the tortuous thinking that went on behind Jerry's decision to come to Oklahoma, but he sized up Tubbs correctly as a boy with enough physical and mental toughness to do anything asked of him. Tubbs is a splendid example of what Wilkinson expects of his boys, and how they respond. In his sophomore year Jerry began the season as third-string center, but moved up to the first team in a matter of days. A sudden weakness occurred at tackle and he was shifted to second-team tackle. The tackle situation became better, and Jerry was brought back to center, this time to the second team. Then another weakness developed. In the Oklahoma defense, the fullback and center are linebackers. There was a question as to whether one of the fullbacks could handle the job. The fact that Jerry had never carried the ball made no difference to Wilkinson. He moved him to fullback. The shift was made a few days before the game with Texas Christian. Tubbs set to work with all his intelligence, diligence, and guts, all three of which he is plentifully endowed with, to learn how to play fullback. The maneuver he found most difficult was the open-field block on the defensive end. It came hard to a man used to playing in the line. Wilkinson himself, who as running guard and blocking back had mastered the maneuver, took over and showed Jerry how to do it.

"I found it kind of embarrassing," Jerry said, twitching with discomfort at the very memory of it. "It had been raining, I remember, and the practice field was wet and muddy. But that didn't bother Coach Wilkinson. You know how personally clean he is. Yet he got out there and threw that block himself, over and over and over, getting down in the mud and picking himself up out of it, until I guess I just felt miserable. Every time I wanted to reach down and pick him up myself. So I guess I tried all the harder to learn it so he wouldn't have to get down in the mud again. It's kind of hard to explain, but here was this man, the country's leading coach, trying personally to show me how to do something, when all the time a great university was giving me an education just to do that anyway. You see what I mean?"

The first time Jerry carried the ball, against TCU, he made six yards. He executed his blocking assignments splendidly. He wound up the season with a six-yard rushing average. Last year he was moved back to center. This year he is expected to be Oklahoma's third All-American linebacker.

Another fine example of a youth of mental toughness is the quarterback, Jimmy Harris. Jimmy also comes from Texas—a town named Terrill. He, too, was All-State, and he had offers from just about every school in Texas, plus a lot more throughout the country. "Everybody in my hometown," he said, "everybody I ever talked to anywhere in the state, kept telling me not to go to Oklahoma. People in my part of Texas not only love Texas, they hate Oklahoma. You have to be from there to understand."

A popular technique among coaches at rival schools is to tell boys they'll never make the team at Oklahoma. Wilkinson thinks this is fine. What those coaches are saying, in effect, is: "You're not good enough for Oklahoma, but you are good enough for me." Some boys fall for it, and those are the very ones Bud doesn't want; other boys bristle at such talk, and they're the ones Bud does want. Such a boy is Harris.

Jimmy had played tailback in the single wing in high school, and he was a standout on defense. When Wilkinson informed him he was going to be a quarterback on the Oklahoma offense, and handle the ball on every play, he jumped at the chance.

He made his mistakes, too. Against California he called a handoff to the right, then he himself went to the left. "I felt a little silly," he said ruefully, "standing there sticking that ball out at nobody."

Another boner he pulled was during a fantastic maneuver Wilkinson expects from his quarterbacks as a matter of course. Many people who saw Oklahoma for the first time on television last New Year's Day expressed even more amazement at the way the Oklahoma quarterback makes his pitchout than at the famed Sooners fast break. Oklahoma quarterbacks, when they pitch out to the halfback running wide on the option play, *don't look where they're throwing the ball.* Wilkinson believes that if the quarterback looks to see where the halfback is, he takes a great deal of the surprise element out of the play. So the Oklahoma quarterback, *any* Oklahoma quarterback, must, while running at top speed, throw the ball sideways and a little behind, with both hands and without looking, at a halfback running as hard as he can.

"I missed Bob Herndon completely against Texas," Jimmy says miserably. "He had to stop, turn around, run back, and fall on the ball. Ten-yard loss."

When first-string quarterback Gene Calame was hurt in the TCU game of 1954, Jimmy, a raw sophomore, went in. TCU was leading, 2–0. Jimmy ran back a punt 69 yards for one touchdown, led a 75-yard drive, and scored himself for another. He broke a halfback loose with a terrific block to set up the third, and saved the game with a great defensive play in the final minute. Oklahoma 21, TCU 16.

Jimmy is one of a series of terrific quarterbacks Oklahoma has had over the years. Learning to play quarterback at Oklahoma beats any annuity yet invented. Within six years after their final season, Jack Mitchell and Darrell Royal were head coaches. Mitchell is now at Arkansas; Royal, who played his last year in 1949, is making a reported $17,000 a year at the University of Washington. Eddie Crowder returned from the service to become assistant coach at Oklahoma this year. Other players under Wilkinson who became head coaches are Wade Walker at Mississippi State and Pete Tillman at Arkansas.

Wilkinson puts in hours of head-to-head work with his quarterbacks. He plays a fascinating little game with them, using what he calls his "little men," three-inch-high figurines of football players. The quarterback takes the blue team, Wilkinson takes the red. He puts a pad of paper in front of him to resemble the football field, makes a mark with his pencil on, say, the quarterback's 30-yard line. That's where the ball is. Then he arranges his own players into one of a dozen defenses—a six-man line, say, with the tackles wide, three linebackers, and a two-man safety. "Okay," he says.

The quarterback now imagines himself standing over center, just before he calls the snap signals. First he looks downfield at the safety. Then he brings his eyes in toward the line of scrimmage, counting the depth of the defense—three deep, two deep, or, as in the goal-line defense, only one deep. Now he looks directly in front of his own center. If there's a man there, the defense is in an odd-man line; if not, it's even. Finally, he looks to see if the ends are covered. And now, quickly, he calls the play. In this case, against the wide-tackle six, he calls his fullback over tackle.

With no hesitation whatsoever, Wilkinson's pencil moves the ball for a loss of two yards. The worst play to call against the wide-tackle six is fullback over tackle. If the quarterback can't see why immediately, he asks, and Wilkinson tells him. After he makes that mistake on paper a few times, he will never make it in a game.

And that's why, in a game, Wilkinson's quarterbacks rarely call the wrong play. They may not call exactly the right one, but it's never the wrong one. And when the Oklahoma team breaks out of the huddle and the quarterback takes his position over center, his eyes always swiftly and automatically scan the defense. Checking his signals and calling another play becomes practically a reflex.

Harris gives additional credit for his own knowledge of quarterbacking to Calame. Gene was a typical Oklahoma quarterback, alert and smart. Yet Gene came to Oklahoma from a tiny town in the state with little football under his belt. Though he weighed just 167 pounds, he made the Oklahoma team in his sophomore year as a defensive right end.

Wilkinson doesn't care how much a boy weighs if he's willing to play the Oklahoma brand of football. He takes chances on high school players other colleges wouldn't touch with a 10-foot pole. A good example was a 5'9", 210-pound butterball named Don Brown. Brown had five scholarship offers from other schools—as a French horn player. The only school that even considered him for football was Oklahoma. Brown is a wonderful example of an old Oklahoma recipe—a boy with guts and a coach with inspirational intelligence. The first thing Wilkinson suggested was for Brown to lose weight. He went on a diet and lopped off 26 pounds, going down to 184.

Brown was further aided by another Oklahoma custom. Each summer Wilkinson and his assistants study movies of football games between other teams. They learn a lot from them. One of the things Bud noticed in the movies of UCLA games was the remarkable grace and fluidity the players showed. Looking for the reason, he found it was due to certain drills. In one of them, for example, a coach stands on a platform and waves his hand forward, backward, to the right, or to the left. The squad, facing him, running at full speed, shift directions according to the wave of the hand. This drill is of such effectiveness that the Oklahoma coaches can actually measure the improvement, in agility and poise, of the first-year man between the beginning and the end of the season.

Brown also had someone else on his side. If it is a coincidence that nine Oklahoma linemen have made All-America, the name of that coincidence is Gomer Jones, just about the best line coach in football. Jones, like Wilkinson, knows full well that playing defense is more difficult and requires faster reactions than playing offense. He has worked out drills that develop instantaneous reflex actions to counter all basic offensive maneuvers. He puts two men head to head and stands behind one of them. Then, with a hand signal, he directs the lineman facing him to perform one of several maneuvers: drive straight forward, take the man to the left or the right, pull, or go into pass defense. The defensive lineman must respond to each maneuver with a positive reaction. After a while it becomes instantaneous.

All of this explains why a 5'9", bowlegged French horn player, weighing 184 pounds soaking wet, played first team the year Oklahoma knocked off the national champions, Maryland, 7–0, in the Orange Bowl. And Brown wasn't a backfield man; oh, no. He played *tackle*. On one play in that game, Brown went right over Maryland's Stan Jones, the 250-pound All-American, to throw Ronnie Waller for a 12-yard loss.

But the wrap-up of all Wilkinson teaches, the result of all these drills, can be seen in two seconds of the movies of the 1953 Kansas-

Oklahoma game. Kansas had the ball. Brown's assignment on the particular defensive play was to make contact with the end. He did so. Then, just as though a coach had waved his hand from the platform during drill, Brown shifted his weight and made contact with the Kansas tackle. Here came the Kansas fullback, and Brown shifted again and piled into him. It took Brown about a millionth of a second to see that the fullback didn't have the ball. He dropped him and got the halfback, who did. On that one play, Brown hit three men and still made the tackle. Kansas made two yards on the play.

On the question of weight reduction, incidentally, the Oklahoma coaches set an example for their boys. Bud is almost as lean and hard as he was when he played football himself. He has never permitted his weight to go over 195 pounds, despite the cold mashed potatoes, gravy, green peas, and bread served on the banquet circuit he is required to make every winter. Jones, who was All-America at 210, is now, 20 years later, 20 pounds under that. "And I wish I'd played at 195," Jones says. "I'd have been faster and better. And I wouldn't have got tired as easy."

The coaches don't ask any boy to take off weight during the season or during spring practice, but rather, to cut down on the food intake in winter and summer. Even so, when a freshman guard named McAdams was advised to knock off a few pounds during spring training this year, he went to work right away. Within six weeks he had trimmed down from 224 to 204. That is a nice weight, incidentally. J.D. Roberts, All-American and Lineman of the Year in 1953, played at that weight. But Roberts came to Oklahoma at 230.

The most demanding position on the Oklahoma football team is that of left end. He is key man in the Oklahoma defense. A few years ago the Sooners squad was blessed with a boy named Carl Allison who could do everything on defense, and do it well. He could play in the line and handle the biggest tackle the opposition could throw at him. He could move back the linebacker and react like a cat. And in the extremely ticklish position of defensive halfback, where one false step can result in the opponent's end catching a pass for a touchdown, he was superb.

Ever after Allison, Oklahoma's left ends have been required to do all three jobs. Last year's Joe Mobra, who had never played end before coming to Oklahoma, was so good at it that he made All-Conference.

Aside from this somewhat unorthodox maneuver of having one man play three different positions on defense, the Oklahoma defense is comparatively routine. It's only on occasion that Wilkinson departs from this. One such occasion last year was against Pittsburgh. Oklahoma was extremely respectful of Pittsburgh last year. Chief scout Lyle described the Pittsburgh offense with awe. Although Pitt ran from the split-T, it nevertheless seemed to generate all the power over tackle and end of the old single wing. Wilkinson decided that his orthodox defense simply would not contain that powerhouse. He gambled with a special defense, devised for Pitt alone.

This was a six-man line. On the right side the end slashed in on a diagonal. The tackle played the Pittsburgh end head-on, trying to drive straight in. And the guard, playing off the Pittsburgh guard, was to knife in between guard and tackle, leaning to the *outside*. This same pattern was repeated on the left side. What it did, in effect, was to put the Oklahoma manpower behind the Pittsburgh tackle.

That seemingly left two openings. One was actual, one wasn't. Because there was no Oklahoma man in the gap from guard to guard, it looked like a good place for a quarterback sneak. Actually, and this is probably the greatest compliment that Pittsburgh quarterback Corny Salvaterra will ever receive, Wilkinson had his two linebackers, Tubbs and Billy Pricer, playing in close to look out for just that eventuality. It was around the ends that the real weakness lay. Only the alertness of the ends, slashing in, and their ability to swerve instantaneously to the outside, protected the Oklahoma flanks successfully.

With such a defense, Oklahoma held Pitt to 14 points. But that was only half the ballgame. So impressed had Wilkinson been by the Pitt defense that he had cooked up one special play to throw at them. This was a reverse that he had first noticed studying movies of Wichita University during the summer, and to which he had added a personal touch.

It's mighty hard to devise a good reverse in the split-T formation. But in the films of Wichita games, Wilkinson had seen that Pete Tillman had managed to cook up a beauty. The Wichita quarterback moved back in a diagonal instead of sliding laterally, and he faked the ball to both the left halfback and the fullback going over the right side of the line. Then he handed it to the right halfback, who took off for the left. Tillman had an interesting pattern of cross-blocking on the left side of the line and pulled his left guard to take out the opponent's right end.

But there was still one thing wrong with this play. Linemen today play keys. If you were the defensive right guard or linebacker, you would see the guard in front of you pull out and skedaddle over to get the end. You would know that, no matter how much faking went on in the backfield, something was going to happen in that direction. You would go there. To circumvent that, Wilkinson put in a very simple little change. He pulled his *right* guard and crossed him over to take out the end. The linebacker on that side of the line would see the guard pull, of course, but for him to cross over was far more difficult. That play paid off for Oklahoma that day. Tommy McDonald scored from 43 yards out, Clendon Thomas scored from the 32, and Bob Burris set up another touchdown with a long run, all off the same reverse.

Put another way, Oklahoma managed to score on Pittsburgh, which the coaching staff considered a more powerful team, through hours spent studying movies in the summertime. The defense came out of conferences that begin at Oklahoma at 6:00 in the morning.

The schedule of a successful football coach is killing, and not just during the season, either. When I visited Wilkinson last spring, I had an appointment, arranged weeks in advance, for some time Monday morning. I dropped into Harold Keith's office at 9:00; Bud came by a minute later, looking for me with an impatience his courtesy almost concealed. At 11:00 he had to leave to drive to Oklahoma City for a conference on a series of television films. He was back at 1:00 in order to be photographed for this and two other magazines. We talked from 2:00 until 4:00, when he left for another appointment. He had a banquet that night and another appointment in Oklahoma City—as head of a Boy Scout drive—at 10:00 the next morning. We agreed to meet at 7:30 AM.

Next morning he was a half hour late. I chided him.

"I'm terribly sorry," he said, "but the athletics director at Nebraska came by to see our training table operation. I couldn't see him last night—I didn't get home until after midnight—so we met at 6:00 this morning. I hope I didn't inconvenience you."

This was the slack season.

But Bud likes the life of a coach, particularly an Oklahoma coach, and he intends to stay. His 10-year contract, at $15,000 a year, doesn't run out until 1962. No one at Oklahoma seems to think he will break it, no matter how much he could get elsewhere. No one seems to think the university would attempt to break it even if Wilkinson had some terrible years. As it stands now, the president of the university, Dr. George L. Cross, is of the opinion that if a university has a football team, it, just like the school of medicine or college of engineering, ought to be a good one.

Everyone except Wilkinson, a natural-born pessimist, expects Oklahoma to have another good season this year. The squad lost five men from the starting team—end Mobra, tackle Cal Woodworth, guards Bo Bolinger and Cecil Morris, and halfback Burris. All made All–Big Seven, and Bolinger made All-America, too. Also, five lettermen were lost, one to the ministry and four who transferred to Edmond, Oklahoma, Teachers College. But 28 lettermen returned. Several of the men on the alternate team were sophomores last year. They were looking great at the end of the season. Some sportswriters at the Orange Bowl said Oklahoma had the *two* best teams in the country.

Look for Oklahoma to continue certain innovations. The fast break, the alternate 11s, and the unbalanced line will all be back again, plus a new spread formation from an unbalanced line. It was used in the first half of the Alumni Game last spring; and Bud and his coaches were pleased with its potentiality. This spread is still another effort to increase the threat of breakaway play, something Wilkinson wants more of this year.

After all, Bud needs everything in the book to get by this year's schedule—North Carolina under its new coach, Jim Tatum; Kansas and Kansas State, two Big Seven foes; Texas at Dallas; and on October 27, Notre Dame at South Bend. Two proud teams, each carrying the tradition of great football powers on their shoulders—whatever happens before or after, that is going to be *the* game. It is to be televised nationally and will attract a tremendous living-room audience. But this will be a game worth viewing in the flesh. A clash of titans always is. See you there.

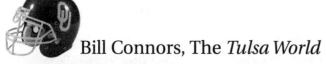

Bill Connors, The *Tulsa World*

DESTINY AND CHARLES FAIRBANKS

When OU head coach Jim Mackenzie died tragically from a heart attack following the 1966 season, Chuck Fairbanks became the Sooners' head coach. Bill Connors wrote the following article on Fairbanks before the 1967 season started.

Destiny has been kind to Chuck Fairbanks. Through trial, temptation, and tragedy it turned his disappointment into happiness, rewarded his loyalty, and, finally, got him what he wanted most, under the most unwanted circumstances.

As a high school coach at Ishpeming, Michigan, Fairbanks was offered his first job on a college staff by Lloyd Eaton at Northern Michigan. Fairbanks happily accepted, but before he could report, Eaton accepted an offer to become an assistant to Bob Devaney, the head coach at Wyoming (where he succeeded Devaney as head coach when the latter moved to Nebraska). Fairbanks shook off his disappointment and reconciled himself to a longer apprenticeship in the schoolboy ranks.

But two months later, Fairbanks's former Michigan State teammate, Frank Kush, was elevated to head coach at Arizona State upon Dan Devine's exit to Missouri. Kush had a job for Fairbanks, and it was a better one than Northern Michigan.

Several years later while an assistant at Houston, Fairbanks was offered a position on Doug Dickey's staff at Tennessee. Fairbanks wanted to accept, but it was midsummer, unusually late to make a move. In a show of loyalty to his boss and good friend, Bill Yeoman, Fairbanks declined the tempting offer and stayed at Houston. Had he accepted, Fairbanks wonders, would he have been in that car that was crumpled by a train a few months ago, killing three Tennessee aides who were en route to an early morning staff conference?

After the season was over, Fairbanks was offered a place on the new staff Jim Mackenzie was assembling at Oklahoma. It was a much better job than the one he had turned down at Tennessee six months previously.

Shortly before last Christmas, Fairbanks was made a tempting offer by Devine at Missouri, with this bonus: Devine would retire within four years and name Fairbanks as his successor. But Fairbanks surprisingly chose to stay at OU, partly because of being elevated to offensive coach (replacing Homer Rice, who landed the head job at Cincinnati) and the subsequent raise in salary that went with the promotion, and partly because he "wanted to stay with Jim and be a part of something big and exciting."

Four months later, the "big and exciting" dream ended for Mackenzie. He was dead at 37, a heart attack victim, and Fairbanks again was the beneficiary, as destiny swept him into the biggest challenge of his life, and into one of the most pressurized jobs in a pressurized profession.

The man who steps into the hot seat as Oklahoma's 15th head coach (third in as many years) is 34, reared and trained in the Big 10, but deep in Southwest conviction and philosophy. Trim, intent, and well-groomed, he has the executive style and organized look that are now as essential to head coaches as booster clubs and quick linebackers. He is 6'1", weighs 190, has brown hair, blue eyes. He usually looks as though he just finished doing a TV shaving commercial.

Fairbanks is ambitious but patient, quiet but aggressive, candid but personable, confident but humble. When OU authorities, for some reason never adequately explained, gave him only a one-year contract and thus greatly magnified the pressure, Fairbanks seemed unshaken. "I plan to get the job done anyway," he said.

Is he Destiny's Darling? Has fate saved him to rebuild the Oklahoma citadel? While a curious public awaits the performance of the team, there are some interesting facts about Fairbanks's background—facts that some may prefer to think of as omens, because they show he has common bonds with OU's most distinguished football alumnus and Fairbanks's two heroic predecessors.

His background and the circumstances of his debut smack of Bud Wilkinson. His postcollege thinking changed like Darrell Royal's. His philosophy and formation preferences are the same as Mackenzie's.

Like Royal, Fairbanks came out of college with views that were geared solely to offense. But coaching quickly gave him an appreciation of defense. Now he is conventional, though less conservative than some of his colleagues. He believes, "You begin to build with a sound defense and kicking. They give you a chance to win." But he adds, "Great backs will win for you. They will do things on their own, sometimes without much help, that win. When I was at Arizona State, we tried to put together a film clip of how we executed a sweep that had been successful for us. We wanted to include all the basic things that made the play effective. We looked at our game films for days trying to find the ideal blocking to use for the clip. We couldn't find it. What we did find was that our great backs were making the sweep go without much help.

"Great backs make the difference. In selecting personnel for positions, I want the best backs to play offense because they win for you there making touchdowns more than they can on defense by stopping touchdowns. But I want the best linemen on defense, because they can win more for you by stopping TDs than making them."

Offensively, Fairbanks desires the same running-passing balance OU displayed last year. "To be consistent over the long haul," says Fairbanks, "I think you must establish something basic and fundamental, something that will challenge your opponent. There are going to be times when you must simply take the ball and drive it down your opponent's throat. You can't do it by being fancy.

"But I also believe you must throw the football to win. I think you must throw some kind of pass real well. I believe if your quarterback is skillful, you can afford to throw the ball from inside your own 30, but I do not believe in being reckless. I think your defense must dictate what you do on offense. If our defense is good enough to stop our opponent and get the ball back for us, we might get a little exotic on offense. But if our defense is weak, then we will be careful what we do on offense."

Fairbanks's coaching philosophy was shaped by four men—Duffy Daugherty, under whom he played at Michigan State, Kush, Yeoman, and Mackenzie. The one thing they all had in common, Fairbanks says, was recruiting. "Each of them worked harder on recruiting than any other area." Expanding on his experiences under these four, Fairbanks recalls: "Duffy was the first man to impress upon me the value of quickness and team speed. When I played at Michigan State [1952–54], we had great quickness and team speed, and we weren't big. I think Michigan State has gotten away from this the last few years and put more emphasis on size. I would not classify myself as an advocate of the present Michigan State system. The first thing I want in a player is speed, over size. But I got that from Duffy. The other thing that most impressed me about Duffy was his sincerity in dealing with all sorts of people. I hope some of that rubbed off on me. He is a man of great integrity. After I turned down the Tennessee job, which he knew I wanted, Duffy wrote me a letter saying he was proud of me for being loyal to Bill. I really value that letter.

"Kush was very blunt, a let-the-chips-fall-where-they-may kind of fellow who was a tough disciplinarian. I am not a hard-nosed disciplinarian, but I can be very demanding. Rather than tell a youngster this is the way it must be done, I would rather instill the desire for a boy to discipline himself, rather than have to discipline him myself. Yeoman was a great organizer and did not believe in doing something that would only help you today. He had vision and worked to build something that would be solid and sustaining."

Fairbanks's association with Mackenzie was briefer than with the others. But he is more like the late Sooners coach than any of his other ex-bosses. There is no similarity in physical appearance to the burly Mackenzie, and Fairbanks is not as outgoing. But he is strikingly similar in other ways. His philosophy is the same. He has the same passion for simplicity, and his conversation is laced with the same slogans: "Don't beat yourself"; "Don't overcoach a great athlete"; and "Do the little things right. You can't expect to do the big things if you don't do the little things right."

Fairbanks, like Mackenzie, is refreshingly candid, both on and off the record, and has thus far handled his press relations impeccably. He says, "I can't be Jim, but I may sound like him, because I believe so strongly in the things he believed in." Fairbanks did not acquire this likeness in the 15 months he worked under Mackenzie. It came over nine years, during which time Mackenzie had a profound influence on Fairbanks's career, dating back to 1958, when Fairbanks recalls, "Kush discovered he had no one who could coach pass defense. He looked at me and said, 'You're elected.' I knew nothing about pass defense, absolutely nothing. I never cared for defense when I was in college, I guess because I was such a poor defensive player. I had never played in the backfield [he was an end], and here I was coaching pass defense.

"I started studying everything to learn it. Believe me, the best teacher is having to do it yourself. I contacted a lot of people. Among them were Jim and Frank Broyles at Arkansas. I went to their spring practice in 1958, and that's where I was first exposed to the monster defense. Broyles and Mackenzie were more responsible for influencing my defensive thinking than anyone. I went back to Arizona State, we put in their defense, and I coached it all the time I was there. We had them come out to Arizona and conduct a clinic. Jim and I became good friends, and we visited quite a lot in the following years. I went to their spring practices whenever I had a chance."

Everywhere Fairbanks has coached, he has developed ball-hawking pass defenses. Arizona State's Joe Zuger led the nation in pass interceptions in 1961, and in Fairbanks's first game at Houston in 1962 Byron Beaver set an NCAA record by intercepting five of Don (Baylor) Trull's passes. OU ranked second in the nation in pass defense last year, allowing only one touchdown pass. Pass defense was the most improved phase of OU's play. Fairbanks also coached the offensive backs at Houston, where he was assistant head coach in 1965. He was in charge of OU's kicking game last year. At both Houston and OU Fairbanks gained a reputation for being a crack recruiter. The 1967 freshman squad has five recruits from Houston, each a result of Fairbanks's work.

"I think," Fairbanks says, "the kind of background I've had has made me a better coach. To coach pass defense you must understand more phases of the game than any other area. And by being where the staff was not always large, I learned how to work. Had I gone to some bigger school and worked with the offense at the start, I might not have become well-rounded enough to become a head coach."

Fairbanks was part of the Michigan State group that has had a sharp impact on the Big Eight Conference. His freshman coach in 1951 was Devine (Missouri). His end coach as a junior and senior was Devaney (Nebraska). From the same staff, Colorado got Sonny Grandelius, and Kansas State got Doug Weaver. Besides Yeoman, who was defensive coach, and Kush, who was a senior when Fairbanks was a sophomore, also on the coaching staff then was Alex Agase, now head coach at Northwestern. Carl "Buck" Nystrom, one year behind Fairbanks, now is OU's offensive line coach. "That was a great staff, but we never sent one out of here that was any better than Fairbanks," said Daugherty the day Fairbanks's appointment was announced.

Fairbanks played two years under Biggie Munn. He was an offensive end on Michigan State's 1952 national champions. In 1953, when limited substitution returned and forced two-way platooning, defensive inadequacies forced Fairbanks to the sidelines. But by 1954, when Daugherty became head coach, Fairbanks had learned to play adequately on defense and won a starting berth.

Fairbanks was married one day before his 18th birthday to Virgeleen "Puddy" Thompson, who was a babysitter for the Devines when Devine was a high school coach at East Jordan, Michigan. The Fairbankses have five children: Charles Jr., 14; Gwenn, 13; Melissa, six; Tyler John, four, and Tobin J., three. Fairbanks was born in Detroit the first year FDR was president. A Presbyterian, son of a retail baker, he graduated from high school in Charlevoix, Michigan, where he competed in many sports but was above average, he says, only in football. He remains an avid golfer. He regrets that he has not had time to sell himself to an unknowing Oklahoma public. But among the alumni and booster club meetings he could schedule, Fairbanks has appeared to impress. The general opinion: Oklahoma came out of a bad situation remarkably well.

He has a shy grin, is a good storyteller at banquets, and is a relaxed speaker. He goes through cigarettes at a fast pace, but is a light eater. He does not hesitate to express his opinion, when asked, on such controversial topics as redshirting and out-of-state recruiting. "I think redshirting can be good in some cases, depending on the boy," Fairbanks says. "A young boy who has not matured as fast or developed as fast as his teammates, and who might be in a five-year course, might benefit from redshirting. I believe in it in these cases. But I don't believe in a blanket, wholesale redshirt program.

"I think we should concentrate our recruiting on boys in the Southwest. But with the great reputation that Oklahoma has, I don't see why we can't go anywhere in the country and get a blue-chip prospect."

In his newly constructed, spacious, red-carpeted office, Fairbanks has quietly prepared for the most important three months of his life, keenly aware of the tradition he inherited and forever mindful of that shocking week last April 28–May 6. During that eight-day span, Mackenzie died; the assistant coaches were pallbearers at two funeral services (in Norman and Gary, Indiana); Fairbanks was selected as head coach, conducted numerous press interviews, and directed the varsity to a convincing victory over the alumni in the spring game.

"I felt," Fairbanks said a few hours after the Alumni Game, "that I aged 30 years the last week. For a while it seemed unreal that Jim could be dead. The first few times I went to the office after his death, I would catch myself about to ask him to make a decision. Then I would realize I must make those decisions." Looking back, four months later, Fairbanks says, "Jim's death cost the coaching profession a man who I believe would have made a great record. But he was more than that. Jim was a great person. I felt I lost a great friend. I have always wanted to be a head coach and have dedicated myself to that goal, but I would give anything for it to have happened under difference circumstances. Someone had to become head coach, however, and I am grateful it was me."

The late date precluded naming an outsider. Elevating an aide and retaining the staff was the only practical decision. The only other aide who was considered was defensive coach Pat James, five years older than Fairbanks and more experienced. This could have created a sticky situation, but they understand and respect each other. Each agreed to stay if the other got the job; Fairbanks's first action as head coach was to promote James to assistant head coach. Their relationship seems sincerely harmonious. When Fairbanks recently returned from a lengthy luncheon interview to find James asleep on his office couch, Fairbanks summoned the other assistants and laughingly said, "This is what our assistant head coach does." Awakened by the laughter, the witty James cracked, "If the head coach can stay out until 2:00 for lunch, I guess the assistant coach can take a nap." In a more serious vein, Fairbanks says, "I've worked with some great coaches, but Pat James is the best, the best I've ever seen on the field."

Fairbanks admits that there has been an inevitable change in his relations with the staff. "We were a real close group when I was assistant," Fairbanks says. "We used to go with our wives to each other's houses. There were no two closer than Pat and I. It was 'Chuck.' Now Pat and the others call me 'Coach,' and they seem to feel they should call or inquire before coming by the house. I guess, though, that's just part of the traditional respect a head coach gets. It goes with the responsibilities, I suppose."

There is a definite tenseness among the staff members about 1967. The squad has a sprinkling of quality, mostly on offense. But overall the squad is not strong, or deep, and the lines are vulnerable. It is generally thought that the Sooners might fall under last season's 6–4 record more easily than they will improve upon it. Fairbanks, however, is not pessimistic. Improved recruiting this year brightens the future.

Fairbanks's situation has a fascinating parallel to Wilkinson's hiring 20 years ago. Wilkinson was 30, with a Big 10 (Minnesota) background, had been on the OU staff only a season, and succeeded a fast-building predecessor, Jim Tatum, who left (for Maryland) after only one exciting season. Then, as now, there was concern about the new coach's ability to sustain the momentum. The momentum of 1947 was so sensationally sustained and upgraded that it cascaded into the tradition and legacy that now cast a giant shadow over Fairbanks and make his job more challenging, more demanding.

Fairbanks has also inherited a problem that has not been a paramount concern to any OU coach since Tatum. It is Oklahoma State. After reeling off 19 straight victories in that series, the Sooners have lost two one-point games to the Cowboys in the last two years. This, to be sure, rankles OU alumni. A decade ago it was Notre Dame and national supremacy that occupied OU. Then, as the decline unfolded, it became Texas and regional supremacy. Now it is OSU and state supremacy, the most important of all.

So the torch has been passed. It is unmistakably hot. But Fairbanks (who says, "I've always been lucky and a winner") calmly accepts his challenge. "I know we have to win," he says. "That's a fact of life. But I'm happy to be a part of a program where the goals are high. Coach Wilkinson built a lasting tradition. I am grateful for the opportunity to work at a university with such a tradition. For however long I am at OU, I want to do things that will be remembered not for just a year or so, but for 30 or 40 or 50 years. I want and intend to contribute to that tradition, too."

Wayne Bishop, *Sooners Illustrated*

BARRY SWITZER, THE COACH

He was brash, bold, innovative, and even lucky. Barry Switzer was also a winner, leading the Sooners to three national titles in his 16 seasons as Oklahoma's top man. Wayne Bishop's profile of Switzer originally ran in Sooners Illustrated *in 1981.*

Oklahoma was trailing Florida State by seven points with only minutes to go in the 1981 Orange Bowl. The Seminoles had not given up a touchdown in the fourth quarter all season. And the Sooners, a running team, had to put the football in the air.

Oklahoma won, of course. Sooners fans knew they'd win. They had "Switzer Magic" on their side.

Barry Switzer: The Boy, The Player, and now The Coach at the University of Oklahoma. Barry Switzer, who has won more football games than any other coach around. Who has won a higher percentage of his games than any other active coach. Who has won back-to-back national championships, coached two Heisman Trophy winners, and a pair of Outland Trophy winners.

Barry Switzer, who is destined to some day be honored in the Football Hall of Fame. Who may end up holding most of the coaching records in the NCAA if he wants to stay in the profession long enough.

But does he? Does this 43-year-old blond from Crossett, Arkansas, plan to stay at Oklahoma and put up with the pressure of winning championships, dealing with an often hostile press, and sacrificing his own private life in order to meet the obligations that the head football coach at Oklahoma University must meet?

"I want to coach at Oklahoma as long as I can coach at Oklahoma," said Switzer on the eve of his ninth season as Sooners boss. "I guess the future dictates just how long that'll be. It's like having a terminal disease ... It'll get you sooner or later.

"You just don't know when.

"I always thought there'd only be two guys who'd ever retire without pressure from the coaching profession—Bear Bryant and Woody Hayes. And Woody Hayes didn't make it.

"I'll tell you this, though: the last two recruiting years—and if we recruit well again this year—we might be in good enough shape to stay around here a little longer."

So the future for Switzer appears to be wrapped up in OU football. But how did he come to be in Norman in the first place? What events led to Switzer having the opportunity to weave his magic for the Sooners, and not for some other school?

In the two previous parts of this series, Switzer's life in Crossett as an outstanding athlete from a modest background to his playing career at the University of Arkansas was presented in detail. And when he graduated from Arkansas and began his hitch in the U.S. Army Reserve, there were few who thought he'd ever again be involved in football as any more than a fan.

But while stationed in Aberdeen, Maryland, in 1961, Switzer was called to the commanding officer's office for a phone call from Dixie White, an assistant Razorback coach.

"I was young, just graduated, and wasn't in a hurry. I was just enjoying life at that time, finishing up my hitch in the service," Switzer recalled. "So I went back to Arkansas thinking I'd work on my masters. I wasn't really thinking about all I was going to do—just let things roll along.

"I hadn't set any goals that I was going to be an executive in a corporation in Little Rock or something like that. I was going to let my connections or the people I knew just fall in place and get into business that way. I wasn't in a hurry."

Switzer and Fred Akers had just finished school at Fayetteville and served as freshman coaches. Then both went into the service.

Akers's stint in the service was extended due to the Cuban missile crisis. But Switzer got out early.

"One of my uncles said he thought Senator Fullbright made a phone call or two when he found out Frank [Arkansas coach Frank Broyles] wanted Barry," said Switzer's brother Don, now an attorney in Vinita. "And all of a sudden Barry was home. That's just my impression, and I certainly don't know that it's the truth, that a few phone calls were made to the right people. Most people, and I included, didn't think it was that big a deal at the time. What was such a big deal about coaching the freshman football team at the University of Arkansas?"

Switzer and former teammate Gerald Gardner drove 30 straight hours back to Memphis, where Barry caught a bus to Stuttgart, Arkansas. That was where Kay McCollum lived. She would soon become Mrs. Barry Switzer.

"I had just ordered me one of those new 1961 Chevrolet V-8s," said Barry. "Turquoise blue, sharp lookin'. And I hitched that up, then drove on down to Crossett. Spent a few days at home, then packed up and went to Fayetteville."

But the football bug had not yet bitten. This was just a vacation from life for Switzer. A chance to get back to the campus he had lived on for the previous five years and to be with the girl he was in love with, while still being able to be around football.

"That's when I really became close to Jim Mackenzie. We had had a player-coach relationship. But suddenly it became a coach-coach relationship. And that's entirely different.

"I lived in the dorm then as a dorm counselor. That was a tough job. When I hire a coach today who wants to do that, I know what they're going through. I probably lived more nights in that athletic dormitory [Wilson Sharp] than anyone else and still might have the record."

It did not sink in with Switzer immediately that coaching was going to be a new way of life for him. Mackenzie made learning not only fun, but a new challenge. Switzer began studying for hours in the film rooms, studying the game he had played only the year before.

"I got swept up in football. It was a good time at Arkansas. They were winning. Frank's program was blooming. And I got involved with some great coaches—Mackenzie, Doug Dickey, Bill Pace, Dixie White, Hayden Fry, Merv Johnson. It was really a great educational experience.

"You're as good as your tutors, I've always said. You go to MIT, you're going to have the greatest technical tutors in the world. You go to Podunk, they're not so good. Arkansas at that time was the MIT of college football when it came to tutors."

Orville Henry, sports editor for the *Arkansas Gazette*, had an early inkling that Switzer would be something special as a coach.

"I know that Barry was conscious of the press. He was always coming up with lines. And if he was around a writer, he'd always leave him with something. Frank would do the same thing. Barry was here last year for the Hall of Fame thing for Jim Mooty, and he dropped two lines on me just like he knew it was my job to get something from him. He always did that. He and Frank are a lot alike.

"They could be sportswriters.

"Jim Mooty was in trouble one spring when Barry was cocaptain, and Frank for the first and last time decided to let the squad determine what the punishment would be. And so they had this meeting, and it was after about the fifth or sixth day of spring practice and Jim had dropped out because of headaches or something. But he also had violated some rule.

"So Barry was cocaptain and he blurted out, 'Why don't we just suspend Mooty until next fall.' Well, that was just what Mooty wanted. It was just something that Barry blurted out without ever thinking. And that's what they did. But after that Frank coached Barry on what to do if they had a team meeting.

"Barry's got the fast motor that coaches have to have. And he also identifies with young people. He has all the confidence in the world, and it was pretty obvious to me that he was going to be a coach, and a good one, from the very start.

"He hung around Mackenzie. I remember in 1965 Arkansas had won 22 in a row and Barry came down the hall at the coaches' office one day and I happened to be there and he told me he had figured out the day, like in 1967, that they would beat TCU and break Oklahoma's 47-game winning streak. Of course, he was laughing."

By 1962 Switzer was making numerous appearances at coaching clinics. And coaches coming into Arkansas to do some brain picking would invariably wind up spending a great deal of time with this young assistant.

"Arkansas was having great success at that time, especially the monster defense. And I was coaching defense with Jim. People would come in from all over the country, and me, being single and free, I could spend hours and hours with them in the film room and at the blackboard. Coaches were always impressed with my knowledge and understanding of the game. I had learned so much from my tutors that I was offered several clinics."

Bob Blackman, who was putting Dartmouth on the football map at the time, spent several hours for three straight nights with Switzer. Barry's brother Don was a freshman at Dartmouth at the time. And Blackman wanted to get the two brothers back together again. He offered Barry the defensive coordinator's job on his staff.

Barry also turned down offers from VMI and several top high schools in Texas. Mackenzie had been tooting the horn for his young protégé.

"And that's how it all got started," explained Switzer. "I got swept up in it at the time. All of a sudden I realized that I knew as much or more than all these college coaches coming around. They were coming to me for answers.

"But I wasn't in a hurry. I knew you got the good jobs by being patient. You didn't just take anything that came along. You had to be selective … and lucky. You're foolish if you think you know it all after your first year as an assistant. It's that way in any profession. The rookie's damn sure not as experienced and as valuable a commodity as the guy who's been there five or six years.

"But all of a sudden I realized that, 'Hey, this might be what I want to do. I see other guys out there that I know as much about what it takes to win in this business as they do, and how to communicate with coaches and players.' So at this time I decided I was going to stay in coaching and see where it takes me."

In 1963 Switzer got the offer he had been looking for and told Broyles he was resigning.

Dickey had taken the head coaching job at Tennessee. And one of his first calls was to Switzer.

"Doug was in New York for the coaches' clinic when he called me and asked me to coach his ends and linebackers. Vince Gibson was going to be in charge of the defense. I had gotten married that summer, so I really considered it.

"At that time I was making about $6,000 a year and the varsity assistants about $12,000 or so. So I went in to Frank when he got back from New York and told him Doug had offered me the job. And I told him I was going to take it, because I'd have more coaching responsibilities.

"But Frank told me, 'Barry, if you don't leave, by this spring I'll have you a varsity position.' And I thought about that, and I knew what was fixing to happen. I knew there was going to be a coaching change—in other words, I was going to replace someone. And I liked everyone on our staff and I was sensitive to what was happening because I knew the guy he had in mind. I liked the guy and he was a good friend.

"I talked to about it, and he said, 'Barry, regardless of how you feel, whether you leave or not, Frank is going to make the change. He's going to replace that coach. So you can't worry that you're the reason it's happening. You're probably making it happen a little quicker, but it's going to happen.' With that rationale, I decided to stay. And Frank did make the move. I got a raise, became a part of the varsity staff."

Once again the Mackenzie influence had played a big part in Switzer's life. But it was to play an even bigger part two years later.

Barry spent the next two years coaching receivers and helping Johnson, now his assistant head coach at OU, with the offensive line. Arkansas went to the Southern Cal "I" offense, and in 1964 and 1965 went unbeaten, being named national champions in one poll the first year.

Switzer turned down more offers. There wasn't a better place to be than Arkansas at that time. He and Kay built a home in Fayetteville in the fall of 1965, just before Arkansas went to the Cotton Bowl to meet Louisiana State.

"Then Gomer Jones resigned at Oklahoma," Switzer commented. "I was very familiar with the Oklahoma situation at the time. You only got Tulsa television in Fayetteville. We speculated a lot about who would get the job—Doug Dickey, Vince Dooley—some of the names that had been thrown around.

"Then all of a sudden Frank Broyles gets Jim Mackenzie an interview. We were in Brownsville, Texas, getting ready for the Cotton Bowl.

It was warmer that time of year than it was in Dallas. Well, Jim gets in one of those puddle-jumper airplanes to go for his interview and he's asleep on the plane when it gets to Oklahoma City. He doesn't wake up until it lands in Lawton.

"So he's got to backtrack while these people are waiting for him in Oklahoma City. He was very embarrassed, but everybody accepted it and the next day he had a great interview with Dr. [George] Cross and the people here and was offered the head coaching job."

The public announcement of the decision arrived in San Antonio, where the Razorbacks had moved their practices, at just about the same time as Mackenzie did.

"All of a sudden, Jim's lifestyle changed. Phone calls and messages from Sooners boosters all over the land. Jim and I knew we were going to leave together whenever he got a head coaching job. And I was with him all the time. We didn't talk about it in front of other coaches, but we knew it was going to happen."

Arkansas lost that bowl game to LSU and two days later Mackenzie was picking Switzer up at the airport in Oklahoma City.

The nucleus for a great coaching staff had been brought together. Switzer was the first addition. Then came Pat James, the defensive mastermind from LSU. Chuck Fairbanks was next, coming over from Houston. Then Swede Lee, Billy Gray, Larry Lacewell.

"We spent the night in Oklahoma City after Jim got me at the airport," stated Switzer, "and the next day he brought me out to the campus. I took a look at the facilities for football and I said, 'You mean I left Arkansas for this? Here is the Oklahoma that I had envisioned with one of the greatest traditions in college football, and it looks like this? How in the world did they win here? How did they recruit players to come here with these facilities?'

"Arkansas looked like the Taj Mahal compared to what they had at Oklahoma at that time. I was thoroughly shocked. We moved into what was then Washington House and started living there with the players. Homer Rice came in and lived there, too. Six or seven of us did."

The facilities weren't the only worries for Mackenzie and his new staff. Bud Wilkinson's dynasty had begun crumbling a bit, and the Sooners were going to battle without superior troops for a change.

"We started our off-season program right away," Barry recalled. "The players had to lose weight. Jim Mackenzie wanted all that jiggle out of the rear ends. We had kids losing 40, 50, and even 60 pounds. And we went out to old South Base, old Stalag 17.

"It was like a concentration camp. These kids today go through an off-season program that's all fun and games. They don't have any idea what it used to be like. But of course that was back when we didn't have a lot of athletes. You made do with what you had. When you recruit nothing but great athletes and good players, you can make it fun. I mean, if you have a guy who runs 4.4 in the 40, how are you going to make him faster? You can't make a Joe Washington a better prospect by making him go out and go through what we were making those kids go through at that time.

"We had to make the kids mentally and physically tougher in 1966. When you have a product that's not as good as the people you play, you've got to do something. But you can't make a kid run a 4.5, or make him gain height. We did other things to give us a chance.

"I remember Eddie Hinton was the only super athlete we had. Eddie used to make things look so easy out there in practice that we used to get onto him for loafing, because everyone else was dyin'. And he looked like he wasn't putting out. But you know what? He was beating everyone in everything. He was first in everything we did. He just made it all look so easy.

"And that's what we've been building toward to get the program where it is today. At that time kids paid the price to play. I wouldn't have gone through it, I'm telling you. But back then the mental attitude was different. Kids loved that ole marine-type discipline. I know the kids who went through that and come back for the Alumni Game each year and still laugh about it. It was a great experience for those who made it through it. Something to cherish today."

That first season for the new staff was an exciting one. Oklahoma upset Texas. The Sooners won their first four games before being buried by one of the most talented Notre Dame teams ever. But they finished 6–4 and Mackenzie earned Coach of the Year honors in the Big Eight.

The coaches decided to turn down a Bluebonnet bid so that they could concentrate on recruiting.

One of the blue chippers still undecided in late April was Monty Johnson of Amarillo, Texas, a standout quarterback. It was April 27 when Mackenzie walked into Switzer's office and told him he was going to Amarillo to try to sign Johnson.

"Jim told me, 'Barry, don't run 'em all off while I'm gone.' We were having a tough spring, and I was back on the defensive staff. My best chance to be a head coach, I felt, was to coach defense. I guaranteed him that I wouldn't run anyone off."

Late that night Switzer and his wife, Kay, were awakened by a phone call from trainer Ken Rawlinson. Mackenzie had died of a heart attack. It was a tremendous shock that Switzer still feels.

Fairbanks was named the new head coach. And in the following six years, he and his young staff put Oklahoma back on top of the football mountain. There was no hint that Chuck might leave the scene when he called his staff together after the 1972 season.

"Chuck was a quiet person. He had told me he had talked to a pro team [New England], but he hadn't expressed any interest. When he told us, we all sat there in shock. Almost fell out of our chairs. Obviously, when a head coach resigns, that means we'll probably all be out of a job, because you can't assume anyone on the staff would be named to head coach. But we had been having ultra success the two previous years, and some people here at the university decided they would try to keep that winning staff together."

With the players on the team supporting him with a petition and the rest of the staff backing him, Switzer was named the new head coach for the 1973 season. That came only a short time after his father was killed in a tragic accident. And it came only a few months before it was announced that the Sooners were being put on probation for violations that occurred under Fairbanks.

Switzer could have been forgiven if it had taken him a couple of seasons to get the program back on its feet. He was, after all, fighting some giant obstacles. And he had a young team with a new quarterback and a new offensive line.

What followed, of course, is history. Oklahoma went 10–0–1 that first season. They were 11–0 in 1974 and national champions, then repeated with a national title in 1975 as they went 11–1 and finally lost a game.

Switzer's teams have won or shared the Big Eight title every year he's been head coach. They've never finished out of the top 10 in the nation. They've won four Orange Bowls and never failed to win more than nine games in a season.

For his career, Switzer will carry a record of 83 wins, nine losses, and two ties. That percentage of .894 is the best in the land. In fact, the all-time high is Knute Rockne's .881 at Notre Dame.

Why? Is it really magic?

"The thing about his coaching is his enthusiasm," says Henry, who has been following Switzer since his days as the state's top high school lineman at Crossett. "And he's still got it! What it turns out he does best is recruit. There is no question in my mind that that's what he does best. And that's what you need to do best at Oklahoma.

"The reason is, he identifies totally with those young kids. And I guess he always will. I don't think he'll ever totally grow up. The kids identify with him, too. Of course, he's going to get some age on him, although he still looks 30. And he talks about how in two years, three years, it may be all for him.

"But what he doesn't realize is what's going to happen to his numbers. As those numbers improve, then before long the investment he has is going to keep him right where he is. Merv will probably keep him in coaching, because eventually they're going to have to coach better at OU. It's not that they can't. They can coach with anybody. They just haven't had to do it. I think probably last year they had to do more coaching than they had done in a long, long time.

"Barry's capable of being as good a coach as anybody, and he can get anyone he wants for his staff. The one thing about Barry is that he will never, ever get a swelled head. He keeps himself in perspective, too. He always sees things exactly as they are. Now he glamorizes things and dramatizes things, but deep down he sees them as they are.

"In a lot of ways he reminds me of Bear Bryant at a similar stage. You know, Barry's had a little trouble with his peers. And Bryant was a pariah. He was an outcast. He was a total outcast in his profession. It wasn't until he had gone back to Alabama for three or four years and some people who liked him talked to him, including Frank.

"Bryant wasn't even a member of the Football Coaches' Association. And Frank got him in there and got him active and he finally became president. But Bear went back and mended all his fences with his fellow coaches. But this was after he had his first national championship at Alabama. When he was in the Southwest Conference, there was only one coach who would talk to him."

Jack Mitchell, who recruited Switzer out of high school when he was the head coach at Arkansas, never had any idea Switzer would end up doing what he's done in the coaching profession.

"You don't have any idea what might happen to someone as a coach. There's no way to know. You gotta be lucky, you gotta hit a place where they got good players. You've got to hit the right school at the right time and give it hell. Everybody can coach. We all can go out there and draw up better Xs and Os than the other guy. They all know the same things.

"Barry has had a wonderful background in his playing and education in football. He was under a great head coach as an assistant, and he has a tremendous staff. He's very aggressive and his aspiration level is high. How many coaches spend the time recruiting that he does? That's where you win. You don't win from September through December unless you win from January through March.

"Recruiting is the key. And when you have a good product to sell and you're a good salesman, you're going to sell lots of merchandise. And that's what it's all about."

Brother Don Switzer points out, "Barry's success in his profession has depended to a large extent on pure chance—at least the opportunity to be successful. But he still had to have the ability to make it work.

"Barry has the type of personality and drive to where he would have been a success at anything he tried. But it just happened that he fell into a particular slot at the right time where he gained tremendous notoriety, which translated itself into financial security and everything else.

"Barry had a lot of distractions when he first took over the job, people saying he was just getting by on someone else's talent. It took him several years to prove to those people that it was not totally chance, but a great deal of ability that led to this success."

There have been the rocky times, too, however. And Don remembers those.

"Pressure ... Barry has said on many occasions, and he believes this is the gospel, that pressure comes from within and comes from one's pride in doing the best he can. He is always trying to do his best, regardless of the record of past successes. And this, I think, is the nature of anyone who is truly successful, whatever that means.

"But he has had his fears in coaching. Back when Chuck was there, you know, the bad year before they switched to the wishbone in 1970. Now that was bad. He and Pat James and those guys were looking for other jobs. And that was fear and pressure then. But I don't think that phenomenon has ever been in the picture since Barry was head coach."

Mooty, his close personal friend at Arkansas when both played football there, and still a very close friend, added his opinions as to why Switzer has maintained such a high level of success in a profession that is so often fickle.

"Let me tell you about Barry. Number one, he's smart. He probably knew more about high school athletes than a lot of college coaches when he was still playing at Arkansas. His enthusiasm over those players was unique. I wouldn't even know who he was talking about, and he'd be telling me about some kid down at Crossroads, Arkansas, who could run a 9.8 hundred and he'd done this and done that and gained 300 in three games.

"He just knew all those stats. He always seemed to have more enthusiasm for other people than he did for himself. I guess one of the things about Barry is he's always been Barry Switzer. He's never tried to be anyone else. He's never tried to copy Bear Bryant or Frank or anyone. He's Barry Switzer, no matter where he's at.

"Barry's greatest ability has been his insight into other people. He's always known what positions kids can play and what they can't play. He can watch a kid and be around him and he knows how to study his heart. This is one reason he's been so successful. A lot of coaches just don't have that ability."

Mooty remembers the time when Switzer came back home for a few days and spent a couple of nights with Mooty in Arkansas. Oklahoma, after a so-so season in 1969, was having problems in 1970 following the switch to the wishbone.

"They had been losing a few games, and I remember how down he was. He was really not sure about what his future was. Then a couple of years later Fairbanks leaves and Barry is the head coach.

"He has a lot of compassion for people. You take kids who graduate from there, whether they played a lot or not, and he never forgets them. And they know this. These kids who leave there are probably among his biggest supporters. He's never forgotten how to be a kid. He knows their problems and tries to work with them. He can't—or won't even try—to hide his enthusiasm over some things in life. I know a lot of head coaches try to be so prim and proper and act like the great adult. And Switzer's the kind of guy who just never tries to conceal his enthusiasm. And he never will change."

Switzer, who used to go out and sit in the rain at track meets or high school football games just to get to know the athletes better ("I wouldn't have gone out in that kind of weather if they had furnished me with a tent," Mooty laughed), admits that being a head coach has been an adjustment.

"I've learned to say 'No.' But it was tough in the beginning. I never wanted to hurt anyone's feelings. I wanted to be everyone's good ole boy. A lot of people have told me I was too honest and too nice. I don't know. Maybe that's true.

"I've turned down some great trips to islands and places like that. I turned down a king salmon fishing trip to Alaska. Last year I finally took one of those trips. You've got to try to smell the roses yourself sometimes.

"Some people think coaching has changed me. I don't know. Deep down inside I think I'm the same person. I think I adjust to certain situations, but when I go back to my hometown or my friends of 20 years ago, I make the transition. I feel very comfortable. I don't have any airs about me."

Switzer, a highly successful businessman in addition to his winning record as a coach, could leave the profession today and be set for life. He doesn't really need it. Or does he?

"I don't know," he said after a long pause. "I've often thought about what I'm going to do when I grow up [laugh]. I'm still wondering what I'm going to be when I grow up.

"I've made some dumb mistakes in my life. And I've done some good things, too. Some people say I'm too hard on myself. I may be my own worst enemy."

Switzer then told of an incident not so long ago in an Oklahoma City office building. He and his "hunting and fishing coach" Bobby Bell were on an elevator when another man got on with his arms full of packages.

"The guy sees me and drops what he's carrying and says, 'Golly, you're Barry Switzer!' And I said, 'Yes.' And he said, 'I *never* expected to see you!' It was really embarrassing. And Bell looked up at me and said, 'Yeah, they let him out of his cage once in a while, and this happened to be one of those days.' And I started laughing.

"You know, if people make you out to be more than what you are, it's their own fault, not mine. That's human nature. My ego has never been that way, and I know my staff realizes that, too.

"What we accomplish here is what *we* accomplish. *I* or *me* never gets it done. Our coaches are due their credit.

"I've seen other coaches around the country try to embellish their reputations and positions off the efforts of others. And I can't do that. That's not why it works. It takes an entire staff of great coaches, a lot of great players, and a tremendous supporting cast like we have in the Oklahoma Sooners fans to make it happen."

Merv Johnson stayed at Arkansas until 1975—10 years after Switzer left the staff there. But the two have been close friends ever since Johnson came to Arkansas in 1958.

"It was obvious that he had an excellent football mind and a tremendous appetite and zest for football—both in recruiting and coaching," said Johnson, who came to OU from Notre Dame. "And the great rapport he has had with his players is something special.

"As far as working for him, he's super. Couldn't be better. He's got great compassion for his assistants. I see a lot of Frank in Barry—so startling similar as far as his makeup, enthusiasm despite success, salesmanship, and voracious football mind. He throws ideas at you so fast it's hard to sort through them. And you see a lot of Jim Mackenzie in him, too. I think he's tried to pattern himself after Jim to some extent."

Has Switzer changed much since taking over as the head coach for OU in 1973? Many of his closest friends see some changes, but nothing for the worse.

"He's not relaxed now," said Billy Holder, one of his lifelong friends who still lives in Crossett. "He spends a lot of time pacing the floor. He's under a lot of pressure. And he's not really relaxed like he used to be.

"He told me he was in some little secluded area across the Bahamas once and there was a son of a gun in there hollerin' 'Hook 'em Horns!' And we were in Canada fishing in a place away from everywhere—no towns close to us—and we go in and there's some fellas from Nebraska fishin' and this one said, 'Hey, Barry, you're out here fishin' and Tom Osborne is down in Kenya recruiting.' And Barry just tells him, 'Hell, we done been down there. They don't have enough speed.' So he just can't go far enough away to get away from football.

"But, no, I wouldn't like to see him get out of coaching. He's got too much goin' for him. A helluva record. When he first became head coach, he told me he hoped he could last 10 years. Barry is at home in Crossett, Arkansas, or in Norman, Oklahoma, or in Houston, Texas. He relates to the kids he recruits. He can communicate."

That Switzer humor is still very much intact. But sometimes it's misunderstood.

"I think at times in my life I've worried about what people thought of me. But not anymore. There are only a few people who are close to you, and it's what they think that matters.

"It's very difficult for me to relax, the kind of pace I have to go at. That's been one thing that's bothered me. I like to relax and have a good time and go places. But I can't do that very often. I'd be going nuts if I didn't have a telephone close by."

When Broyles retired at Arkansas, one of the first things he did, according to Henry, was to call Barry and ask him if he was interested in the job.

"Barry said he'd have to think about it, then told him the next day he had too much going for him at Oklahoma," Henry continued the story.

"Somebody once asked me, and I told them that Barry would like to be head coach at Oklahoma and head coach at Arkansas at the same time. And that's just not possible. He can never leave Oklahoma. There's no other place. After you get to Oklahoma, that's it. You don't want to go anyplace else unless they run you out of the profession."

It's hard to run a man out of the profession when he wins as often as Switzer does. And the way he does.

"Have you seen the number of games he wins in the last minute or two minutes?" queried Mooty. "A lot of people think it's a fluke deal. They can't believe he can pull so many out like that. But let me tell you something: he works on that."

And Switzer, who relishes his success against Nebraska perhaps more than any other accomplishment, feels good inside about his 1980 team—more so, perhaps, than any other.

"Coming back after being two and two like they did, winning the Big Eight and the Orange Bowl. And the criticism J.C. Watts took. Then he comes back to lead us to another title and is named the MVP in the Orange Bowl for the second straight year.

"That's when you like to tell 'em to stick it. We know what we're talking about, and you don't."

But Switzer doesn't have to tell anyone that. Football fans across the nation already realize that Barry Switzer is THE COACH.

Matt Hayes, *The Sporting News*

SOONER THAN EXPECTED

It had been more than a decade since the Sooners held the national spotlight as one of the country's top football programs, but at the end of the 2001 Orange Bowl, OU was again the king of college football. Bob Stoops took his team to the top faster than anyone had anticipated and has kept them there. After Oklahoma won the national championship for the 2000 season, The Sporting News *ran this article on the Sooners' head coach.*

Oklahoma needed only two years under Bob Stoops to win the national championship. And if the coaches and players are right, these Sooners won't be one-hit wonders.

Josh Norman didn't see it coming. A television reporter was about to treat him—and Oklahoma—like part of a sideshow at the Orange Bowl.

That's right. The nation's number one team was a national championship novelty, a one-hit wonder led by the quarterback with the funny name. When the talk was Florida State, it was football and titles and dynasty. When the talk was Oklahoma, it was *everything* else.

Norman, the roommate of Heisman Trophy runner-up Josh Heupel, was an easy target. Actually, he expected plenty of questions, asking him over and over about Oklahoma's two-year journey from laughable to improbable to indescribable.

The reporter closed in.

"You're Josh's roommate, right?"

"Yes," Norman replied.

"Does he, well ... does he, you know, flush the toilet after he goes?"

If you're looking for symbolism or any form of deeper meaning, don't waste your time.

"Some people," Norman says, "just don't get it."

Wake up, America. There's still plenty of room on the Sooner Schooner. If you thought that 13–2 dissection of heavy favorite Florida State in the national championship game was impressive, wait until you get a glimpse of what's next. The Sooners return 14 starters and, believe it or not, they will have a quarterback with as much potential and promise as Heupel had when he walked on campus two years ago.

All three candidates—Nate Hybl, Jason White, and Hunter Wall—are more physically gifted than Heupel, the senior All-American with the baby-face grin and killer instincts. And whoever wins the job will have all of this season's receivers back as well as a majority of the offensive line.

"I feel good about the situation," says offensive coordinator Mark Mangino. "We're in good shape."

More than anything, Oklahoma is in good shape because of Stoops, the 40-year-old architect of the magnificent metamorphosis in Norman.

TSN's Final Power Poll
(Preseason ranking in parentheses)

1.	Oklahoma (17)	13–0
2.	Miami (6)	11–1
3.	Washington (16)	11–1
4.	Oregon State (—)	11–1
5.	Florida State (2)	11–2
6.	Virginia Tech (13)	11–1
7.	Nebraska (1)	10–2
8.	Oregon (—)	10–2
9.	Kansas State (5)	11–3
10.	Florida (8)	10–3
11.	Michigan (12)	9–3
12.	Texas (7)	9–3
13.	Purdue (14)	8–4
14.	Georgia Tech (—)	9–3
15.	South Carolina (—)	8–4
16.	Colorado State (—)	10–2
17.	Clemson (23)	9–3
18.	Notre Dame (22)	9–3
19.	Iowa State (—)	9–3
20.	Auburn (—)	9–4
21.	LSU (—)	8–4
22.	Wisconsin (4)	9–4
23.	Northwestern (—)	8–4
24.	TCU (18)	10–2
25.	Tennessee (10)	8–4

Preseason pretenders: Alabama (3); Southern California (9); Georgia (11); Ohio State (15); Mississippi (19); UCLA (20); Texas A&M (21); Michigan State (24); Southern Miss (25).

Dropped out (from season-ending poll): Ohio State; Louisville; Toledo.

The TSN Power Poll is determined by TSN staff members.

Stoops has no ties to the tradition at Oklahoma, but he has an unmistakable crimson-and-cream aura. In just two years Stoops has made believers of everyone associated with the program. Most importantly he has his players believing they can accomplish anything. After years of wallowing under three miscast coaches who ran from the past, the Sooners found it all with a coach who chased after the school's football history—then added another chapter.

"He has them believing they can win," says Florida State coach Bobby Bowden. "That's where the battle is won."

These guys were double-digit underdogs against Florida State. Never had a number one team been so discarded. At halftime—with the Sooners leading 3–0—ABC was grilling Miami coach Butch Davis about the Hurricanes' claim to the national title. The entire week leading up to the championship game was flush with talk of the Bowl Championship Series and its problems—and if Miami or Washington would have the biggest gripe about not getting a share of the national title.

The Sooners? They dodged questions about personal hygiene. But when everything was said—and done—they got to dance all over the field.

Undefeated. Untied. Undisputed. Don't bother with the recount.

But wait. The inevitable came shortly thereafter: Stoops was asked if Oklahoma is the real deal.

Real deal? The Sooners went 13–0 for the first time in school history. They rolled through the best conference in the nation and dismantled one of the best offenses in recent memory in the national championship game. And they did it with a team that included 23 freshmen and sophomores on the two-deep roster. The foundation is firmly in place. The deal is real.

"A lot of teams that have not played so well through the years want to talk about how young they are and how they're developing," Stoops says. "You don't hear that about a team that has just gone 13–0, but we are a young football team."

To understand Stoops is to understand the makeup and mentality at Oklahoma and why the future looks so promising for the Sooners. Bob Stoops was the son of a coach in Youngstown, Ohio, a father who lived for the competition and camaraderie of the game. Ron Stoops also died with it, right there on the sideline, from a massive heart attack. Ron Jr. was on the other sideline that Friday night, coaching against his father.

Ron Sr. roamed the sidelines of Cardinal Mooney High School for 28 years as defensive coordinator, his sons learning lifelong lessons and the game of football with each passing fall. Dee Dee and Ron Stoops had four sons and two daughters, and anyone who knew the family knew the boys were photocopies of their father.

Ron Stoops would have loved the postgame scene at the Orange Bowl last week, when Bob stood on the podium surrounded by his family and players and with the Waterford crystal Sears Trophy.

For the last decade, Florida State turned college football sideways with its wide-open, fast-break offense, blitzing into the new millennium with the pizzazz and persistence of a new generation. All those All-Americans, all that glitz and glamour swaggering into south Florida.

Ron Stoops always taught his boys that anyone could score points. When you stop teams from scoring, that's when you win championships. For all the flash of Oklahoma's pass-oriented offense and the hoopla over Heupel, the defense was the reason the Sooners won the national championship. When was the last time someone held Nebraska to 14 points? Remember Torrance Marshall's interception return for a touchdown at College Station, when things looked bleak for Oklahoma's struggling offense against Texas A&M?

Poor Ben Panter. He might be the only Oklahoma player who can't fully celebrate the national championship. If his snap hadn't sailed over the head of punter Jeff Ferguson, the Sooners would have shut out the Seminoles. But even Ron Stoops could have understood that. Besides, the man who literally died coaching defense probably had the best seat for the game.

"He was very special to me and my brothers," Bob Stoops says. "The good Lord has a good coach up there."

Ron Stoops left a pretty good one behind, too. By offering Bob the job at Oklahoma, when the Sooners' proud football tradition was in shambles, athletics director Joe Castiglione made a daring—and some thought desperate—move. Stoops was well-respected in the coaching fraternity, but hiring a 38-year-old with no head coaching experience for a job with such tradition and high expectations was clearly a gamble. Unless, that is, you know the story of Bob Stoops.

"You could see it in college," says Chuck Long, Oklahoma's quarterbacks coach and a teammate of Stoops's at Iowa. "He was born to coach."

Once an overachieving, All–Big 10 defensive back, Stoops always has had the charisma and leadership to mesmerize and energize. He was a key factor as defensive coordinator in the Kansas State revival. He took a talented but fragmented Florida defense and turned it into one of the nation's most dominating units as coordinator from 1996 to 1998. The Gators beat Florida State for the national title in his first season, and Stoops no doubt used that knowledge of the Seminoles in delivering Oklahoma its first national title since 1985.

The Sooners dominated the offense of the 1990s like no other team had, using five or six defensive backs much of the game and confusing Heisman Trophy winner Chris Weinke with different coverages and blitz packages. A majority of that defense—including All-American linebacker Rocky Calmus, standout safety Roy Williams, and emerging cornerbacks Derrick Strait and Michael Thompson—will be back in 2001.

"The kids believed in the scheme because we had a guy who won a championship doing the same thing four years ago," says Brent Venables, Oklahoma's co–defensive coordinator. "They believed in us from Day One, and that's a credit to Bob and what he has brought to this program."

When Stoops accepted the job, he said the Sooners would compete for championships—not in three years or with that all-encompassing five-year plan coaches like to talk about, but immediately. Players were heaving and losing their breakfasts in Stoops's first practice two years ago. By the end of the season, the program that hit rock bottom with three head coaches since the ugly exile of Barry Switzer had led at some point in all 12 of its games.

A year later the Sooners completed a remarkable turnaround with one of the most impressive defensive showings in a championship game in years. What makes anyone think they can't get better?

"From where we were to where we came, it's hard to describe," says senior safety J.T. Thatcher. "No one knew what to expect. They know now. Look what coach Stoops has done, and he's only been here two years. Who knows how good it could get? I think people are finally realizing what we have here."

No kidding. Before the Sooners had 24 hours to digest it all, rumors circulated that Ohio State was looking at Stoops as a prime replacement for fired coach John Cooper. Stoops says he's happy at Oklahoma, and he recently received a contract extension that pushed his salary to $1.4 million a season.

But that doesn't mean the Sooners' staff will stay intact for long. Bob is pushing his brother, Mike, Oklahoma's co–defensive coordinator, for the Ohio State job. Venables interviewed with Missouri in December, and the young staff is loaded with potential head coaches, including wide receivers coach Steve Spurrier Jr. and Long.

If the novelty finally is wearing off, that one-hit wonder tag can't be far behind.

"This isn't just some one-year fling," Norman says. "We've got it back."

Moments after the win over Florida State, Heupel stood in front of the Oklahoma band directing the "Boomer Sooner" fight song.

Go ahead and sing along. If you know the title, you know the words. But you'd better hop on that schooner before it fills up.

"We accomplished a once-in-a-lifetime dream," Heupel says. "But better things are on the way for this program. This is just the beginning."

Sooners football has been the mainstay for Oklahoma sports fans for generations, dating back to 1895.

Section V
THE MYSTIQUE

C. Ross Hume, *Sooner Magazine*

HUC' CUM WHAT THEY SAY AND WEAR

Time-honored traditions have a lasting resonance for a reason, and this article, which ran in November 1930, explains the beginnings of a few of the Sooners' more storied ones.

One of the First Two Graduates of the University Tells How the University's Yell and Colors Were Chosen

Bill Jones was a long, lank freshie from the Kiamichi mountains. His dad, Sam Jones, had come from McCurtain country to be present at Dad's Day celebration. In a seat on the west side of the stadium he was watching the crowd gathering for the football game, and the many yells and colors were a puzzle to him. The writer was sitting close by and after a while Sam turned and burst out, "Huc' cum what they say and wear?"

How many others have been puzzled by the same question, why they yell "Hirick-ety" and wear cream and crimson?

The story goes back 35 years to the fall of 1895 and the beginning of football and other activities at OU. The 1895–96 catalog in my hand shows five sophomores, five freshmen, 12 specials, 121 preps, and five pharmics, a total enrollment of 148 in the university, and a faculty of six professors and one librarian.

One of these special students was John A. Harts of Wichita, Kansas, who had been a student the previous year at Winfield College, and who organized and coached the first football team. Other students started the oratorical association, and it became necessary to have a yell and colors so the vast student body would be able to recognize a friend and discover a foe.

The football team practiced until early December before it had its first and only game of the season, being defeated by Oklahoma City High 34 to 0. The oratorical association had its contest during the holidays, when Maude DeCou won the first intercollegiate contest.

President Boyd selected a committee consisting of Miss May Overstreet, an instructor, as well as Ruth House, L.W. Cole, and Ray

Hume, students, to choose colors, and the committee chose cream and crimson. Of course special shades were chosen, but when we went to get colors, all shades of red and from white to yellow could be seen. The colors have never been changed.

Cole had been a Sigma Nu at Winfield College, and others were from there, and the first yell suggested was a variation of a fraternity yell:

"Hi-rick-e-ty-whoop-to-do,
Terra-ga-hoo, hell-a-ba-loo,
Uni-Uni-Uni-U."

The last line alone was changed from "What's the matter with Sigma Nu."

This yell was accepted and I recall trying to yell it at games and other contests until I could hardly speak.

We realized that it was too long, and did not express the spirit of the school, and during the year 1897–98, a number of members of the glee club, which at that time was practicing for a tour, suggested retaining the first line of the old yell and adding a new line, and at chapel service the new yell was given as follows:

"Hi-rick-e-ty-whoop-to-do,
Boomer, Sooner, O. K. U."

In the files of the historical society I examined the files of the *People's Voice* of December 26, 1897, and found that "University correspondent" stated that on November 22, there was a grand piano recital, and that the new yell given was as stated above. The only change is "Okla. U."

I was of the impression that it was about three months later but accept the above contemporaneous evidence as correct.

No one individual is entitled to the credit for either the colors chosen in 1895 nor for the yell adopted in 1897, but the following besides Cole, who chose the first line, had a part in the second line: C.C. Roberts, Roscoe, Helvie, now deceased, Harry Ford, and myself.

There was agitation and dispute in 1915 as to each, and at that time the testimony of several members of the faculty and student body was taken and is published in the 1916 annual.

It has been suggested that every syllable is significant of the history of Oklahoma, and I prepared the following legend to show how we have retained this for all time to come.

Legend
HI noon of the opening day for the race came; along the border the

RICK-E-TY creaking rigs rushed across the plains; where before only the war

WHOOP of the wild Indian and the howl of the lone coyote had been heard. The purpose of those sturdy pioneers was

TO DO, or die if they failed to get a claim. Whether the

BOOMER, who had sought the opening long and earnestly; or the

SOONER, who had slipped in before the crack of the gun; or the later settler, who came to this "Land of the Fair God": all had visions of churches, schools, and homes: and in time they hoped that their children could go to dear old

OKLA U., whose name and yell are heard around the world.

Sigfrid Floren, *Sooner Magazine*

SPORTS TRADITIONS

Sooner Magazine *again explains the OU football traditions, this time in an article that was originally published in September 1940.*

Many of the university traditions are connected in some way or another with intercollegiate sports, and particularly with football.

Football was first played at the University of Oklahoma 45 years ago—in the fall of 1895, when the university had five sophomore students and about 10 freshmen, the rest of the student body consisting of four pharmacy students and music and preparatory school students. However, only one game was played that fall.

The next year a football team was organized and two games were played with Norman High School.

With the rapid increase in student interest in football, the adoption of university colors, yells, songs, and pep meetings was inevitable. Consequently Dr. David R. Boyd, first president of the university, appointed committees.

Members of the committee on colors were: May Overstreet, an instructor, and three students, Mrs. Ruth House Daniels, '02, now deceased; L.W. Cole, '99, recently retired professor of psychology at the University of Colorado; and Ray Hume, '01, pharmacist, doctor and surgeon, now deceased.

The committee chose cream and crimson as the official university colors. Various deviations of these exact shades have appeared through the years in the form of pennants, banners, streamers, and so on, but through 45 years the official colors have remained the same.

The first yell suggested was a derivation from a Sigma Nu fraternity yell. After several revisions, the yell was standardized as follows:

Hi rickety whoop-to-do

Boomer, Sooner, Okla. U.

With the exception of the change from "Okla. U." to "O. K. U.", the same yell is still used by student crowds at football and basketball games. Many others have been originated through the years but none has seriously challenged this one as *the* Sooners yell. Since it has lasted nearly half a century, it seems to be one tradition that deserves the name.

The story of Sooners pep songs is quite different. As was related in a recent article in *Sooner Magazine*, dozens of OU songs have had bursts of popularity, but most of them have quickly sunk into obscurity.

The "Boomer Sooner" song of recent years probably has more tradition about it than any other. Its history, however, is rather obscure and its future is somewhat endangered by the frequent objections to the tune, which is the same as that of Yale University's "Boola Boola" song.

"Boomer Sooner" is doing very well at present. It is sung or played regularly at football and basketball games. Every OU touchdown is a cue for the band to strike up "Boomer Sooner" with a contagious enthusiasm. Student and alumni loyalty to the song is indicated by the general observance of the custom of rising to one's feet whenever it is played.

Pep celebrations in connection with football games came into vogue at an unknown but early date. Huge bonfires have long been the nucleus for such celebrations, beginning before the turn of the century. Along with them developed the "chain" or shirttail parades in which students marched through the student residential area and downtown in Norman.

There was a period of years when pregame pep meetings resulted in student parades that closely resembled riots. Mobs of students would storm the doors of the theaters or perhaps jam their way into a campus shop. Prudent managers would post a lookout and lock their doors when a "parade" came in sight. Frequently property damage caused by raiding students amounted to a considerable sum. University officials, finding that an official ban on such activities had little effect, resorted to strategy and managed to have the pep rallies handled in such a way as to discourage violent demonstrations. In recent years the Friday night pep rallies have been colorful but not riotous.

A hot issue 10 years ago—but virtually dormant today—is the traditional contest for possession of the clapper from the old A&M College bell. The large iron bell hung in the tower of Old Central Building on the A&M campus and was ceremonially rung after every intercollegiate victory. Several courageous Sooners, deciding that the victory bell should not be heard following the 7–0 Aggie triumph over OU in 1930, robbed the bell of its clapper.

A party of Aggies drove to Norman, lured the clapper's guardian away on a "ghost" date, but could not find the clapper. Between halves at the Aggie-Sooner basketball game later in the year the OU '89ers Club paraded it before the crowd. Afterward the Aggies proposed that the clapper be put up as a permanent trophy to the winner of the annual A&M-OU football game. It was so agreed.

Enthusiasm over the bell clapper has died down in recent years, partly due to the fact that the Aggies have not beaten OU since 1933.

The Sooners regained the clapper in 1935 and held it. Whitley Cox, '36ex, a university sprinter from '32 to '35, now a Tulsa salesman, became the recognized custodian of the clapper for OU. At last report he still had it.

Homecoming of alumni on the occasion of one of the major football games in early November is a tradition of many years' standing. C. Ross Hume, one of the first two Bachelor of Arts graduates of the university, believes that he is the first Sooner "homecomer." Mr. Hume, now an attorney in Anadarko, graduated from the university in 1898. That summer he was elected teacher in the Newkirk public schools. He was the only man on the faculty there, and that fall he introduced and coached football there. He returned to Norman for the Thanksgiving Day game with Texas Christian University in the fall of 1898.

On October 30, 1915, he attended the first formal Homecoming for university alumni. Faculty members had been talking about such an event as early as 1912 and the Missouri game in 1914 was classified as the Homecoming game by the student newspaper of that time. Since the first official Homecoming celebration, held on the occasion of the Kansas game in 1915, the occasion has become more outstanding each year. Student houses are elaborately decorated in honor of the visitors and a lively parade is presented for the crowd. A reception for the returning alumni is held in the Union Building following the game.

A colorful addition to the Homecoming tradition was made about 1927 when the Indian Club began its all-night tomtom ceremony. At sundown the pledges of the Indian Club begin beating the tomtom at a chosen spot on the university campus and continue until sunrise of Homecoming day, a ceremony that is the final rite in initiation of the club's pledges. Tradition holds that any break in the steady beat of the tomtom throughout the night is likely to endanger the success of the Sooners football team the next day.

Sooner Magazine

ONE MAN, ONE TEAM, PRIDE

What does OU football mean to its fans? In an article that originally ran in 1958, several OU alumni explain why football has been so important to them and the university.

Much has happened to Oklahomans' pride in the '30s. Some prominent OU alumni have definite ideas as to why.

> "Them Okies? They're all hard-looking!... Well, you and me got sense. ... Okies got no sense and no feeling. They ain't human. A human being wouldn't live like they do. A human being couldn't stand it to be so dirty and miserable. They ain't a hell of a lot better than gorillas."
> —*The Grapes of Wrath*

Perhaps John Steinbeck had no intention of saddling the residents of one state with an inferiority complex and a slurring nickname when he wrote about the migrant workers who fled America's Depression-wracked Dust Bowl in the mid '30s. Intend or not, *Okie* stuck. *Okie* became as insulting as a great many other four-letter words.

But times change. Today Oklahomans forget to cringe at the sound of *Okie*. Indeed—by some Oklahomans—the word *Okie* is used as the stark slogan for a resurging sense of self-confidence. Today Oklahomans are proud of their state.

What has brought about this switch? There are many reasons for the new attitude. But one of the most apparent reasons is a football team and its coach.

A number of distinguished Oklahomans were asked to evaluate the effect OU football has had upon the people of Oklahoma. Here are their comments.

Jenkin Lloyd Jones, Editor, *The Tulsa Tribune*
"A great football team can't make a great state, any more than it can make a great university.

"But it can remind some people of truths they may have overlooked. One truth that has been generally overlooked among Oklahomans is that this *is* a great state. We are great bickerers among ourselves and apologizers to strangers. It is wise to be conscious of one's shortcomings, but Oklahoma has overdone it. We have too often had the gnawing fear that maybe we *are* Okies, after all.

"The Wilkinson teams helped dispel this delusion. An invincible backfield and an impenetrable line can be appreciated by even the dumbest citizen, and we all threw out our chests a little.

"Secondly, the favorable publicity about the Wilkinson teams was second only to the delightful musical *Oklahoma!* in peddling to the world the impression that Oklahoma must be quite a place. The image of shiftless sharecroppers riding around in jalopies covered with mattresses didn't tie in well with 11 smart lads running circles around the nation's great teams under the guidance of one of the most articulate and obviously one of the most gentlemanly football coaches in the business.

"The BIG RED has done a fine job for us all."

Mike Monroney, '24 BA, United States Senator

"For some 30 years Oklahoma talked about means of properly publicizing our state. The exploits of the 'Pretty Boy' Floyds, the impeachment of governors by pajama sessions of the legislature, the Dust Bowl migrations—all cried out for counteracting publicity.

"We lacked the money and the news peg for the big publicity push to place our merits—instead of our demerits—before the world.

"Then came our two great breaks—the Rogers and Hammerstein musical show and movie *Oklahoma* and the Big Red football team. Both served to rescue us from the glaring headlines of crime, poverty, and instability.

"Throughout each year, the millions who read the sports pages (and more read these than the straight news stories) follow Oklahoma as the supreme leader of America's number one sport. Eighty-four million TV viewers marvel at the speed, the versatile play, and the sportsmanship of the Big Red in the network telecasts of our games.

"Oklahoma has become a favorite with the world's fans not only because of its many victories, but because of the clean, intelligent type of young men who play and the heads-up, rapid-fire style given them by coaches Bud Wilkinson and Gomer Jones. A state that can produce this kind of team *must* be good!

"For sportsmanship in victory or defeat, the Big Red tops all the hundreds of college teams. They not only win like the champions they are, but in the Notre Dame game they proved they could lose like champions too.

"The great reputation won on the playing fields at Norman has given Oklahoma a new international reputation unmatched by any other of our 48 states."

Robert S. Kerr, '16, United States Senator

"The development of football at Oklahoma under Coach Bud Wilkinson and his associates has made a contribution to the university and the state of tremendous proportions.

"Oklahoma is more highly respected in the nation and, for that matter, in the English-speaking world because of the great and sustained success of Oklahoma's Big Red under Wilkinson.

"To my mind the most important contribution he has made has been to the youth of Oklahoma, not only to the young men on his team but also to the young men throughout the state. He has put the emphasis on character, self-reliance, teamwork, and discipline. It has resulted in those who come under his influence wanting to improve themselves not only physically, but also mentally and morally.

"As an Oklahoman and one interested in the growth and development of our people, I am and shall always be tremendously grateful to Bud Wilkinson for his effective leadership."

D.A. McGee, President, Kerr-McGee Oil Industries, Inc.

"Almost from the time Bud took over, victorious OU teams have served as a symbol of state pride. Most persons, if asked the official colors of the state of Oklahoma, would probably answer, in all sincerity, 'red and white.' It is difficult to tell at which point the Sooners cease to be a part of Oklahoma as a whole and become an athletic team from one of her colleges—or if there even is such a point.

"Just the fact that the Sooners team has won consistently would have provided a rallying point for state pride, but other teams and other schools have won for the state of Oklahoma before. The personality of Bud Wilkinson has been the basic ingredient in building pride in the Big Red team, with its consequent effect on state pride.

"The quiet and authoritative personality of Wilkinson has had its impact on Oklahoma in many ways. His alumni are among us, especially in the oil industry. He has taught Oklahomans a great deal about how to handle success and how to take defeat.

"He prepares his players in a straightforward manner to do their best to win. In victory, he praises the attempts of the opponent: in defeat, he comments only that the other team played better. Then he turns to the task of winning the next game.

"Oklahoma, as a young state that is hustling to grow, has found a valuable lesson in Wilkinson and his football team."

H. Milt Phillips, '22, Editor and Publisher, *The Seminole Producer*

"The University of Oklahoma's Big Red football team has indeed made a fine contribution to Oklahoma in many, many ways, not the least of which is a surge of state pride among our own citizens.

"The ability to win football games has, of course, brought attention to Oklahoma throughout all of the United States. The schedules of the teams have been of advantage because they have included games from Boston to the West Coast, and from Indiana to Florida.

"This Oklahoma football record has been noted, favorably, in every section of the country by people in almost all walks of life—because football, especially college football, has attracted the interest of people in every stratum of business and social life. Thus Oklahoma has benefited because our state's name has become known to untold thousands who heretofore would have been unable to pinpoint the geographic location of Oklahoma without searching over a map.

"But the winning of football games is not the only benefit Oklahoma's fine football teams have brought to our great state. The conduct and attitude of Oklahoma players and coaches has made a deep impression on millions of football fans.

"The teamwork of the players, the humility blended with confidence—all leave a favorable impression, even on those who are extremely partisan during football contests.

"Businessmen, industrialists, leaders in the economic fields of our nation, and those in other professions or occupations who influence investment and determine business and industry policies, are favorably impressed with the name *Oklahoma* through knowledge and contact with our splendid OU football teams.

"Yes, University of Oklahoma football teams have made a fine contribution to our state over the past 10-year period. They represent success. They represent fine individual qualities of Oklahomans. They represent teamwork. What finer qualities could anyone seeking a new home or considering business expansion desire from the citizens of a prospective state? People make up a state—and Oklahoma's Big Red has shown the nation the finest group of citizens they could find in any state in the Union.

"These contributions, although perhaps intangible, are of far greater importance than most Oklahomans realize."

Dan Procter, '36 M.Ed, '43 Ed, Former President of Oklahoma College for Women, Now Vice President for Star Engraving Company, Houston, Texas

"As Paul once said, 'I'm Saul of Tarsus, a citizen of no mean city.' In reference thereto, Abraham Lincoln said, 'Yes, it is good to be proud of your hometown, but it is better to so live that your hometown will be proud of you.'

"Bud Wilkinson has 'so lived' that Oklahomans are proud of him and his 'works.' Everyone loves a winner *if* he abides by all the rules of fair play, and Wilkinson does just that! As Darrell Royal, head coach of Texas University, said, 'Bud Wilkinson has the respect and admiration of his players because of his insistence upon every player adhering to a code of ethics that will build high morale for any team.'

"Having known Wilkinson personally for the past 10 years, having worked with him in Boy Scout finance drives and other youth projects, I have learned some of his personal qualities that inspire those who work with him. His quiet, unassuming manner, his cleanliness in speech and living habits, and his magnetic smile are an inspiration to all who associate with him.

"Yes, Wilkinson and his Big Red football teams have won the hearts of Oklahomans—at home and abroad—and especially those who live in Texas, the state that boasts of the 'biggest and mostest' of everything but football!"

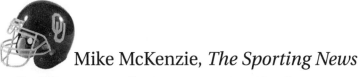

Mike McKenzie, *The Sporting News*

OKLAHOMA: WHERE THE WINS COME WHIPPING DOWN THE PLAIN

A winning tradition is never about just one thing and takes decades to develop. The Sooners were the defending national champs when Mike McKenzie put together this August 31, 1986, article tracing the history of OU's winning ways.

Norman, Oklahoma—Oklahoma. The word evokes images of "black gold" gushing from manmade derricks. Or it's the place where the wind comes whipping down the plain, and there's a surrey with a fringe on top. Think of Oklahoma and you think of Will Rogers, Boomer Sooner, Big Red, kill 'em dead football.

Since World War II, football at the University of Oklahoma has been a standard for state pride, defining the term *success* for all of collegiate football.

The changing face of college sports—high-powered, TV-era budgets and recruiting, beefier and speedier athletes with specialized skills, parity brought about by NCAA rules—has created no decline in the talent attracted to Oklahoma.

For 21 consecutive years the Sooners have won more games than they've lost, and only twice since 1947 have they experienced losing seasons.

Why? How? Who?

Some say it's state pride. Some say coaching. Everyone says it's talent. All of these answers are correct.

The coach now, a complex man given to bluntness, gives one-word answers to a multifaceted puzzle.

As Barry Switzer's coaching career developed at Oklahoma as an assistant from 1966 to 1972, he turned down several opportunities to become a head coach at other major institutions.

"Why? Simple," he says. "Couldn't win there. I won't say where. And they aren't winning there today."

After 13 seasons as Oklahoma's head coach, Switzer has the best winning percentage among active major-college coaches. His record is 126–24–4, an .831 success rate.

Switzer said recently he never truly believed he would have an opportunity to steer Oklahoma's program.

"The only time I envisioned it, ever, was one night in 1973 when Chuck [Fairbanks] called me into his office and said he was going to take a pro job, and I about fell out of my chair," Switzer said.

Switzer knew one thing most certainly, though. He knew whoever coached Oklahoma would win.

That's all Oklahoma has done since World War II, all but twice. That's all Switzer has done, and he expects to continue to do so.

"Why? Simple," he said. "One word: talent. Great players go where great things happen."

Talent, then, feeds off tradition. It's an age-old cycle in any sport, and certain unique state university football programs in America—Alabama, Nebraska, Oklahoma—reflect the cycle year in, year out. Everybody knows they will certainly win, will probably vie for the conference title, and will possibly have a shot at the national championship.

When talk turns to Oklahoma tradition, that means Bud Wilkinson.

When Bill Hancock was a boy in Hobart, Oklahoma, all he lived for, he said, was Sooners football.

Today, as an assistant commissioner in the Big Eight Conference, Hancock recalls a time in the third grade when he ran home from school to bring his parents bad news.

"My friend Billy is going to flunk," he announced. "He doesn't know anything. He doesn't even know who Bud Wilkinson is."

"Bud made it easier for all of us," Switzer said, referring to the four coaches who have followed the success of the Wilkinson era, 1947 to 1963.

In those 17 seasons Wilkinson's teams won at an 83.3 percent rate. The record was 145 games won, four ties, 29 losses. The Sooners won the conference championship 13 times, and were national champions three times—in 1950, '55, and '56.

Some measure of Oklahoma football tradition existed before Wilkinson arrived from Minnesota, an outsider, not yet 30, smooth with people and remarkably adept in exacting effort from young men in his charge.

Oklahoma splashed into national headlines with probably the most significant date in its history, January 1, 1939. The Sooners took on Tennessee in a battle of undefeated, untied regional giants, and the

Orange Bowl media guide credits the game with establishing the bowl as a nationally significant event rather than a scrap among Southern powers. Tennessee won, 17–0, but Oklahoma's course was set.

"After the war then," said Mike Treps, the Oklahoma sports information director, "school officials and politicians decided to use the Sooners football team as a beacon to promote the state."

Wilkinson was an assistant coach on Jim Tatum's staff in 1946, and the school president, George Cross, handpicked Wilkinson to succeed Tatum when Tatum took the coaching job at Maryland.

Oklahoma has produced 82 consensus All-Americans since 1913. Nearly three-fourths of them have played since 1950.

Wilkinson had a Heisman Trophy winner in halfback Billy Vessels in 1952 and two Outland Trophy winners, tackle Jim Weatherall in 1951 and guard J.D. Roberts in 1953.

Two more Heismans have followed: fullback Steve Owens in 1969 and halfback Billy Sims in 1978. There have been two more Outland Trophy winners, Lee Roy Seimon in 1975 and Greg Roberts in 1978. And last year, nose guard Tony Casillas was named the winner of the Lombardi Award as the nation's top lineman and Brian Bosworth won the initial Dick Butkus Award as the nation's best linebacker.

The most incredible mark of the Wilkinson era, however, stands in the NCAA record book. From 1948 through 1950, the Sooners won 31 consecutive games, now the fourth longest streak in college football history. Then, from 1953 to 1957, Wilkinson's Sooners won 47 in a row—the longest streak in college football history.

Switzer's first teams, while on NCAA probation because of a violation when Fairbanks was coach, ran up 28 straight victories from 1973 to 1975. That's the eighth longest streak in the NCAA record book.

Oklahoma wasn't allowed to go to a bowl in 1973 or '74, but Switzer has taken the Sooners to a postseason game every year since then, except for 1983, when OU played a December game in Hawaii and Switzer decided not to subject his 8–4 squad to another game.

Wilkinson had 13 conference champions in 17 years. Switzer has fielded 10 in 13 years.

"We've had a hell of a job trying to keep up with the monster Bud created," Switzer said. "It's a double-edged sword—it makes the job easier, and harder.

"But thank him, anyway."

Roberts tells the story. The scene was the Orange Bowl game, January 1, 1954, the opponent number-one-ranked Maryland. The Sooners were ranked number three at the close of the 1953 regular season. "In our minds we had a chance for the national championship," Roberts said.

The night before the game, the Orange Bowl parade appealed to the players. Many of the Sooners were married and their wives were on the trip. Maryland's players were attending, so Oklahoma's cocaptains went to Coach Wilkinson to express the players' wishes to go watch the parade.

Wilkinson called a squad meeting. "The parade is beautiful and worth seeing," he said. "But it takes your minds off what you came here to be: champions." He said the players could go if they wanted to. But, he noted, champions always did what it took to win, and he didn't see any way that watching the parade would help OU win, and some factors might prevent it.

Wilkinson left and the squad voted. "I'd say before his talk probably 70 percent of the players wanted to go," Roberts said. "Not a single guy voted for going. We won the game, 7–0. I never saw the parade, and I don't regret it."

Wilkinson developed a reputation for drawing the strongest of effort from football players. Some of his former standouts speak of fatherly talks, of a soft method of correcting mistakes, of getting their minds right, of a steel will to win.

"There was a Wilkinson image, and we were expected to represent the university that way," said Roberts, once the coach of the New Orleans Saints and now a sales manager for Milo Park Drilling Fluids in Oklahoma City. "He had the knack for getting the most out of us, and that set the precedent that still stands."

Today the 70-year-old Wilkinson helps operate PEBSCO—Public Employee Benefit Services Corporation—in St. Louis. He quit coaching at Oklahoma to make an unsuccessful run for the U.S. Senate. Later, he was an analyst on college football telecasts and he returned to coaching with the NFL's St. Louis Cardinals in 1978. His NFL record was 9–20 when he was fired late in the 1979 season.

What does he think of the college game now?

"It's such a different world in college football today, I don't know how to translate the 20 or 30 years," Wilkinson said, taking an overview of Oklahoma's ability to maintain the program he wrought.

"We played one-platoon football all the time I coached," Wilkinson said. "Conditioning patterns, substitution patterns, recruiting—everything was totally different. We had decent talent, but in one-platoon you learn to do things you don't naturally do; you subject yourself to that discipline.

"Morale, conditioning, belief in the team—that kind of makeup of a player—was probably 80 percent more vital back then. But nobody could foresee what we built, because results come from preparation game by game, and you just see how it develops after one year or three."

Or 17. Those were the roots. Wilkinson recruited almost solely from a 300-mile radius around the campus in Norman, sweeping through parts of Texas, including Dallas.

Roberts said even a large majority of players from Texas had Oklahoma backgrounds, such as he did growing up in Dallas but spending summers in Oklahoma City with grandparents.

That regional scheme, a "family" atmosphere, bled into the tradition. The state was hooked on its football beacon. Kids grew up with fantasies of wearing the Red.

"I was always Tommy McDonald in our kid games in the yard," said Hancock. "I never played football except in my mind, but I lived and died Sooners football. It pervaded every facet of life in Oklahoma."

He even credits his love for the Sooners for giving him his career. Hancock's father published a newspaper, the *Hobart Democrat–Chief*, in a town of 4,000 about 120 miles from the Oklahoma campus.

"The Sooners taught me at an early age how to read a newspaper, because from the age of four to 12 that's all I thought about," Hancock said. "Reading about them got me hooked on journalism." He went on to receive a journalism degree at Oklahoma and entered public relations.

Clendon Thomas was an All-American back under Wilkinson, leading the nation in scoring in 1956 just ahead of McDonald as they led the Sooners to a second consecutive national championship. Today, Thomas owns a chemical manufacturing company in Oklahoma City. He has a son, Brad, 16.

"It's the same with kids in our state today, growing up wanting to play for Oklahoma," Thomas said. "Brad loves OU football. But it's even more difficult today to make it. I didn't dream I'd ever get the chance, because such a minute group got to.

"Anybody who'd think he'd be one of the fortunate few, his elevator doesn't go much past the first floor, does it? I figured I had about as much chance as becoming a state senator.

"The players today, I have to admit, are better and the coaching is good, if not better. We didn't have the programs and the training that compounds the chances of year after year having great teams.

"But we had the same rawboned kids, and Bud had an admirable ability to get us to play."

The roots. Always, it goes back to tradition and the talent it produced.

"When we were winning national championships 11 and 12 years ago," Switzer said, "our players now were in grade school. They grew up seeing us win 10 Big Eight championships. The fathers and mothers of those kids saw Bud Wilkinson do the same thing.

"You grow up living Oklahoma football. We don't recruit by saying, 'Why wouldn't you come to OU?' That sounds arrogant. But if you were a great football player, wanted to play in this area [Big Eight], and knew without question you were not going to sit on the bench, which two schools would you choose from?"

After Wilkinson, whose only losing season was 1960 (3–6–1), Gomer Jones struggled. His teams were 6–4–1 and 3–7. Jim Mackenzie followed with a 6–4 mark in 1966, but he died of a heart attack during the last week of spring practice in 1967.

Chuck Fairbanks restored the Oklahoma tradition, producing six teams that had an aggregate record of 52–15–1. His staff also landed Oklahoma on probation before he skipped to the pros, leaving Switzer with no television appearances or bowl games until his third season. The Sooners went 10–0–1 (a 7–7 tie with Southern California) his first year, 11–0–0 his second year, and 11–1–0 in 1975, including an Orange Bowl victory over Michigan.

In subsequent years Switzer, an outspoken man, has endured public controversy over an array of subjects: his personal life, rumors of cheating, drinking-and-driving citations, stock market dealings.

But he has thrived in a state that loves one thing: winning. This is the state that drove Oklahoma City sportswriter Frank Boggs from his home with threats because he dared report that the Oklahoma football program was under investigation.

Thomas, who has stayed abreast of the Sooners' program, said, "Three years ago, I was on Barry's case pretty hard. But he's straightened out his act.

"And I'm convinced that his background has much to do with his success—a bootlegger's son whose dad was shot to death, whose mother committed suicide in the backyard, and then Barry carried her into the house in his arms.

"I believe the reason he's so good at dealing with some of the black players is that they can't whine, because they can't top his story."

The great black athletes—another large item in the progression of Oklahoma football: Sims, Heisman Trophy; Selmon, Outland Trophy; Joe Washington and Greg Pruitt, All-Americans who went on to outstanding professional careers.

When Wilkinson arrived in Norman the Sooners had no black players. Wilkinson's background in Minnesota had been filled with racially integrated teams. In the mid-1950s he recruited a black athlete.

Prentice Gautt grew up in Oklahoma City, son of a mechanic with an eighth-grade education. Gautt's mother helped his uncle operate a tavern/café.

As a lad Prentice would walk four miles to a hotel where the Oklahoma team stayed the night before home games and he'd collect autographs.

One weekend in the ninth grade, he and some friends rode the bus to Norman, walked to Owen Field, jumped the fence, and "ran up and down the field where Billy Vessels ran until we were exhausted." On the way back to the bus they were confronted by a man who told them to get moving, because they couldn't, by law, be in Norman after sundown.

A few years later, after the Supreme Court decision outlawing racial segregation in education, Gautt went to Oklahoma with a desire to become a doctor on a scholarship provided by a black medical group in his community.

Instead, Wilkinson put him on athletic scholarship. Gautt, in 1957, became the Sooners' fullback—Oklahoma's first black player—and went on to play in the NFL. Today, he is an assistant commissioner in the Big Eight Conference in Kansas City.

"Bud had a way of letting you know your destiny was in your own hands," Gautt said. "I certainly had some concerns when I went there. Trying times? Oh, gosh. Does the sun rise? Bud stuck his neck out. Cautiously, I like to think those are ghosts—the 'you can't, you can't.'

"I didn't see it as anything at the time, but I'm sure it has helped Oklahoma down the line, recruiting the better blacks in an atmosphere created under Switzer of getting the best out of yourself without thinking about the tangential things of [Oklahoma] not being conducive to minorities."

From hardy lads off the farms and oil fields of Oklahoma and west Texas, to the fleet-footed players from all across the country, Oklahoma football has thrived for 40 years.

Roberts, who sold soft drinks and programs in Dallas so he could watch Oklahoma play Texas, witnessed the boom from which present-day fans have prospered.

"Think about it," Roberts said. "We came into the limelight in the late '40s and the '50s. There was Bud Wilkinson and Oklahoma football, always in the news. Every day you'd read about 'The Oklahoma Kid,' a great young baseball player who made the New York Yankees. And what hits Broadway and stays through the whole '50s?

"Every time you picked up a paper you'd read about Mickey Mantle. Every time you turned on a radio, you'd hear the theme song from *Oklahoma!* We had a record in our dorm, and that damn thing must have played half the day!"

Roberts added, "It was always in front of you that if you were going to put on the red jersey, you were going to play hard, and you were going to win. Fairbanks used it well, kept it in front of the kids, and Switzer has done a great job in a state that has unbelievable support and tremendous pride."

The fever grew, and there is no end in sight.

The stadium bulged from its prewar 37,000 to 61,000 in 1949, and to 71,800 in 1975, and to 75,004 in 1980. In '87, new luxury boxes will be in place, and there's a waiting list for donors who will pay $10,000 just for the right to buy a seat in a new addition to Owen Field.

"There's no other game in town," said Treps. "So Oklahomans will give up that extra pair of pants, or eating out once a week, to get the ticket to a game. Death and moving are the only way anybody on the season-ticket waiting list gets one."

"As long as we're winning," Switzer said, "we'll be full. We don't take anything for granted. Players and families resent it when you present yourself in a light of bigger and better than other folks.

"You go in with your hat in your hand, humble. They already know the main thing: We win."

Edgar L. Frost, SoonerSpectator.com

BEDLAM'S BEGINNINGS

The Bedlam Series with Oklahoma State first started in 1904 and has been a long, classic rivalry. Edgar L. Frost wrote about the beginning of the series for SoonerSpectator.com.

It all started on a cold November day in Guthrie.

They weren't known as the Sooners and Cowboys, but when the schools that would later be called by those names first met on a football field—November 5, 1904—they started something that would become a permanent part of the college football landscape.

More than a century later, the two schools in question are preparing to square off for the 100th time. On November 26, 2005, at Norman's Owen Field, Oklahoma and Oklahoma State will renew a little interstate feud known as Bedlam.

It all began in Guthrie, then the capital of Oklahoma Territory. People still recount the stories about that first battle and about a play that will live forever. More about "The Play" a little later—let's focus on the landmark game for now.

Oklahoma won that day, 75–0, and the series remains almost as one-sided as that initial final score. In spite of some more recent Cowboys' successes, OU leads the overall series by a substantial 76–16 margin. There have also been seven ties.

The Sooners have carved out a 36–8–2 edge in Norman, own a 34–6–5 lead in Stillwater, and hold a 5–2 advantage in games played at Oklahoma City. And of course, there's that 1–0 edge at Guthrie—a mark that isn't likely to change.

The first game remains the most lopsided in series history, and the 75 points are the most ever tallied by either team against the other, though OU came close in a 73–12 rout engineered by Jim Tatum's Sooners in Stillwater in 1946.

Guthrie remains the only place other than Norman, Stillwater, and Oklahoma City where the two state universities have played each other on the gridiron. It is a town that has embraced its place in history, and last year, to mark the passing of 100 years since the launching of the series, it erected a fitting monument to the event.

211

Sponsors collected donations from supporters of both schools and conducted a Centennial Monument Celebration on November 5, 2004, in Guthrie's Mineral Wells Park.

A visit to the site, surrounded on three sides by the waters of Cottonwood Creek, explains why the spot was once known as Island Park. Technically, maybe it's a peninsula rather than an island, but the idea is clear.

At the bottom of the handsome monument, cut from granite by Willis Granite Products of Granite, Oklahoma, is an arrow pointing to the actual site of the game. It leads straight to the water's edge, and amidst huge old trees that appear to have been there forever, it is easy to stand on the site and picture it as it was when "The Play" occurred.

The play in question unfolded when the ball was punted and got caught by a healthy gale, which pushed it straight up and blew it back toward, and then into, the creek. Instantly, since the ball was still in play according to the rules of the time, the chase was on.

It is necessary at this point to interrupt the narrative and postpone a description of the game's most famous play. The question arises as to why the game was played in Guthrie in the first place.

Why, indeed? Maybe it had something to do with the city's spirit. It's really a small town, but Guthrie has never acted like one. Everybody there seems to be an extension of the chamber of commerce, talking up the place. That type of pride and ambition were apparently born long ago.

In his book, *Oklahoma Kickoff*, Harold Keith explained, "The territorial capital stood approximately halfway between Norman and Stillwater, and its live-wire commercial club had sought and obtained the game."

Keith also pointed out that Stillwater had no railroad at the time. The Payne County town was not an easy place to get to, and it would have been a long trip to Norman. Guthrie was eager for the match and a logical compromise situated between the two campuses.

Take a trip to Guthrie now and stop at 315 West Oklahoma Avenue and you'll find the Oklahoma Sports Museum and its chief cook and bottle washer, Richard Hendricks. A former school teacher and coach, the personable Hendricks provides further background on the OU-OSU series opener at no charge, although you can make a suggested $3 donation to the museum if you wish.

As a trolley trundles by on one of Guthrie's quaint streets outside the museum, Hendricks describes how OU's squad came by train for the first game and the team from Stillwater arrived by horse-drawn wagons. Listening to Hendricks, one can easily be transported back to 1904 and that errant football bouncing crazily down the banks and into the frigid waters of Cottonwood Creek.

And so, the ball was in the creek and both sides wanted it. The Tigers—later the Aggies and then the Cowboys—had punted from near their goal line and the ball had exited the playing area, sailing back over the end zone and into parts beyond. They needed to secure the ball to prevent an OU touchdown.

In those days, whoever retrieved a ball that had left the field—and returned to the field with it—gained possession. With the stakes high, players from both squads plunged in after the elusive pigskin. Among their numbers, according to legend, was one Aggie who had forgotten he couldn't swim—and the water reached as deep as seven feet.

Miraculously, neither he nor anyone else was drowned, though all who entered the creek came out soaked and freezing in the howling wind. The scant written accounts of the game vary in their details, but evidently there was some ducking and hair pulling and a veritable water polo scrum in the murky waters.

First one player and then another would grab the ball and then lose his hold on the cold, slippery object, and in the absence of a rule providing that the water could not cause a fumble, the melee continued until OU's right halfback, Ed Cook, put a stop to the craziness.

As Keith described the action, "Cook, who could swim like a bullfrog, finally reached the ball, convoyed it to the bank, and touched it down in the sand for the oddest touchdown a varsity man ever scored."

All of that, and the reward was only five points, which is what a touchdown was worth at the time.

Doris Dellinger's book—*A History of the Oklahoma State University Intercollegiate Athletics*—reported that Cook "finally secured [the ball] after a 10-yard swim," which presumably was not included in Oklahoma's stats for the game.

The stats, however, did record the fact that every man on OU's team scored a touchdown that day.

Some 50 years later, in November 1954, before the Bedlam game in Stillwater that season, 10 survivors of the series' initial match showed up to share dinner, reminisce, and compare accounts of the distant and, at that point, legendary contest. Five Tigers returned, along with five Rough Riders, as the Sooners were known in 1904.

On the day of the 50-year celebration of that first game, the main order of business was the contest between Bud Wilkinson's Sooners and J.W. Whitworth's Aggies, a match Wilkinson's troops were destined to win 14–0 on their way to an all-victorious season.

But probably at least as vital to the 10 Tigers and Rough Riders who journeyed to Stillwater was their reunion over lunch to discuss the long-ago happenings along the banks of—and in—Cottonwood Creek. The Aggie player who had authored the fabled punt [Keith listed him as B.O. Callahan, while Dellinger gave his initials as O.P.] had died in Oklahoma City more than a year before the reunion, according to *The Daily Oklahoman*. But Cook, the stalwart swimmer who planted the ball on dry ground for five points, was able to attend. Also among the survivors and attendees was Dr. Roy Waggoner, who, in an odd twist, had played for OU in the tilt and later became a doctor in Stillwater and served as the Aggies' football trainer. He was given an honorary letter at A&M and thus had one from both schools.

The Bedlam Series, which got its name later on, has had a few other "interesting" moments over the years. There was the ball ricocheting off a Cowboy's helmet, allowing OU to escape 21–20 in 1983, and the Sooners' 13–0 win in 1985's Ice Bowl before 44,000 frozen fans. But the 2005 game will have to go some to top the antics from 1904.

After all, they don't play the thing next to a creek anymore.

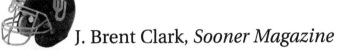

J. Brent Clark, *Sooner Magazine*

SOONER CENTURY: 100 GLORIOUS YEARS OF OKLAHOMA FOOTBALL

In 1995 J. Brent Clark chronicled Oklahoma's storied and tradition-rich football history for Sooner Magazine.

No collegiate football program in the country, with the possible excep-tion of Notre Dame, can lay claim to a richer tradition of football excel-lence than the University of Oklahoma. In keeping with OU's decades of football dominance, it was inevitable that as a part of Sooners football's centennial celebration, a carefully written, pictorial history of Oklahoma football would appear. J. Brent Clark, a 1971 honors gradu-ate of OU and a 1975 graduate of the OU College of Law, had won the 1994 Oklahoma Book Award in nonfiction for his first book, 3rd *Down and Forever. Clark was commissioned by the University of Oklahoma Foundation, Inc., to research and write a comprehensive history of Sooners football, chronicling all 100 years of gridiron exploits. The Touchdown Club of Oklahoma and* The Daily Oklahoman *provided additional financial support. The result of this multiyear project is* Sooner Century: 100 Glorious Years of Oklahoma Football, *excerpts from which are offered here by author Clark as his tribute to those Big Red stalwarts who have brought so much excitement to sports fans everywhere.* —Editor

The auctioneer raised his aged wooden gavel over his head and slammed it down on the Formica tabletop with authority. "Sold to bidder number 55!" he barked. With that, the distinctive old Town Tavern football scoreboards that had hung, seemingly forever, above the heads of the great, the near great, and merely mortal, in Campus Corner's venerable meeting place, had found a new owner. On this day, the Town Tavern was closing its doors forever. Later in the evening, long after the last bidder and curiosity seeker had wandered away from the corner of Boyd and Asp, an old Town Tavern counterman, his face lined with deep creases, sat down one last time in a corner booth and gazed up at the scoreboards.

The ancient plywood panels began reflecting Sooners football game scores in 1947, the year Sooners legend Bud Wilkinson took over the reigns of the Sooners program. The old counterman lit up a Camel and, as smoke curled overhead, reflected back over the years of Oklahoma football glory. He had witnessed a few of the truly great games personally. Others had taken place long before he had peeled his first potato at the Tavern. He had, however, heard Norman natives talk about how football had arrived on the OU campus.

Let's Get Up a Football Team!

The old style game, a kind of controlled chaos, is what young V.L. Parrington had observed while at Harvard, and that is the game he introduced to a few brave souls in Norman, Oklahoma, in the fall of 1897. Actually, the first football team representing the University of Oklahoma was organized in September 1895 by a handsome, confident lad with compelling gray eyes. His name was John A. Harts. Fancying himself an athlete, and with more than a smattering of bravado, Harts had played football on a college team in Winfield, Kansas, and as a schoolboy growing up north of Wichita, Harts undoubtedly was aware from newspaper accounts that the first organized football game in Oklahoma Territory had taken place a year before, in November 1894, between Oklahoma High School (later Oklahoma City Central High) and a rowdy group of townies billing themselves as "the Terrors." The Terrors had taken a terrible beating in that game.

In any event, when Harts's fellow students brought out an old Spalding football on a golden fall afternoon in Norman, they discovered Jack Harts the athlete. It came as no surprise, then, that the long-haired, brazen young man thereafter declared from his seat in Bud Risinger's barbershop, "Let's get up a football team!"

Harts became the team's first captain and coach. Few of the students attending the university in the fall of 1895 had ever seen a football game, since the Oklahoma Territory had only a mere handful of high schools. Of the 148 students registered at the university that fall, 121 were taking high school work. The game of football was a curiosity only, but Hart's glib tongue ensured a representative attendance at the one and only university game of the 1895 season.

Harts himself, in an overabundance of enthusiasm, had suffered a knee injury in practice and could only hobble along on the sidelines, yelling instructions and encouragement. A North-South gridiron had been laid out on a field of low prairie grass just north of the lone university building. Today the site is slightly north and west of Holmberg Hall. A single strand of wire fence was strung around the playing rectangle.

Team members Joe Merkle and Jap Clapham volunteered teams of horses to haul wagonfuls of dirt to fill the field's buffalo wallows.

On the eve of the contest, Harts discovered he was still two players short of a full team. At the last minute the resourceful Harts enlisted the barber, Risinger, and Fred Perry, a 26-year-old married man who drove Norman's street sprinkling wagon. Risinger and Perry, representative of Oklahoma pioneers, could not resist Harts's exhortations and leapt into the fray. Neither, of course, was enrolled in the university.

The opponent was from Oklahoma City and was composed of high school students, a few students from the Methodist College there, and a couple of town toughs. Most importantly, the varsity team had played a prior game or two. The visitors drubbed Harts's valiant men, 34–0. The university's first football team, in its first game, neither scored a point nor made a first down. The disconsolate university players trudged back to Risinger's barbershop, where they washed up, dressed their wounds, and discussed the merits and demerits of football. "I went home and climbed in bed," Clapham remembered. "I was too sore to do the chores, but I sure slept good. I was feeling kind of blue, but I had liked the rough physical contract."

The old counterman found a heavy ceramic coffee mug and brewed himself a cup of coffee before setting down again in the corner booth. He had his own painful recollections of the 1930s. Work was hard to find in those days. He counted himself lucky to find steady work on Norman's bustling Campus Corner. His musings carried him back to the year 1935. A new football coach had arrived in Norman, he recalled.

Biff Jones Arrives

Lawrence "Biff" Jones had attended West Point, graduating in 1917. Jones was a blunt-spoken, hard-nosed military man. He had coached Army football from 1926 to 1929. As the head coach of Louisiana State in Baton Rouge, he had refused a request by the "Kingfish," Governor Huey P. Long, to address Jones's Bayou Tigers at halftime of a football game. Thereafter, Jones became available to coach the Sooners.

Gene Corotto, a sophomore-to-be in the spring of 1935, recalls Jones's arrival on campus. "We'd already had one spring practice under Lewie Hardage. When Biff Jones arrived, we had another one."

Reflective of Jones's no-nonsense approach, instructions to the players were typewritten and distributed. New wooden lockers replaced coat hooks in the dressing room. Jones looked out for his players. In exchange he demanded discipline and respect.

"Most of the boys were scared of the guy," Corotto recalls, referring to the 6'3" coach. "When he hollered at you, you didn't jump once; you jumped three times."

While there was renewed interest in the fortunes of Sooners football, inhabitants of Oklahoma were struggling to cope with the effects
of the Dust Bowl. "We'd practice in dust storms so thick, you couldn't
see the sun. By the end of practice, we were covered in thick dust,"
Corotto recalls.

Conditioning and toughness were the hallmarks of Jones-coached
squads. Popular offensive formations of the day were the single-wing
and the double-wing. End sweeps by fleet halfbacks complemented
punishing dives by fullbacks. The quarterback received the ball from
center some four yards deep, then turned his shoulders toward the line
of scrimmage to conceal the ball and induce deception. The Sooners
featured outstanding tackles in J.W. "Dub" Wheeler and Ralph Brown.
Backs Nick Robertson and Bill Breedon would join them in earning All-
Conference honors.

The season opened with blankings of two opponents, Colorado,
3–0, and New Mexico, 25–0. Then came the annual showdown in
Dallas. With the smallest crowd ever on hand at Fair Park Stadium for
the annual meeting, 16,000, the Sooners fell 12–7. Jones's squad played
fiercely all season long, shutting out five of its nine opponents. The
Sooners' six wins were the most since 1920. The general feeling among
Oklahomans was that Jones would be able to produce victories in very
satisfying numbers in the days to come.

The Town Tavern was a regular meeting place for all kinds of
people after the trauma of World War II. The OU campus was bursting
at the seams with new students seeking a diploma to validate their
endless optimism. By the fall of 1947, the year the first Town Tavern
scoreboard went up, a regular customer, Charles "Bud" Wilkinson, had
become OU's new football coach.

The Wilkinson Era Begins

The casual observer might conclude that a brilliant sun shone contin-
uously on Wilkinson from the day he emerged from a low-slung
Hudson automobile onto the OU campus in the winter of 1946. Such
was not the case. In fact, Bud knew better than anyone of the necessity
to win football games at Oklahoma. He set about to do just that. He
insisted upon perfection, according to his players. He had an acute eye
for detail, which was reflected in everything—even his wardrobe. On
game days, he paced the sidelines in a gray flannel suit, white oxford
cloth button-down shirt, a red necktie, and a gray fedora. His message
was clear. To play at Oklahoma, one must be serious-minded, disciplined, and prepared.

One of Bud's first tasks was to engage a line coach. He had been
favorably impressed by the coach at Nebraska, a young Ohio State
product named Gomer Jones. Jones was a husky, bespectacled fellow,
purposeful yet given to broad smiles. He fit Bud's vision for success

perfectly. "Dutch" Fehring was held over from the '46 staff. Four other men, including Bill Jennings, completed the staff.

Most fortunately, Bud and his coaches could count on a field general second to none to run the breathtaking, risky split-T formation. He had earned the moniker of "General Jack" Mitchell. Thirty-one of Bud's top 33 players were war veterans. Among the youngest was a kid from Hollis, Oklahoma, named Darrell Royal. Royal had grown up eagerly awaiting the Saturday afternoon radio broadcasts of OU games.

"I'd put a radio on our front porch and have me a solo game in our front yard," Royal recalls. "The play-by-play wasn't so important, but that 'Boomer Sooner' played by the Oklahoma marching band sure was. It lifted me right out of my socks."

By the late 1960s the old counterman at the Town Tavern thought he had seen it all. Now, however, as he gazed over the scoreboards, he stopped to reflect upon the scores of 1969. A young Sooners football player who had grown up in Miami, Oklahoma, had found the Town Tavern a comfortable place to rest that fall, and he had been a very busy young man, indeed. For his labors, he secured collegiate football's highest individual honor.

Owens and the Heisman

Steve Owens sat in the stands at Super Bowl XXVIII in Atlanta, Georgia, when he was recognized by a stranger who urged his young son to ask for an autograph from the 1969 Heisman Trophy winner. "The kid didn't know Steve Owens," Owens recalled. "But he knew the Heisman."

Winning the Heisman means membership in one of sport's grandest fraternities. The day Owens went to New York City to receive his award, he was told, "Your life's never going to be the same." The observation proved accurate, from the autographs to being dubbed "Harry Heisman" as a Detroit Lions rookie to the personal relationships with fellow winners like Roger Staubach and O.J. Simpson. But those are not the faces Owens sees when he looks at one of the planet's most famous pieces of hardware.

"I see the faces of my teammates," said Owens. "That's why it means so much to me. I think of Mike Harper and Steve Zabel and Jack Mildren. I think of Chuck Fairbanks and Barry Switzer and all the guys." It's safe to assume they often think of him.

Owens did not lead Oklahoma to a national championship, and his Heisman-winning year was one of the more disappointing seasons in Sooners history, with a 6–4 record and no bowl game. But Owens won more than the Heisman with his sterling performance in 1969. He won a reprieve for a coaching staff that included Fairbanks, Switzer, Larry Lacewell, and Galen Hall.

Owens had already been announced as the Heisman winner when the Sooners played Oklahoma State at Stillwater on November 29. However, OU was 5-4, and a loss to the Cowboys would not bode well for Fairbanks and his staff. The previous three times the Sooners had ended a season with a loss to their Bedlam Series rival—1945, 1965, and 1966—had been the final game for OU's head coach.

"To save our coaching staff, we really needed to win that game," Owens said.

The Sooners won it, 28–27, thanks to a failed two-point conversion by OSU in the final 1:15 and a yeoman effort by their Heisman-winning tailback. Owens carried the ball an incredible 55 times that day, an NCAA record, and gained 261 yards. In the third quarter alone, Owens carried 20 times, still an NCAA record for one period, and gained 97 yards.

During that excruciating third quarter, when the Sooners turned a 21–14 deficit into a 28–21 lead with 13:56 left in the game, Owens was exhausted. In the quarter, he had carried seven straight plays during one stretch and six straight during another. He asked Mildren, OU's sophomore quarterback, to call timeout. From the press box, Switzer, then the offensive coordinator, barked over the headset, wanting to know who called timeout. Mildren told Switzer that Owens was tired.

"Well, I'll tell you what," Switzer says he told Mildren. "You go inform that big stud he ain't supposed to get tired. Tell him to saddle up ... because we're not going to a bowl, so he can rest 'til spring."

Owens didn't hold a grudge. After a successful six-year career with the Lions, Owens returned to Norman. "The day I retired, I told my wife, 'Call the moving van,'" he said. "'We're going back to Oklahoma.' I've enjoyed this university and this city so much. Playing here meant so much to me."

Darkness was descending on Campus Corner. The old counter-man poured himself a half cup of coffee from the Town Tavern's huge old Bunn-O-Matic. He had nearly completed his sentimental journey, savoring tiny fragments of Oklahoma's rich football tradition. By 1987 the last days of the Tavern loomed ahead, but my, what a splendid team Switzer was fielding over at Memorial Stadium.

"You Will Shock the Nation"

In 1987, the Sooners were simply dominant. They had five Associated Press All-Americans—tight end Keith Jackson, defensive end Darrell Reed, linebacker Dante Jones, safety Rickey Dixon, and offensive lineman Mark Hutson. None of their first nine opponents came within 19 points. OU walloped Texas by 35 points for the second straight year, 44–9. The Sooners scored at least 59 points on four opponents.

However, on November 7 against Oklahoma State, the magnificent Jamelle Holieway suffered a career-shattering knee injury. Ripping an anterior cruciate ligament in the open field, he hobbled into the arms of OSU head coach Pat Jones. The Sooners' chances now rode on the slender shoulders of redshirt freshman Charles Thompson from Lawton, whose speed and quickness surpassed Holieway's. The Sooners struggled against OSU—winning 29–10 only after fourth-quarter interceptions by Troy Johnson and Dixon were returned for touchdowns—and against Missouri, winning 17–13 with Scott Garl's fourth-quarter interception holding off the Tigers.

On November 21 at Lincoln, OU and Nebraska staged Game of the Century II. The Huskers were number one, the Sooners number two, and both were 10–0. Oklahoma appeared vulnerable without Holieway, and for once it was Nebraska that was brash, with linebacker Broderick Thomas promising victory. Switzer pointed out that the Huskers had scored only three offensive touchdowns in three years against OU. Privately, he told Thompson, "You will shock the nation." Thompson and the Sooners did.

OU outgained Nebraska 444–235 in total yards and dominated the game. Fumbles handicapped the Sooners in the first half, but Dixon's interception set up Anthony Stafford's 11-yard touchdown run, which forged a 7–7 tie in the third quarter. Patrick Collins raced 65 yards for a touchdown with 1:39 left in the third, and R.D. Lashar nailed a clinching field goal with 7:40 remaining. Collins, backup fullback Rotnei Anderson, and Thompson all rushed for more than 100 yards, and OU had accomplished its first perfect regular season since 1974.

It was time to go now. The old counterman shuffled over to the coat rack and gently lifted his jacket. How is it, he wondered, that Oklahoma football had managed to play such an important part in his life? Perhaps, he thought, there was always hope for a few moments of shared glory whenever the Sooners of Oklahoma took the field. Whatever it was, it had made him feel warm inside to have witnessed so much of Oklahoma's football glory, and for that, he was grateful. The old counterman turned off the lights, locked the door, and headed down Asp Street toward home, whistling a tune vaguely resembling "The Orange Bowl March."

NOTES

The publisher has made every effort to determine the copyright holder for each piece in *Echoes of Oklahoma Football*.

Reprinted with permission of The Associated Press: "Skein Ends at 47" copyright © November 17, 1957.

Reprinted courtesy of The College Football Hall of Fame Research Library: "Letter to the College Football Hall of Fame," by Bennie Owen, November 30, 1956.

Reprinted with permission of *The Daily Oklahoman*: "Longhorns Defeated by Sooners on Boyd Field," copyright © November 14, 1908; "Sooners Take Valley Title in Final Game" copyright © November 26, 1920; "Check Signals? Why, That's So Easy!" by Harold Keith, copyright © November 17, 1948; "OU Bound for Sugar Bowl after Holding Off Aggies 19–15 in Football Thriller," by Pete Rice, copyright © November 27, 1948; "Vessels Wins Heisman Trophy," by Harold Keith, copyright © November 26, 1952; "Little Big Man," by Berry Tramel, copyright © April 14, 1999; "Welcome Back, Oklahoma," by Berry Tramel, copyright © December 3, 2006.

Reprinted with permission of *The New York Times*: "Bosworth: Getting Better Means Getting Tougher" by Malcolm Moran, copyright © August 24, 1986; "Oklahoma Rallies and Earns Berth in Orange Bowl," by Roy S. Johnson, copyright © November 23, 1986; "Rising Star from Texas Plays for the Other Guy," by Pete Thamel, copyright © October 9, 2004.

Reprinted with permission of *Sooner Magazine*: "Soonerland's Undefeated Elevens" by Harold Keith, copyright © November 1928; "Just Say 'Bennie'," by Charles H. "Chuck" Newell, copyright © February, 1930; "Huc' Cum What They Say and Wear," by C. Ross Hume, copyright © November 1930; "Sports Review–1939 Orange